D0065464

KEATON
The Man
Who Wouldn't
Lie Down

The Balloonatic, 1922. Eleanor Keaton.

KEATON

The Man
Who Wouldn't
Lie Down

TOM DARDIS

Charles Scribner's Sons

New York

For Francis, Anne, and Tony,
who have heard it all from the beginning,
and for Ellen, who helped a lot

Also by the author:
Some Time in the Sun

Copyright © 1979 Thomas A. Dardis

Library of Congress Cataloging in Publication Data

Dardis, Tom.
    Keaton, the man who wouldn't lie down.

        Bibliography: p.
        Includes index.
        1. Keaton, Buster, 1895–1966.   2. Moving-picture
actors and actresses—United States—Biography.
3. Comedians—United States—Biography.   I. Title.
PN2287.K4D3   791.43′028′0924 [B]   79-857
ISBN 0-684-16150-8

"Buster Keaton Takes a Walk" by Federico Garcia Lorca,
published by arrangement with New Directions,
copyright © 1979 New Directions.

1 3 5 7 9 11 13 15 17 19 V/C 20 18 16 14 12 10 8 6 4 2

Printed in the United States of America

CONTENTS

ACKNOWLEDGMENTS

Eleanor and Louise Keaton have been extraordinarily generous with their time and have shown great patience in dealing with my endless questions about Buster. So too have Buster's old friends: Marion Byron Breslow, Louise Brooks, William Collier, William Cox, Carol DeLuise, Jane Dula, Leopold Friedman, Harold Goodwin, Charles Lamont, Garry Moore, Ben Pearson, and Gilbert Roland.

The following have most generously shared their knowledge of Keaton's work with me: Rudi Blesh, Kevin Brownlow, Frank Capra, Jean-Paul Coursodon, William K. Everson, Alan Hoffman, Lewis Jacobs, Jay Leyda, Dwight MacDonald, David Robinson, Pierre Sauvage, and Alan Schneider.

For permission to see and make use of material I thank the following individuals and organizations: Herbert S. Nussbaum and Richard Kahn of Metro-Goldwyn-Mayer; Jerry Edwards, John Meehan, and George Stephenson of Twentieth Century–Fox Film Corporation; Leopold Friedman, formerly Secretary of Buster Keaton Productions, Inc.; Charles Silver and Emily Sieger at the Film Study Center of the Museum of Modern Art; Mary Corliss of the Museum of Modern Art Film Stills Archive; Steve Maser at the Wisconsin Center for Film and Theater Research; Gillian Hartknoll at the Library of the British Film Institute; Anne Schlosser and James Powers at the Charles K. Feldman Library, The American Film Institute in Beverly Hills; The Library of the University of Southern California; The Library of the University of California at Los Angeles; The Theater Division of the Research Collections of the New York Public Library at Lincoln Center; The Oral History Project, Columbia University, New York; Sam Gill of the Margaret Herrick Library of the Academy of Motion Picture Arts and Sciences.

The following individuals have allowed me to see films that I could not otherwise have seen: William K. Everson; Jeremy Bolton of the National Film Archive (London); Marshall Deutelbaum and George C. Pratt of George Eastman House; Herbert S. Nussbaum of MGM; Douglas Lemza of United Artists; Bob Borgen of Los Angeles, and Maryann Chach.

And my special thanks to Joan and Bob Franklin for placing their tape of a long interview with Keaton in 1958 at my disposal, as well as giving me permission to quote from their interviews in 1958 with A. Edward Sutherland and Adolph Zukor. The transcripts of these interviews are on deposit in the Oral History Project of Columbia University, New York City. My thanks are also due to Patricia Cristol, who originally commissioned this book, and particularly to its final editor, Caroline Sutton, who displayed great patience and care, and to Faith Evans and Ellen Ervin who performed speedy miracles of super editing, and to John Cushman who makes all things possible. The following have also contributed significantly: Jennifer Mulhern, Christopher Brunel, and particularly Arthur Manson, without whose help this book would never have materialized. William K. Everson read the manuscript and offered useful corrections.

Think slow, act fast.

—Buster Keaton

Laughter alone does not respect any taboo; the comic alone is capable of giving us the strength to bear the tragedy of existence.

—Eugene Ionesco

Buster Keaton's bicycle hasn't a caramel saddle and pedals of sugar, of the sort that wicked men might wish for. It is a bicycle like any other, except that it is the only one that's permeated with innocence. Adam and Eve would run in terror if they saw a glass of water, but on the other hand they would stroke Keaton's bicycle.

—Federico Garcia Lorca

PREFACE

It was not until the late fifties that Buster Keaton was rediscovered and acknowledged as Chaplin's only serious rival among the great masters of silent film comedy. Since then Keaton has emerged in the eyes of many as at least Chaplin's equal, if not his superior. His now legendary reputation rests mainly on the work he did in the short time span of 1920 through 1929, a period of incredible creative achievement in which he made twelve feature films and nineteen two-reel comedies, nearly all of them superb by any standard. This rediscovery of Keaton has also had its miraculous side, for many of his films, believed lost forever, were found only as late as 1960.

After twenty-five years of neglect, Keaton has been totally rehabilitated as a great comic actor and discovered as one of the great filmmakers. In the 1960s and 1970s the incomparable comic gloom of Keaton's art has seemed extraordinarily contemporary in spirit. His fame has produced a flourishing Keaton industry, and half a dozen books have been published about a man who had been almost completely forgotten by the end of the 1930s. American universities give courses entirely devoted to Buster's films, while hundreds of articles have appeared that deal with the infinite subtleties to be found in his best work. Unlike Chaplin, Keaton always refused to identify himself as an artist, preferring to be regarded as a technician of laughter, a master of pratfalls. To Keaton, who attended school for only one day in his entire life, artists were people with an education.

Perhaps the most disconcerting thing about Buster Keaton was the deadly seriousness with which he undertook the art of being funny. Unlike other famous comedians, Buster was convinced that humor is a very serious business. His work was always the greatest single passion of his life.

Buster possessed all the wrong character traits for a successful comedian. He was pathologically shy, he detested what he called low comedy, and he had a terror of crowds. He was totally uninterested in money; although he made an immense amount of it, he lost every penny. His first two wives were absolutely unsuitable, and he was very much his own worst enemy. He exhibited a curious mixture of extreme shyness and testy arrogance in his dealings with the world. Buster was a truly private person, and none of his close friends ever claimed to know what he really felt about anything except his work. The "Great Stone Face" was an enigma to everyone who knew him well.

Charles Samuels attempted to tell Buster's story in his 1960 "as told to" book, *My Wonderful World of Slapstick,* but he was severely curtailed by his decision to obtain all of his information only from Buster himself. Rudi Blesh wrote his *Keaton* as early as 1955 but could not find a receptive publisher for it until 1966, after the Keaton revival was well under way through the pioneering work of James Agee, Walter Kerr, and Andrew Sarris. Blesh's book is justly famous for its evocation of Buster's childhood on the vaudeville stage, yet it makes little of the continual violence that Buster encountered from the hands of his drunken father. It also gives the impression that Keaton's life came to an abrupt end in the winter of 1929 at the time of the triumph of the sound film. Both Samuels and Blesh were sharply restrained by Buster's deep reluctance to discuss sensitive subjects such as his alcoholism and his relations with women. They were also hampered by the fact that many of the chief participants in Buster's life were still alive at the time; his first two wives and his producer, Joseph M. Schenck.

I have been allowed access to the Keaton files at MGM and Twentieth Century–Fox, as well as those of Keaton's own production firm. The information from these sources clears up many matters that have been either misunderstood or ignored until now. There is quite a lot about money in this book, for it was the financial failure of Buster's best work that stifled his creative freedom at the beginning of the sound era. It has been widely believed that Buster's sound films for MGM were financial failures compared with his great silent films; in fact, the reverse is true. There have been several myths about the reasons for Buster's fading into obscurity in the 1930s at MGM, and this book attempts to set the record straight, an enterprise to which he would doubtless have given his approval.

1

BORN WITH A SHOW

[1]

Maybe you think you
were handled roughly
when you were a kid—
Watch the way they
handle Buster!
—Ad for "The Three Keatons" in Myra Keaton's Scrapbook, 1905

Ginger is Buster's watchword and he owns a Ginger
plantation right in Gingersville which sends him a
fresh supply twice a day.
—Scrapbook, 1907

Joseph Frank Keaton literally crawled his way onto a stage for
the first time at the age of nine months. He had escaped from
the theatrical trunk that served as a backstage crib and scuttled
out to the stage where his father, Joe Keaton, was warming up
that night's audience with a flow of comical chatter. Joe suddenly
noticed that the audience had really begun to laugh its head off;
he felt a strong tug on his right leg and looked down to see his
infant child sitting between his legs, staring out, wide-eyed, at
the laughing crowd. Joe immediately held the child up in his
arms to take a bow, receiving a wild round of applause.

In the next three years there was nothing the Keaton parents
could do to keep their child from getting back on that stage. By
the age of four he had become a regular part of the Keaton family's unique vaudeville act, had special costumes designed for
him, and was the talk of American show business. Audiences
couldn't get enough of this strange nonsmiling kid who made
them laugh so much. Buster soon became a real professional at

the rate of ten dollars a week, appearing regularly in the knock-about comedy act that his father had designed for his unique talents. Or, as Buster later put it, "I'd just simply get in my father's way all the time and get kicked all over the stage." By the time Buster was five he was appearing at Tony Pastor's famous vaudeville theater in New York; by the age of six he had played the entire Orpheum theater circuit all over the United States.

Throughout his life Buster loved to talk about his childhood on the vaudeville stage, relating in great detail amazingly vivid tales of disastrous encounters with fires and storms, regularly punctuated by terrifyingly close calls with violent death. It is more than likely that many of these marvelous stories are apocryphal, or the products of his father's inspired imagination. But Buster firmly believed in them, and they soon became a central part of his life. In contrast, he was reticent about the brutality he received at the hands of his father, who was frequently drunk. When Keaton recalled these years, he did so in a mood of complete detachment about the regular beatings he received both on stage and off; they too had become an accepted part of his life. Early photographs reveal a sullen face that glares back at the camera with the expression of someone who has undergone a terrible violation. It is a face that asks to be left alone.

Some of the old tales about Buster's early life have become as legendary in their own way as Parson Weems's account of George Washington and the cherry tree. One of the most famous of all the Buster Keaton stories is about how he got his name. Shortly after his birth in the tiny town of Pickway, Kansas, on the fourth of October, 1895, young Buster at the age of only six months topples down an entire flight of stairs in the theatrical boarding house where his parents are staying with a traveling "medicine show" troupe. Another member of the troupe is the man who later became the supreme magician of the age, the famous magus himself, Harry Houdini. The great Houdini is fated to be present at the very moment when the tiny infant rolls down the stairs. After quickly picking the baby up, Houdini is deeply shocked to discover that it is not only totally unharmed but is actually *laughing*. Houdini gasps at the apparent miracle; he tells the anxious parents, Myra and Joe Keaton, what they have just seen with their own eyes: *"That's some buster your baby took!"* Most versions of this story conclude with young Joseph Frank Keaton being promptly dubbed Buster by his father.

There are a number of other equally miraculous events that reportedly took place during Buster's earliest years, and the element of intense physical danger is present in nearly all of them. When Keaton is a baby, not quite a year old, he is nearly suffocated when the lid of a large steamer trunk, his only crib at the time, suddenly falls shut over his head. Buster's mother providentially enters the backstage dressing room only seconds after the lid has fallen and saves him from certain death.

The most action-packed story of all is said to have taken place just before Buster's third birthday, in the "twister" country of central Kansas. In the course of this one long, hot afternoon, young Buster loses part of one finger in a clothes wringer, severely injures his head with a rock he has thrown up in the air, and ends his day by being blown out of a second-story window into the eye of a cyclone that suddenly sweeps down over the town. Once again a miracle: Buster's frantic parents find the child sitting peacefully in the middle of a street three blocks away from their boardinghouse, surrounded by debris created by the storm. The torrential force of the wind has carried him safely through the air to deposit him on the ground without a single scratch.

Buster was always consistent in his recounting of these tales, as if he were describing events that had been thoroughly documented. In fact, many of the specific details of Buster's close encounters with death had already appeared in print more than once by the time he was only eight years of age, in 1903. These curiously fascinating stories about this "exception among the modern prodigies," as he was sometimes called, began appearing with some regularity in newspapers all over the United States shortly after Buster's first triumphant success as the main attraction of the Keaton family's comic vaudeville act, "The Three Keatons." In nearly every one of these newspaper accounts the individual supplying the facts about the sheer wonder of this boy was the proud father himself, Mr. Joe Keaton. He was a brilliant public relations man.

Buster's mother, Myra Keaton, kept a press scrapbook for the better part of twenty years, in which she regularly pasted all the feature stories about the Keatons, as well as all the ads for the family act, which often appeared in the same paper. There are many variations in the tales about his childhood. One account maintains that his birth took place in a country church in the middle of the night at the full height of still another raging cyclone. In this version of the story, Harry Houdini is present at Buster's birth, lending his own considerable presence to the seriousness of the occasion. By about 1905 all the details about the fall down the stairs, the clothes wringer, the steamer trunk, and the cyclone are to be found combined in one newspaper story; Buster's past is nearly complete.

Joe Keaton loved any sort of publicity. In 1906, he arranged a kidnapping hoax involving his second son, Harry, or "Jingles," Keaton, which was exposed very quickly for what it really was: a publicity gimmick for "The Three Keatons." Joe never traveled very far without taking along his huge old battered typewriter, an ancient German make called a Blickensderfer. On this machine he regularly typed out all the recent, newsworthy events he had discovered about Buster for the local newspapers, whose editors printed them with enthusiasm.

Perhaps Buster's fall into the waiting arms of Harry Houdini took place initially on the keyboard of that old but quite dependable Blickensderfer. Whether or not the story is actually true makes little difference, for it has taken on a life of its own. It is precisely the kind of thing that should have happened in the childhood of the man who made films like *The Navigator* and *The General*.

---

[2]

Tell me, little Buster, are there any more at home like you?

NOT!!! There is only one *Buster,* and that is BUSTER KEATON

—Scrapbook, 1908

Joe Keaton was a full ten years older than the tiny young woman he married in 1894. Myra was the seventeen-year-old daughter of Frank Cutler, who produced and managed a number of traveling "medicine shows" in what was then known as the Old Wild West. She had been appearing in them since she was twelve.

These shows were a curious hodgepodge of tent-show entertainment, ranging from performances of the standard English melodramas of the day to broad farce comedies, all of them supplemented by stern, admonitory lectures on health problems. They were called medicine shows because various patent and nonpatent "medicines," nearly all of them alcoholic in content, were dispensed to the thirsty crowds attending them. The medicine was sold between the acts and after, and when Houdini was with them he usually perfomed all the dramatic roles in addition to his magic act. Joe Keaton followed him with what he called his "eccentric/grotesque" comic dancing. After their marriage, young Myra performed the functions of a soubrette who played the alto saxophone, an instrument that was quite a novelty at the time. Myra also played the piano, bass, fiddle, and cornet, and took "old maid" parts in plays like *East Lynne.*

The early professional years of Myra and Joe Keaton were mostly spent on the extreme edge of poverty. Engagements were often hard to come by; there were long and desperate periods of unemployment. They traveled all over the Far West, some accounts of the places they worked in sounding very much like the stark and glacial Fort Romper described by Stephen Crane in his story "The Blue Hotel." These little lost towns in the wilds of Minnesota were deadly cold in the winter, and the elixirs served at "The Keaton and Houdini Medicine Show" at least kept the audiences warm in their seats. Traveling endlessly from town to town this way promised no bright future. For reasons now unknown, Joe Keaton and Houdini finally parted company when Buster was still quite small, each to seek out his fortune in more hospitable areas of the country.

A reporter, Guy G. Frittz, recalls the agonizingly hard times experienced by some of the famous performers he had known in their early days, among them the Keatons:

I recalled the time when they, like many others, were fighting hard to get a foothold. My home is in Pittsburg, Kansas, and I first met the Keatons there in 1897. . . . Joe and his wife drifted in there looking for an engagement and got work at the park. Joe did his acrobatic act and his wife appeared in a saxophone speciality. Both played parts in the dramas they were putting on. . . . At the close of the park Joe Keaton went away to join the J.T.R. Clark medicine show and it wasn't long until he got an engagement for his wife Myra and wired her to join him. "Buster" Keaton, who is well known here, was a mere babe at the time. He was sick and Mrs. Keaton couldn't take him with her. My mother took charge of the youngster and kept him until he got well enough to join his parents. While the Keatons were with the medicine show they toured the mining towns of Kansas. . . .

The Keatons were Irish, or at least Joe Keaton always said they were, but Buster's sister Louise insists to this day that the name is an Indian one and that all the Keatons resemble Indians: "Just take a look at those cheekbones! Those eyes!" It is pretty certain that Joe Keaton spent at least some time in Indian Territory. He was born in 1867 in the community of Dogwatch, a hamlet on the outskirts of Terre Haute, Indiana. Like Huck Finn before him, Joe "lit out" for the Oklahoma Territory as a homesteader, or "boomer" as they were called, at the time of the Oklahoma land grants of 1889—or at least he claimed he did in the stories he later wrote for *Variety*. He liked to tell a long tale about taking a total of eight dollars with him on his first trip to Oklahoma, with one dollar intended for bacon and eggs and the remaining seven for ammunition as a defense against claim jumpers.

Besides *Variety*, Joe was also a frequent contributor to the *Dramatic Mirror*. The stories he wrote for them are in a style similar to that used by his famous friend from Oklahoma, Will Rogers, with perhaps a bit of W. C. Fields thrown in for added flavor. There is a tall-tale quality to many of these stories, several of them featuring Joe's exploits in hostile Indian territory, armed only with the trusty Winchester given him by his father. Buster Keaton grew up believing all these stories to be absolutely true.

By about 1890 Joe gave up his prospecting for the joys of the stage. Buster once described his father's theatrical talents by saying that he was "a natural dancer . . . a great pair of legs to do eccentric work . . . a natural clown." Joe was the only tall Keaton, five feet eleven inches. His life-long specialty was an incredibly high kick, which he used not only as an essential part of the family's act but also as a savage offensive or defensive weapon while offstage. He always liked to claim that he "took nothing from anyone," and he had an awesome reputation for being strong tempered, frequently falling into violent disputes with booking agents and theater managers. The famous comedian Ed Wynn appeared on many vaudeville bills with "The Three Keatons," and his considered judgment of Joe was that he was "a totally undisciplined Irish drunk." Joe did indeed drink, heavily and steadily for most of his years on stage, creating professional problems that steadily worsened over the years. When drunk he became violent and totally unbearable.

Joe's drinking, his fights, and his generally irascible personality as reported by his children, Buster and Louise, seem strangely at odds with photographs of him taken in the early 1920s. They show a beautifully dressed man, apparently in his mid-fifties, wearing a small gold watch chain that curls its way across his vest. A tiny Knights of Columbus or Elks pin appears in his lapel; he looks like a bank president.

Myra was an enthusiastic, nonstop talker and cardplayer nearly all her life—pinochle at first and then bridge. She often smoked a pipe, and she loved good bourbon. Just as sharply critical and outspoken about things as Joe, she possessed an immense, tireless flow of energy that never left her. In spite of her small stature—she was only four feet eleven inches, and Joe always referred to her as "The Little Woman"—she was quite imperious in her demands. In the early days of the Keatons' act her diffident playing of the saxophone was intended to add a touch of class to what was really an extremely rough and rowdy form of entertainment.

Things improved dramatically for the Keatons shortly before the turn of the century, largely due to the overwhelming audience response to Buster. As Buster recalled, his first professional appearances were simply those of a cute toddler who wished to join his parents in the fun out there on the stage. In a very short time his role became that of "the living mop": a child who was dropped, shaken, and thrown around the stage by his father like a rag doll. Some sort of appropriate costume was necessary.

> My father put grotesque clothes on me, similar to the ones he was wearing. So I had big pants, and big shoes on immediately, and they started playing me in matinees only when I'm around three years old. Time I got about four some manager says, "You keep him in for the night show and we raise your salary ten dollars." So from then on I was in, and starting at ten dollars a week. . . .

Buster's talents were quickly recognized by the leading theatrical papers of the day, and *The Dramatic Mirror* and the *Dramatic News* both started to give him extensive coverage shortly after his

Buster at five. *National Film Archive / Stills Library*

first appearance as the third member of "The Three Keatons." "The older folks are clever in their way, but they have to 'go back upstage' when their young and hopeful 'Buster' gets the attention of the audience." Buster was only seven when this appeared. As early as 1905 the *Dramatic News* reported:

> Joe and Myra Keaton act a background to their little godsend, in the literal sense of the word, for Buster Keaton certainly is the breadwinner of the family. . . . His future would seem to be better assumed if his knack of mimicry were cultivated and developed, instead of relying on the guffaws of the "lowbrows" in making tiresome use of the child's body for the wiping of the stage floor.

The Three Keatons. *Museum of Modern Art / Film Stills Archive*

Two more children were born to the Keatons, in 1904 and 1906: Harry, or Jingles, as he was known when a small child, and Louise. Joe managed to incorporate them in the act for a few years, relying again on their cuteness, but neither Harry nor Louise ever displayed any of Buster's startling talents and their theatrical careers were quite short.

In the brief time that Louise and Harry were part of the act, the Keatons were usually billed as "The Man With a Wife, Table, and Three Kids," with Joe utilizing as his main prop a sturdily built oak table. Before Buster became the main attraction, Joe would throw himself up, down, and around this table in an intricate series of jumps and leaps. After Buster's rise to fame, the table, as well as Myra and her saxophone, became progressively less important.

In time the act became a unique kind of improvised physical exchange between Buster and his father, a roughhouse dialogue involving a breathtaking series of violent encounters in which Buster either hit his father or was hit by him. In order to make audiences accept this brutality as "funny," Buster had to secure some sort of comic mask to prevent the audience from thinking that the rough treatment could hurt him. This mask became the grave face that never smiled, Buster Keaton's identifying mark as a performer for the next sixty years.

[3]

They call my first years on stage as training. Well, you wouldn't really call it training, you'd call it experience. . . .

—Keaton, 1958

BUSTER is not a midget performer, but a revelation in eccentric juvenile talent . . . a miniature comedian who presents irresistible comedy, with gigantic effects. . . .

—Scrapbook, 1909

Buster had a simple explanation for his deadpan expression or his "Great Stone Face" look: "I developed the stone face thing quite naturally. I just happened to be, even as a small kid . . . the type of comic that couldn't laugh at his own material. I soon learned at an awful early age that when I laughed the audience didn't. . . ."

The truth is that a great deal of agonizing work went into the perfect control of his facial muscles, a control that effectively concealed pain as well as mirth.

> If something tickled me and I started to grin the old man would hiss, "Face, Face!" That meant freeze the puss. The longer I held it, why, if we got a laugh the blank pan or the puzzled puss would double it. He kept after me, never let up, and in a few years it was automatic. Then when I'd step on stage or in front of a camera, I *couldn't* smile. . . .

While still in his twenties, Buster allowed his name to be used as the author of an "as told to" article in the *Ladies Home Journal* entitled "Why I Never Smile." It emphasized Joe's constant, excruciatingly painful pressure on Buster to suppress his feelings.

> In this knockabout act, my father and I used to hit each other with brooms, occasioning for me strange flops and falls. If I should chance to smile, the next hit would be a good deal harder. All the parental correction I ever received was with an audience looking on. *I could not even whimper. . . .*

That last line has the ring of unmistakable truth, for Joe had taught him that he literally couldn't ever afford to smile. It is likely that being knocked about on the stage every night of his life left indelible psychic scars on Buster. The curious passivity that is found in his relations with women and employers in later years may well have stemmed from this early training, which demanded total obedience. These early years also had much to do with the formation of the superb spirit of comic gloom that suffuses his great films of the twenties.

*Emphasis added.

In 1907 one unfriendly critic described "The Three Keatons" as follows:

> The two chief performers, representing themselves as a proud but very abusive father and a solemn child, possessed by the devil and provided with a suitcase handle between his shoulders so that he can be flung about the deck without tearing his clothes, keep the audience, or at least the male part of it, heartily amused. For instance, the father starts making a very poor speech to the audience, while the solemn son, with a basketball at the end of a clothesline mounts on a table and swings his weapon through the air. The rope isn't long enough. The speech continues. The solemn and still unseen son carefully gets down, pulls the table six feet nearer, revolves the basketball and clothesline with great violence and at last knocks the parental hat off and at the next revolution bounces the ball severely against the parental skull. Can you laugh at that sort of thing? Then you can get no end of fun out of the Keatons. . . .

Joe and Buster made up an endless series of variations on this kind of behavior. In one, Joe is shaving with a straight razor to which is attached, unknown to him, a long thin piece of rubber tubing. Buster would begin to stretch the tubing farther and farther, agonizingly far, until it would finally snap, causing Joe's razor to fly across the stage.

The nightly violence onstage was not all one-sided, for Buster gave it back to Joe just as hard as he could. To protect himself from Buster's blows, which kept getting stronger all the time, Joe had a steel cap made that fitted snugly under his bald wig. One night, after drinking a bit more than usual, Joe forgot to place the protective cap on his head. Buster banged away energetically on his father's head with the broom handle as usual and was surprised to find his father strangely still on the stage floor; he had knocked him completely unconscious, and the curtain had to be quickly lowered.

Joe Keaton emphasized the danger and violence in some of his extremely bizarre publicity stunts on behalf of the act. One was a full-page ad that he ran several times in the vaudeville trade press; it took the form of a mock letter addressed to the GERMAN-AMERICAN STAFF OF PHYSICIANS AND SURGEONS INSTITUTE, claiming that it was their work alone that had saved his young Buster's life:

New York, N. Y. Jan. 1, 1903

Dear Sirs: Replying to your inquiry regarding Buster's health, will say I feel it a duty I owe you and the afflicted to advise all in need of medical assistance to seek your aid. Before consulting you, our little son had been given up to die by eight physicians. They said he could last but a few days at most. His limbs were almost fleshless, and his stomach was bloated nearly as large as that of a person three times his size; he ate nothing for several days, and to tell the truth, there never seemed to be one little chance for saving his life; but I can truthfully say that within forty-eight hours after commencing your treatment a decided change was noticeable, and in a few weeks little Buster was as sound as a dollar, one of nature's own rosy-cheeked boys. We play at Forest Park, Kansas City, week of September 7th.

Yours gratefully,
JOE KEATON
"The Man With the Table."

The law took a dim view of "The Three Keatons," especially Buster's role in the act. The authorities would attend a performance, be appalled by the shocking violence accorded young Buster, and proceed to drag Joe into court to defend himself against the charge of gross brutality to his own flesh and blood. Often Buster had to disrobe in front of a judge in his chambers and demonstrate that while he might be known professionally as "Mr. Black and Blue," his body in fact was untouched by either color; Buster had mastered the fine art of taking a fall at a very early age.

Rumors that Buster Keaton was not really a child but a talented midget began to flourish as early as his seventh year, for it seemed quite unlikely that any normal child could be prevailed upon to endure passively this endless battering. Joe was perfectly willing to spread these midget rumors all over the country, for he knew this was one way to prevent the law from coming down on him. Right from the start he had been trying to establish Buster's age as several years older than it really was. Today, Buster's stage activities would come under the scrutiny of those who enforce the child abuse laws; at the turn of the century this function was performed by an organization called the Gerry Society, whose agents vigorously enforced the newly enacted child-labor laws. These laws in effect prevented a child under seven from appearing on a stage in any capacity whatever; only those over sixteen could in any real sense of the word "perform." But if Buster couldn't perform, there was, as he recalled, "nothing that said you couldn't kick him in the face or throw him through a piece of scenery."

Since Buster was the real breadwinner of the family, it was an absolute economic necessity to avoid these threatening work restrictions. If they thought Buster was a midget, let them go on thinking it; so much the better for everybody. Joe did everything he could to encourage the midget idea: he had professional photographs taken of Buster wearing a little "Dapper Dan" suit especially made up for him, carrying a tiny valise and cane, the whole ensemble topped off by a minuscule derby. Buster later remarked, "In Massachusetts, for instance, they thought I was a midget. They took it for granted. But we were arrested many times because we always managed to get around the law because the law read, no child under the age of sixteen shall do acrobatics, walk wire, play musical instruments, trapeze, and it names everything. . . ." The lawmakers had never imagined that steady violence could be the mainstay of a vaudeville act.

Buster at eight. *Museum of Modern Art / Film Stills Archive*

The vaudeville world, or variety, as it was known in England, of the Keaton family, was the most eagerly followed form of mass entertainment in both countries for nearly three decades, roughly from 1900 through 1930, when it was displaced by the advent of radio and the sound film. It was in vaudeville that all of the great film comedians got their start: Harry Langdon and W. C. Fields as well as Eddie Cantor, Will Rogers, and the Marx Brothers. The list includes all the legendary names.

An absolutely ideal evening of American vaudeville in about 1910 consisted of seven or eight acts, each running from ten to twenty minutes. If you were extremely lucky, you might see on a single bill Al Jolson singing four or five of his songs; W. C. Fields doing his world-famous bent cue-stick number; Weber and Fields with their famous Jewish dialect comedy act; and Will Rogers twirling his lasso, drawling out his topical humor in a rich Oklahoma accent. Somewhere on this bill of attractions, almost never at the top, but rarely at the bottom, would be "The Three Keatons" and their whirlwind comedy act of a naughty boy and his maddened father. Theater managers had problems with where to place the Keatons on the bill: if they came too early, the effect might be disastrous for the next "serious" performer; if too late, it became difficult to get the audience to leave the theater.

In the days of their greatest success the Keatons knew all the big names in show business. In these early years Buster and his father worked alongside the great figures of the day: Bert Williams, Fred Stone, Lillian Russell, and Eddie Cantor. Buster loved to talk about his family's part in these days of the triumph of American vaudeville:

> See, I saw the great days of vaudeville. I got in just in time to see vaudeville go from the ten, twenty, and thirty cent admission fees to the two dollar and in fact, The Three Keatons, that's what we were called, we held Hammerstein's Theater record for playing it the most times. You were only supposed to play there twice a year. We used to average four to six times a year. . . .

To fulfill their bookings, the Keatons did an enormous amount of traveling all over the United States and Canada in the early years of the century. Buster's home was often the interior of a hot, dusty, day coach making its bumpy way from Chicago to Duluth, or else in the endless round of theatrical boarding-houses usually situated within a short walk of the main theaters. The Keatons' home in New York was one of these, a Mrs. Ehrich's on West Thirty-eighth Street. There were extended stays there between bookings. On one of these Buster was given a "Browniekar," an expensively made car for children that actually worked. Photos of Buster sitting at the wheel of his Browniekar show him dressed impeccably, with not a hair out of place. The car may please, but he is not smiling for the camera.

On extended tours of the country, Joe Keaton kept up his habit of writing the ad copy for the trade press. Sometimes it was curiously self-mocking, coming from the father of the breadwinner: "Without doubt the worst act that every played St. Louis. The old folks should be ashamed of themselves of living off a little kid. I'll bet Buster is not their son all right; they have just picked him up somewhere. (What a lucky find). I don't see how they stayed the week out. Oh, I guess they don't get much salary. I know they don't because they don't wear any diamonds or good clothes."

Buster at thirteen. *Museum of Modern Art / Film Stills Archive*

Joe never tired of finding new approaches to identify his Buster as an altogether unique personality in American show business. He liked to experiment with teasing tag lines to get people's attention. One such line appeared in hundreds of papers all over the country in 1909: KEEP YOUR EYE ON THE KID KEEP YOUR EYE ON THE KID KEEP YOUR EYE ON THE KID. He tried to interest the females in the audience with the announcement that Buster was "the cutest little bundle of jollity that ever wriggled into the hearts of audiences."

[4]

Some people fall quite hard in this world
it really is quite sad,
But when I fall it's soft for me
and I never use a pad
I always was a bouncing boy!
'Till one day he bounced me
on the stage
and I've been bouncing ever since!
          —Scrapbook, 1909

As the "cutest little bundle" advanced in age, his father's act became ever more wild and unpredictable. Audiences looked forward to seeing almost anything happen when the Keatons appeared on stage: there was nothing like them in show business. There were times when the improvised nature of the act got completely out of hand: one night in New Haven Joe used Buster as a human cannonball to throw at a group of rude young hecklers from Yale who were sitting in the front row of Poli's Theater. The smashing impact of Buster's seventy pounds broke one student's nose and cracked the ribs of another. Once a flying kick from Joe Keaton's powerful left foot left the ten-year-old Buster lying unconscious for eighteen hours. Buster got his own back by pure chance: on one occasion, as part of a freak accident, he shot Joe in the face with a gun containing blank cartridges, causing him considerable pain and discomfort from powder burns.

Buster received almost no formal education, for there was simply no time for it. He always liked to tell people that the reason he'd only spent one day at school in his life was the teachers' violent objections to the stream of puns, one liners, and punch lines that he delivered to his delighted classmates: he'd been sent home in disgrace. He claimed that Myra and Joe had hired tutors for him as the family played its bookings across the country, and recalled Myra's teaching him to add and subtract while the family was waiting to get out on the stage. But his formal education remained very scanty; his real classroom was the theater, and he loved that rough and tumble world.

> You'd call it pantomime although my father kept talking all the time. He never said the same thing twice. He just tried to convince the audience that there was only one way to bring children up and that was to make them mind. Be gentle and kind to them, but make them mind. By that time I'd knocked both of his feet from under him with a broom. . . .

The vaudeville season came to an end in June, and Buster spent his summers after the vaudeville season in Michigan. By 1907 the act had become so successful that Joe was able to buy a summer home for the family right on the lakefront of Lake Muskegon. Here Buster spent eight idyllic summers. Like Ernest Hemingway, who also spent childhood summers on a lake in Michigan, Buster early became an extremely proficient duck hunter and a skillful fisherman. He continued to follow both these pursuits all through the twenties. And it was at Lake Muskegon that he developed his lifelong passion for baseball.

Though he made the most of his all-American-boy summers, the remaining nine months of Buster's year were spent on the road or in the wings of theaters. It was about now that he began to acquire that quiet, withdrawn air that remained with him all his life. This is the quality that always puzzled so many of his friends, the mysterious feeling he gave of being somewhere else a lot of the time, simply *not there*. Always strangely impassive, he would stare at his friends with his bright brown-eyed regard, puzzling them with his long silences.

In 1909 Joe proudly announced to a waiting world that Buster had finally reached the proper legal age of sixteen and could now perform with no further restrictions. The ads for weeks on end read: BUSTER IS SIXTEEN BUSTER IS SIXTEEN BUSTER IS SIXTEEN. He actually wasn't; he had not yet reached his fourteenth birthday.

For the past two years the interference of the Gerry Society had been slowly but surely destroying Buster's status as a midget. This had been a losing struggle, for by the age of twelve Buster had become entirely too big to pass for one much longer. At this point the eyes of the society fell upon him more sharply than ever. His final undoing as a professional performer at this time came about through an act of charity on Joe's part.

During the Thanksgiving season of 1907 Joe was persuaded against his better judgment to allow the entire Keaton family to perform in a benefit show for needy children at the Grand Opera House in Brooklyn. They performed with great success, but Buster's illegal appearance in Brooklyn was observed by the law and on the twenty-third of November Joe was hauled into court and fined $300, an enormous sum in those days.

The resulting rash of newspaper stories made the situation even worse, for it was soon clear that Buster could no longer work safely either near New York or in other places where the Gerry Society held sway. Conceding defeat, Joe made Buster enter a period of semiretirement that lasted until May of 1909, when Joe reluctantly accepted an offer to appear in a theater three thousand miles from New York. Alfred Butt, the manager of the world-renowned Palace Theater in London, had offered the Keatons the sum of forty pounds, or two hundred dollars, for a week's engagement. A rip-tooting, "America-is-first" patriot his entire life, Joe Keaton had no desire to see England or the English, but work was work and pounds could be exchanged for dollars. He finally agreed to go, stating that "only the brimming tears in Buster's eyes had driven him to accept the offer."

A number of interesting photographs were taken of the entire

Keaton family while on board the S.S. *Washington* en route to Southampton. One, of Buster and his father, shows that fourteen-year-old Buster has not yet totally accepted his "stone face" but displays instead a hostile gaze that seems to reject the intrusion of the camera. Joe is quietly and elegantly dressed; he sports a newly acquired mustache.

Joe wrote a long account of his mishaps in England for *Variety*. As with most of Joe's newspaper stories, he places himself at the center of everything and can see only the wrongs he endured at the hands of the English. Things had started off badly when Joe got drunk the night before they sailed:

> That night around the "42nd Street Corners" I met old pals, with cheering words, and took in quite a load of Ehret, neglecting to check my luggage. I did this on purpose. "The Boys," thinking they were doing an Old Pal a favor, hurried our trunks to the pier and carried me up the gangplank. I started a fuss when on board; anything to get thrown off. I even auctioned off Louise. I commenced the thing by saying: "Before this boat sails I am authorized to sell this orphan child. What am I offered?" The bids opened up well and I sold Louise to a bright-looking little fellow for seventy-five cents. I demanded the money before I would turn over the baby. The boy's father told his son I was only fooling. That was the beginning of a scrap. But they wouldn't put me off the boat. Instead they told me if I tried to auction off any more babies they would put me in irons.

From the moment of the Keatons' arrival in London there was a steady succession of these scraps, most of them alcohol-inspired, with Joe managing to antagonize nearly everyone he met. A tense situation prevailed at their first rehearsal at the Palace, for only then was it discovered that the Keatons had not brought props with them from New York and the theater staff could not provide any.

The English audience, after a few minutes of shocked disbelief, quickly warmed up to the peculiar magic of the Keatons. But after the performance, Joe angrily recounts that they were not permitted to take more than one bow, despite the enthusiasm of the audience. Alfred Butt instructed his stage manager to prevent the Keatons from receiving any further applause.

The Keatons on board the S.S. *Washington*, 1909. *Pierre Sauvage*

The Keatons in 1908. *Pierre Sauvage*

"Fine applause. Why don't they allow them a bow?" Mr. Butt replied to his stage manager: "It isn't on the level." The next night Butt moved us up so early there was no one to speak of on the lower floor or in the stalls.

What really seems to have been bothering Alfred Butt was Joe's brutal treatment of Buster. The next morning Joe was summoned to the office of Butt, who had only one question for him:

"I shall ask you. Is that your son or an adopted one?" I told him Buster was my own son. "My word" said Butt: "I imagined he was an adopted boy and you didn't give a damn what you did to him." The next day I purchased three tickets for the next boat sailing. . . .

This was the Keatons' one and only trip abroad, but Joe never forgot Alfred Butt and the ill-conceived trip to England. Three years later he wrote these lines:

> In dear old London
> It is a fine old town.
> The PALACE, Oh!
> the Palace, where the
> Keatons went to
> clown.
> We opened on a
> Monday. On Saturday
> we shut.
> We certainly had a
> lively time
> BUTT——BUTT——
> BUTT——
> —Scrapbook, 1912

The Keaton family's professional difficulties in the next few years were mainly caused by Joe's wild and drunken behavior, especially his high-handed treatment of the people who employed him, among them the owners of the larger vaudeville circuits. There were many people who found Joe Keaton simply intolerable. Harold Goodwin, Buster's close friend, still recalls how

Joe behaved when he met someone in a restaurant. Joe would stick his thumb in the person's cup of coffee and hand it to him, saying tersely: "This yours?" Another friend, Buster Collier, remembers Joe as a living horror that his son had learned to endure over the years. Buster was fond of his father when he was sober, but found his drunken state as painful as everyone else.

One of Joe's particular hates was Martin Beck, a reigning monarch of the American vaudeville circuit. Joe found in Beck a natural target for all the enmity in his soul and berated him publicly on every possible occasion. An explosion came suddenly one night when Joe spotted Beck standing in the wings of his own theater in New York, just as Joe was about to finish his act on stage. Beck shouted out to him on stage, "Make *me* laugh, Keaton!" Joe stopped dead and began to chase his employer out of the theater. Beck ran out into the street in deadly fear for his life. After that the act was banished to the hinterlands: no one else would hire them.

Joe's drinking obviously had a good deal to do with the final breaking up of the act. The act demanded absolutely perfect physical coordination, almost impossible to achieve after the massive doses of alcohol that Joe consumed every night. His constant drinking not only made the act exceedingly dangerous for both him and Buster but did nothing to improve its quality. Moreover, the success of "The Three Keatons" had always depended upon Buster's talent and youth. He was twenty-one in the fall of 1916, and at five feet four inches he weighed only 140 pounds; this was a lot of weight for Joe Keaton to whirl around a stage twice a day.

In the *Ladies' Home Journal* piece, Keaton's ghost writer had some difficulties in describing the final days of "The Three Keatons." Until this point the article had Buster speaking in the first person; with no explanation the next section shifts to the third person, which may indicate that Buster insisted on this oddly sad note.

As this boy who wore the clothes of an old man and always felt old, grew older, he became too big to be used as the butt of his fa-

ther. He could no longer be thrown around and other things had
to be thrown into the act, which was about played out anyway. . . .

From what Buster's sister Louise can recall—she was ten at the
time—it is clear that Joe's abusiveness to the world in general
had by then extended into the Keaton home and that Myra and
the two boys were subjected to a steadily increasing barrage of
invective about everything. It was just a matter of time for the
end of the act and, eventually, the marriage of Myra and Joe as
well.

In early 1917 the United Booking Office finally came through
with an offer for "The Three Keatons" to play the Pantages
Theater in Los Angeles. This was good news, except that they
were supposed to perform three times a day, and the sheer
amount of physical energy employed in their act made this impossible. Joe wanted to accept the offer, but Myra and Buster
were totally opposed to it and did not turn up to meet Joe in Los
Angeles. It was the end of the act. It was also the end of Buster's
apprenticeship in the theater: he was now ready to begin his real
work.

2

THE BIJOU DREAM

[1]

> I went to Pittsburgh where I saw a lot of men trying
> to get into a place that was charging five cents admis-
> sion. I wondered what it could be that was so inter-
> esting to them, and I paid my nickel and joined
> them. . . .
>
> —Adolph Zukor, 1903

It was the wonderful new nickelodeon that Zukor, the future
founder of Paramount Pictures, had discovered that day in Pittsburgh. The nickelodeons were the crude and noisy precursor of
the motion picture theater, the place where an absolutely different kind of popular entertainment flourished. These pictures
that *moved* delighted the American public to an astonishing degree. In the early years of this century, the nickelodeon craze
swept over the entire length and breadth of the United States
with speed and intensity that remained unrivaled until the dawn
of television. Nickelodeons were frequently thought of as the
"jack rabbits" of the entertainment business and were described
that way in the pages of *The Billboard* in 1904:

> They multiply so rapidly. No one is in a position to estimate the
> number of these exhibits which are now in operation, for an es-
> timate today would be worthless tomorrow. In all the big cities
> they seem to be on every business block. In the middle-sized
> towns locations are being eagerly sought and no one can tell what
> the amount will eventually be.

As early as 1905 somewhere between 10 and 20 million Americans had become regular patrons of the nickelodeons. They
went to them several times a week, for the bills were usually

changed daily. One historian of early American film has described the staggering impact of the immense success of these shows on the entire entertainment world, as in this comment in a trade paper: "It was something incomprehensible, incredible, fantastic. It could not be real—or if, by any chance, it was real, it could not endure. . . ."

Besides being totally new, these "living pictures" also had the great advantage of being cheap. Until the advent of film, all the major forms of theatrical entertainment in America (plays, opera, ballet, and vaudeville) were pretty much attended and supported by only some 10 percent of the population, leaving the remaining 90 with little to enjoy but traveling circuses and black minstrel shows. Orchestra seats at most theaters cost about two dollars at a time when factory workers were paid the traditional dollar for a day's work. As Benjamin Hampton observed, to millions of Americans the nickelodeon was truly "a new world—for a nickel."

The nickelodeon had rapidly evolved from the earlier "peep shows" that in turn had sprung from Thomas Edison's original Kinetoscope of 1889, the primary source for all forms of "living pictures." The peep shows had often been located in the penny arcades of the day; they were wooden cabinets containing fifty feet of film, which one operated by inserting a penny and turning a crank. The customers for these peep shows often were eager to view the same footage over and over again; the demand for the new product was immense. Among the early proprietors of some of the penny arcades in New York City were William Fox, Marcus Loew, and Adolph Zukor, the future founders of the Fox Film Corporation, Metro-Goldwyn-Mayer, and Paramount Pictures, respectively. They were quick to note the public's insatiable appetite for moving pictures and decided to create theaters that could easily accommodate all their eager customers at the same time.

The basic form of the nickelodeon then developed quite quickly: a converted arcade or storefront filled with either benches or cheap wooden kitchen chairs, a crude screen that was as often as not a simple bed sheet, and the projection equipment. The number of chairs was rarely more than the magic number of 199, for above that required having a regular theater license, costing the relatively high sum of $500. But there were several early manager/owners who had the foresight to take the plunge and invest in the license.

In the very beginning it was the sheer spellbinding novelty of this form of entertainment that was responsible for its phenomenal popularity. When a high-speed locomotive appeared to be heading directly into the laps of a closely packed audience, they felt an unparalleled, terrified delight that frightened them in a lovely new way, a sort of communal *frisson.* Speeding locomotives were only extreme instances of what most appealed to these audiences: almost anything would do at first, *as long as it moved:*

> The second picture represented the breaking of waves on the sand, and as they struck, broke into tiny floods, just like the real thing. Some of the people in the front rows seemed to be afraid they were going to get wet, and looked about to see where they could run to, in case the waves came too close. . . .

The reviewer here was describing the effect of what was advertised as Edison's "Vitascope" on an audience attending Koster and Bial's Music Hall, a Herald Square vaudeville theater on the present site of the R. H. Macy Department Store in New York City. The bill of attractions that included the Vitascope material was first shown on the night of April 23, 1896, the date many American film historians have accepted as the first public exposure to the new visual sensation. There have been many other claimants for precedence, for several countries have written their own versions of early film history. The fact is that feverish experimentation with the new discovery was going on all over Europe at exactly the same time as it was taking place in the United States. The Lumière brothers had shown their first films in Lyon, with sensational results, on March 22, 1895, and an Englishman, Robert Paul, had revealed his results in London on February 28, 1896. There are also German claimants for the honor of having been the very first to introduce the thrill of "living pictures."

Although Thomas Edison's highly potent name was used on the Vitascope pictures shown that night at Koster and Bial's, the projection device was actually the work of Thomas Armat, who had gone on experimenting with film after Edison had lost interest. Nevertheless, virtually all the basic patents governing both the taking and projecting of pictures were eventually assigned to Edison and became the chief weapon of the later-day infamous Motion Pictures Patents Company.

A great many new words were quickly coined to describe the new processes, many of them deliberately chosen to have a bookish ring to them in order to give them dignity, such as *bio-scope, bio-graph,* and *theater-graph.* The word *nickelodeon* itself succinctly combined the word for the American five-cent piece with the Greek word for theater: thus, a nickel theater.

The early nickelodeon shows ran uninterrupted for about twenty to thirty minutes: the theater managers apparently believed that this was the outside limit of their patrons' interest. The barkers in front of the shows used to tell their prospective customers: "If you don't like the show, they can only inflict fifteen minutes of it on you!" The customers were, however, cordially invited to stay for as many shows as they desired, and many of them took up the offer.

It was only a short time before the demand for films with some sort of story arose, but in order to make them it became crucial to increase the length of the films. At the very outset most films ran to only about 100 feet or so, a length giving little opportunity for any real story development. When lengths of 250 to 400 feet (four or five minutes) were achieved, it then became possible to make simple, crude "chase" films. It was during the years 1903 through 1907 that lengths of 500 and even 1,000 feet were first attained, resulting in films that could accommodate a plot. A 1,000-foot film made up one reel, which took about ten minutes to project. Among the more famous films of this period was Edwin S. Porter's *The Great Train Robbery,* released at the end of 1903. It contained fourteen "scenes" in a length of 740 feet and succeeded in enthralling audiences all over the world, demonstrating that a story could be told in film as in no other way. *The Great Train Robbery* was only the beginning; the appetite of the new and ever-widening audiences became insatiable for these films with "stories," as a studio manager of 1907 explained:

We've got to give them a story; they won't take anything else—a story with plenty of action. You can't show large conversation, you know, on the screen. More story, larger story, better story with plenty of action—that is our tendency.

By the following year the nickelodeon fever had become so widespread that it began seriously to invade the borders of Buster Keaton's beloved vaudeville world. The first real film trade paper, *Moving Picture World,* reported that Keith and Proctor's Twenty-third Street Theater in New York, until then given over almost exclusively to vaudeville, would become a full-time motion picture theater on December 6, 1907: "Admittance will be five cents and ten cents. No seats will be reserved. . . . With the change in style of amusement, the theater's name will also be changed. *Thenceforth it will be the Bijou Dream. . . .*"

The new Bijou Dream had been one of "The Three Keatons' " regular stopping places on their tours back and forth across the country. Buster vividly recalled the gradual introduction and final takeover of these "living pictures" at this theater and at many others. When the flickering early films were first introduced, it was as the last attraction of a long evening of live acts. They were intended as "chasers," items on the bill of attractions that would serve to clear out the theater after the last regular act. The plan didn't work, for the audiences loved the films and wouldn't leave until the projectionist turned off his machine.

As a child of twelve, Buster saw hundreds of these early films on his trips across the United States at the beginning of the century. Family tradition had it that "The Three Keatons" were offered a chance to appear in a film as early as 1912, but refused the opportunity. Buster's sister, Louise, recalls her father going on and on about "those terrible movies." He disliked them right from the beginning and, even later, he agreed to work only in films that were directed by Buster. The movie offer had come from William Randolph Hearst, who wanted Joe to play the part of Jiggs, the harassed father, in a film to be based on George McManus's immensely popular comic strip *Bringing Up Father.* The strip was distributed by King Features, a Hearst subsidiary, and its owner was eager for the added publicity a film would give to the property. Joe Keaton's reply to Hearst, as well as to other filmmakers at this time, was to ask: *"The Keatons—for ten cents? For ten lousy cents on a bed sheet—the Keatons?"*

---

[2]

Keaton: "I've never even been in a studio."

Arbuckle: "Come on down and play a scene with me and see how you like it."

The most important day in Buster Keaton's life occurred as a result of a chance meeting in the street with Roscoe ("Fatty") Arbuckle on a rainy day in New York in late March of 1917. Buster was just twenty-one and pictures taken of him at this time show a handsome young man of almost classical beauty. The critic David Robinson found in that unsmiling face a strong resemblance to a Jean Cocteau drawing.

Buster and Arbuckle already knew each other's work, for Roscoe had seen "The Three Keatons" perform on many occasions and Buster had followed Arbuckle's film career from the beginning. He described him as his first and last teacher in the art of filmmaking, and for many years thought of him as his best friend. The meeting that day also indirectly led Buster to his first wife, Natalie Talmadge, and to her brother-in-law, Joseph M. Schenck, who was to be the most vital figure in Buster's professional life for the next decade.

Buster may well have felt a sense of surprise at meeting Arbuckle on a New York City street that day, for until then nearly all of Arbuckle's films had been shot entirely on the West Coast. There were some interesting reasons for shifting his productions to the East Side of Manhattan in the spring of 1917. These reasons require a look into what had been happening to the American film industry in the year or so before Buster's meeting with Arbuckle.

In 1917 the motion picture business was growing at a furious rate. The building of new theaters solely devoted to the showing of films gives some idea of how deeply serious the passion for movie-going had become. Starting in April of 1914, with the wildly successful opening in New York City of the Mark Strand Theater, which had been built with a seating capacity of three thousand on two floors, the construction of ever larger and more opulent theaters proceeded all over the country. The number of paid admissions per week soared into the millions. If any single person can be held responsible for this ever-increasing, consuming interest in films it was surely D. W. Griffith, whose final triumph in mastering film narration during his days at Biograph Studios in the period 1908 through 1913 was summed up in his *Birth of a Nation* in 1915. It was not uncommon for people to see this film repeatedly; Buster claimed that he'd seen it at least three times shortly after its opening. Everybody saw it, for it was truly the "coming of age" movie for the entire industry.

Although the film business was booming in 1917, there were serious economic problems accompanying its growth. The cost of making feature films had become extremely high: in 1916 features had reached an average negative cost* of between $10,000 and $30,000. By 1918 they had soared to as much as $30,000 to $75,000, and even as high as $100,000 and $125,000 if the film included stars of the first rank. The greater part of these additional costs in filmmaking arose because of the huge salaries demanded, and obtained, by the actors.

In 1910 Biograph Studios had refused to reveal either the names of the leading players in their productions or their directors. Early foes of the cult of personality, the owners of Biograph were all too well aware of the Pandora's box they would be opening if they were to indicate the names of the actors and actresses on the credits of their films. The public soon began to be curious about their identities, but the Biograph executives remained adamant in their policy of secrecy. It was not long before the stars and the directors, including Griffith, went elsewhere, for this curiosity could not be appeased. The film audience demanded to

*The complete cost of a film through the last day of production, excluding the additional costs of making prints, promotion, etc.

know the real names of "Little Mary" (Pickford) and the Funny (or Nasty) Little Tramp (Chaplin), and they were also avid for information about their private lives. The stars soon became fully conscious of just what their names might be worth in the open marketplace of the film industry. In the eyes of that industry the two worst offenders were Mary Pickford and Charles Spencer Chaplin, both of whose demands for money had no end.

When Mary Pickford began working for Adolph Zukor in 1913 (with her name on the credits) and the Famous Players–Lasky Studios, she was paid what was then considered the astronomical figure of $1,000 a week. By the beginning of 1915 this figure was increased to $2,000 a week, plus one half of the profits of the film. Within another year her mother, Charlotte Pickford, demanded that her daughter's basic salary be increased to $1,000 per day, plus a fifty-fifty share of the profits. She eventually settled with Zukor for a short-term contract at $10,000 a week plus profit sharing, the package amounting to more than a million a year.*

Chaplin was equally successful in raising his original rate of pay from $150 per week, while working for Mack Sennett at the beginning of 1914, to $1,250 per week in January of 1915 when he began working for Essanay Film Corporation. He was then approached by a group proposing a merger of Paramount with some smaller firms and was asked what he wanted in the way of salary. Chaplin's answer was immediate: $10,000 a week. A working agreement was signed, but the Mutual Film Corporation then came through with an offer of $10,000 a week plus a "signing-on" bonus of $150,000, an offer Chaplin accepted without delay.

The news about salaries of this size got around the industry, and all costs involved in the making of films escalated sharply. But the growth boom continued, and as profits soared the battle to obtain the services of the biggest stars began in earnest. There was no letup until someone was found who would pay the price, whatever it might be. Roscoe Arbuckle was one of the superstars

*It should be noted that all dollar figures of this time must be multiplied by at least ten in order to convey any sense of what they might mean today.

Roscoe Arbuckle, London, 1919. *National Film Archive / Stills Library* who, like Pickford and Chaplin, found himself in tremendous demand.

Arbuckle's early films, like Chaplin's, were made for Mack Sennett's firm, the Keystone Film Company, whose pictures were distributed through Mutual. As perhaps the quintessential Keystone Company personality, Arbuckle had appeared in twenty-nine one-reel comedies for Sennett in 1913, mostly roughhouse stuff, and the amazing total of forty-six films, mostly one-reelers, in 1914. That was the year that Arbuckle began directing his own films, many of them co-starring Mabel Normand, with several appearances in them by Chaplin and at least one by Harold Lloyd. Arbuckle turned out another nineteen of these in 1915. His final year with Sennett was 1916, in which he completed nine two-reelers, most of them shot out in Fort Lee, New Jersey, which enjoyed a short-lived success as a filmmaking center. Arbuckle's energies, and his productivity, were astonishing.

By the spring of 1916, Arbuckle's last year with Sennett, his comedies were immensely successful all over the world, and he

was nearly as popular as Chaplin. All his films exploited his physique: he was a jolly fat boy, Dickens's Joe brought to life, a large man who could move with astonishing speed and grace. His actual weight was 260 pounds, although he was always publicized as weighing at least 360. The poundage was definitely not all fat, for Arbuckle was an extraordinarily powerful man, strangely, even eerily, graceful in his movements. Mack Sennett, in his "as told to" autobiography *King of Comedy,* recalls how Arbuckle struck him at their first meeting in 1913:

> A tremendous man skipped up the steps as lightly as Fred Astaire. He was tremendous, obese—just plain fat. "Name's Arbuckle," he said, "Roscoe Arbuckle. Call me Fatty! I'm with a stock company. I'm a funnyman and an acrobat. But I could do good in pictures. Watcha think?" With no warning, he went into a featherlight step, clapped his hands, and did a backward somersault as gracefully as a girl tumbler. . . .

Sennett always had an eye for talent and hired Arbuckle on the spot. Comparatively few of Arbuckle's feature films have survived, and it is now difficult to assess his talents accurately. The films are, on the whole, crude action comedies, centering on the violent and unpredictable buffoonery of the entire cast. Although truly inventive, they are not in a league with Chaplin's or Keaton's own comedies made just a few years later. But they are full of humor, most of which emanates from Arbuckle himself. It is still a great pleasure to see him perform his celebrated feat of producing and lighting a cigarette with only one hand in a matter of split seconds.

Like Buster Keaton, Arbuckle suffered many physical batterings as a child, for his father thrashed him regularly because of his refusal to remain in school. He also went on the stage at a very early age. There was a curious childlike quality to everything about Arbuckle, a sweetness of character, an innocence that later served to make Buster and him very close friends.

Arbuckle came East in the spring of 1916. He realized then, for the first time, that he could easily command a lot more money than the $500 a week that Sennett had been paying him. Thronging crowds followed his every movement in New York and convinced him that he did want a lot more. Arbuckle was also enjoying the comparative freedom in the East to make his pictures the way he wanted them to be made—totally outside Sennett's pervasive influence. At this time he first met Joseph M. Schenck, the man who was to produce all of Buster's films in the 1920s, and Schenck talked Arbuckle into producing his films in New York.

Joe was the older of the two Schenck brothers. His first efforts at film production included a low-cost film starring the ill-fated beauty Evelyn Nesbit Thaw, but by the beginning of 1917 he had become the sole producer of the popular films of his wife, Norma Talmadge. With stars like Pickford, Douglas Fairbanks, and Chaplin tightly under contract elsewhere, it was not surprising that Schenck should have turned his attention to Arbuckle. His offer was in the same range as the deals with Pickford and Chaplin: $365,000 a year plus 25 percent of the profits, amounting to about a million dollars a year. Schenck also created for him the Comique Film Corporation, the firm that in time became Buster's production company for his films. When they concluded the agreement with a final handshake, Arbuckle found a small key in his hand; a Rolls-Royce was the signing-on bonus for the deal.

It is not clear why Schenck wanted Arbuckle to make his pictures in New York. It may be that he preferred the East because he could keep in close touch with the progress of his productions as well as the source of the money he needed to finance his operations. Schenck was clearly going against the tide, for fewer and fewer major production units were to be found in New York. His wife, Norma, the oldest of the three Talmadge girls, may have preferred to remain in New York with the rest of her family. Joe had married Norma in late 1916 while he was still working for Marcus Loew as general manager in charge of booking films and vaudeville acts for the Loew chain of theaters. After his marriage to Norma, Schenck decided that his future lay in producing films, and before quitting his job with Loew's he became her producer. Buster knew little or nothing about what had brought Roscoe Arbuckle to New York on that rainy day in March 1917, but he soon found out.

[3]

Tell me from nothing. Go ahead, what should I
know about comedy?
—Joseph M. Schenck, 1917

Shortly after the breakup of "The Three Keatons" in February
1917, Buster came east in search of a job. When asked forty
years later about his coming to New York, he chose to say absolutely nothing about his family's personal problems:

> In the spring of 1917 vaudeville wasn't quite as good as it used
> to be, and I went to our agent and told him I wanted to get out
> and he said, "All right. Send your folks to your summer home in
> Muskegon, Michigan, and I'll put you at the Shuberts."

Buster's agent was Max Hart, who also represented Arbuckle
at the time and who kept his promises. He got Buster a job almost immediately with the Shubert brothers' *The Passing Show of
1917,* an annual variety show that successfully competed with
Ziegfeld's *Follies.* When they hired Buster, the Shubert brothers
were not at all sure what he would do to earn the $250 per week
they agreed to pay him for his role in the show at the Winter
Garden Theater, but they were confident he would work out
something satisfactory. It would be his first time alone on the
stage, and Buster immediately began seeking out that new something.

At this crucial time he met Arbuckle in the street, accompanied by Lou Anger, a "Dutch" vaudeville comedian he had
known on the road. This was in late March, just a week or so
before rehearsals were due to begin for *The Passing Show.* Buster's account of the meeting indicates that Arbuckle got down to
business immediately:

> I had about ten days to wait for rehearsal when I met Roscoe
> Arbuckle on the street on Broadway and he says: "Have you ever
> been in a motion picture?" And I said, "I've never even been in a

studio." He says, "Well, I'm just startin' here for Joe Schenck. I've left Sennett . . . and Schenck's puttin' me up here to make pictures in the Norma Talmadge Studio." He says, "Come on down and play a scene with me and see how you like it. I'm startin' tomorrow."

Buster did not hesitate and agreed to meet Arbuckle the following day at 318 East 48th Street, a loft building between First and Second avenues, where Schenck had set up production facilities. Buster walked into a new world that day, a world of surprise and discovery. He encountered the passion that was to occupy most of his waking hours for the next twenty years; he fell helplessly in love with every aspect of filmmaking. When Arbuckle suggested that Buster play a scene with him, he meant just that. Within an hour or so after his arrival, having completed a grand tour of the building conducted by Arbuckle himself, Buster found himself performing in the film in progress that day, *The Butcher Boy*, in fact, the first Arbuckle picture under his contract with Schenck.

Buster loved every moment of his day's work and came back for more the following day. When the film was completed a day or so later, Arbuckle asked Buster to continue with him and tried to talk him out of his commitment to *The Passing Show* and the Shuberts. Arbuckle was offering Buster a future in films, and he did not need much persuading to give up vaudeville:

> As long as I had a few days to spare, he carried me all the way through the picture. Then he talked to me like a Dutch uncle. He says, "See if you can get out of the Winter Garden. Stick with me." . . . So that was it.

Buster always found his refusal to honor the contract with the Shuberts extremely funny and was still laughing about it as late as 1958:

> I . . . went back to my agent and says, "I want to get out of the Winter Garden." Says, "Go ahead," he says, "I'll just tear up the contract." I says, "Well, what's Shubert got to say about that?" He says, "We'll tell him afterwards!"

The technical as well as the creative aspects of filmmaking appealed to Buster right from the start. He loved all of it:

> The mechanics of it. The way of working . . . fascinating. One of the first things I did was tear a motion picture camera practically to pieces and found out the lenses and the splicing of film and how to get it on the projector . . . this fascinated me.

In the days and weeks that followed, Buster underwent what amounted to a complete course in filmmaking under Arbuckle's guidance and he was insatiably curious: "The first thing I did was make a friend with the cameraman and get in the cutting room . . . and find out how I get trick photography and things I could do with a camera that I couldn't do on the stage."

In the best days of "The Three Keatons," Joe and Buster had loved the perfect freedom they had to improvise their act, to make it new virtually every night. When Buster began working with Arbuckle, he once again found this kind of freedom; he could do almost anything that came into his head:

> There was no script. We simply talked over what we were goin' to do and we got our ideas and went to work. Arbuckle was his own director and I'd only been with him probably about three pictures when I was his assistant director. . . . Arbuckle would turn you loose. Because he didn't care who got the laughs in his pictures. He wanted 'em in there. . . .

Joe Schenck's policy with Arbuckle was simple: leave him alone and let him make his comedies whatever way he wanted. He disclaimed any knowledge of the art himself. Joe took to Buster immediately, recognizing his extraordinary talents, and Buster, for his part, formed a high regard for Joe as one of the shrewdest men in the film business.

Buster's work that day in *The Butcher Boy* is an impressive first appearance and can still be enjoyed as a curious glimpse into what Buster would later develop so richly on his own. David Robinson in his *Buster Keaton* has noted that from the very first second of Buster's appearance in the film it is quite apparent that his *way* of doing things, the very tempo of his movements, is

Coney Island, 1917. *National Film Archive / Stills Library*

absolutely different from all the other characters'. In contrast to
their frenzy, Buster displays a commandingly austere dignity.

The film takes place in what is supposed to be a turn-of-the-
century general store. The entire cast is seen engaged in performing all sorts of "comic" business. Arbuckle, the butcher boy
of the title, displays his dexterity with knives and sausages and
dons a huge raccoon coat every time he enters the store's cold-
storage area. Buster's entry is quite subdued, and he looks as if
he had stumbled accidentally into this busy store. He is mildly
curious about what he sees before him. After plucking some of
the straws in a broom, "testing it," he notices a barrel filled with
molasses, which appeals to him. He manages to get his foot stuck
in the sticky pool at the bottom of the spigot, then he proceeds to
lick the finger he has applied to his shoe. He attempts to purchase twenty-five cents' worth of the molasses, which entails Arbuckle's filling up a small pail with the stuff. Missing the pail,

Arbuckle pours the molasses into Buster's hat, the quarter is lost at the bottom of the pail, and a mêlée ensues in which a number of people get covered with molasses from head to toe. This sequence was accomplished in a single take, a feat of which Buster was always immensely proud.

Buster didn't object to the comparatively low salary he received from Arbuckle, $40 a week. He thought of himself as an apprentice earning an apprentice's wage. It was a lot less than the $250 he was turning down at the Winter Garden Theater. But the net loss of $210 was no real loss at all, for he had found his life's work.

[4]

I can only reply "humanly and honestly," film folks are just folks! They are recruited from families all over the United States in precisely or approximately the same way my girls were recruited from Brooklyn.

—Margaret L. Talmadge, 1924

Nineteen-year-old Natalie Talmadge was also present that first day at the studio on Forty-eighth Street, working there in a secretarial position for the Schenck companies shooting in the building. Throughout most of her life Natalie, the middle Talmadge sister, lived in the shadow of her two famous sisters, Norma and Constance, believing they were both prettier and far more talented. She made no effort to get into films and chose to attend a business school after completing high school. Photographs of all three Talmadge sisters indicate that tastes have changed: many today might see Natalie as the prettiest of the three, particularly in the pictures of her taken by James Abbe in the early twenties, but in 1917 she was considered the ugly duckling of the family. The Talmadge girls were raised in

Brooklyn by their ambitious mother, Margaret Talmadge, or Peg, as she preferred to be called, a woman totally dedicated to the success of her talented daughters. Their father, Fred Talmadge, was a heavy drinker; he is usually described as shiftless and improvident.

Buster was drawn to Natalie from the first moment he spoke to her. He found the entire Talmadge family fascinating and quickly became acquainted with Natalie's two famous sisters. Norma, the oldest of the three, had begun working in pictures at the age of thirteen in 1910 at the old Vitagraph Studios in Brooklyn. Or she may have been fifteen or seventeen that year, depending on which date was the correct year of her birth. Film stars of the twenties had their birthdates moved forward in time at regular intervals by the studio publicity departments. By 1915 Norma had reportedly appeared in at least 250 short films, but it was Joe Schenck's production of *Panthea* at the beginning of 1917 that established her as a major dramatic personality. From then on, she played suffering women in a dozen feature films that put her on a par with Mary Pickford and Gloria Swanson in the ratings. Norma was the serious one of the three sisters: she was darkly intense about her career and placed it above everything.

The other star of the family, Constance, was an extremely gifted comedienne who bore little resemblance to her two sisters. Taller than Norma and Natalie by several inches, Constance was blond, blue-eyed, and witty and seems to have charmed nearly everyone she ever met. Her first break in films came from D. W. Griffith when he cast her as the tomboyish "Mountain Girl" in his *Intolerance*. From then on she played in dozens of light comedies that were consistently popular all through the twenties. She became one of the golden girls of the decade, and when F. Scott Fitzgerald's daughter, Scottie, was born in 1921, her joyful father sent Zelda's parents a telegram which read: LILLIAN GISH IN MOURNING CONSTANCE TALMADGE IS A BACK NUMBER A SECOND MARY PICKFORD HAS ARRIVED. Fitzgerald claimed that he had been "half in love with her" for years, and he wrote an unproduced screenplay for her on his first visit to Hollywood in 1927. She was also unsuccessfully courted by the most eligible bachelor in Hollywood, Irving Thalberg.

Convinced that she could never compete with her sisters, Natalie adopted a Cinderella stance and tried hard to be a good secretary, only occasionally appearing in bit parts in the films being shot in her brother-in-law's studio. Peg Talmadge, in her incredible ghost-written biography of her three girls, noted that Natalie was not at all like the other two.

> She was the serious type, of studious bent, with contemplative eyes and soft voice. She was an orderly little thing too. She loved to keep her section of the toy closet "just so." . . . We used to call her the "Just-So Girl."

Buster liked the "Just-So Girl" as much as Peg did. Thirty years after his first meeting with Natalie, Buster recalled,

> She was working with the Arbuckle unit as a combination secretary and script girl. She seemed a meek, mild girl who had much warmth and great feminine sweetness. Shortly after our first date I met her mother and the rest of her family. I thought they were all wonderful. They were gay and vital and full of good humor. . . .

By April of 1917 Buster Keaton was a very happy man. That was the month of the release of *The Butcher Boy*, about two weeks after the United States declared war on the Central Powers in Europe. In the very first week of its release there were two hundred theaters running the film, thirty-five of them in New York City. Keaton's initial screen appearance was singled out by the leading trade paper of the day, *Moving Picture World:* "Buster Keaton does some excellent comedy falls . . . a whale of a comedy." This review may not have heralded the arrival of a new cinematic genius, but it did clearly mark Buster as a notable addition to the Arbuckle company. In that same issue of *Moving Picture World*, Paramount Pictures ran a full-page ad for all the Arbuckle films they were currently distributing. It showed his cherubic face perched on the snowy summit of their recently created "mountain" logo.

Arbuckle, Al St. John, Buster at Coney Island, 1917. *Museum of Modern Art / Film Stills Archive*

The public couldn't get enough of these Arbuckle comedies, and Paramount wanted to be able to release at least one a month, which is about the way they were produced for the next year or so. The importance of comedies in the film industry at this time was tremendous, for there were many people who went only to see Chaplin or Arbuckle and were quite often indifferent to the sufferings of Norma Talmadge in the feature film on the bill. The producers of these two-reel comedies knew perfectly well that their comedies were the lure that brought a lot of the ticket buyers into the theaters and felt they were not getting their fair share of the proceeds. Their feelings would pave the way for the great shift from two-reel to feature-length comedies in the early twenties.

The first six of Buster's films with Arbuckle were all produced in and around New York; most of *Coney Island* was actually shot there. Buster smiles in this film, for he had not yet realized that he could make much of his frozen face in pictures. *Coney Island* was the last of the films to be shot in New York; Arbuckle had finally convinced Schenck that there were no real economic advantages to shooting the films in New York. Besides, he preferred the open air of California, as Buster explained. "It was a little too tough to try to do those chases and scenes around the studios in New York. So Arbuckle made Joe Schenck ship us to California after we made about six two-reelers. . . ."

The entire Comique Film Corporation departed for Long Beach, California, in October 1917. The orange groves of Hollywood were only twenty minutes away on the electric trolley line.

3
AIR LIKE WINE

[1]

When I got to Hollywood in 1915, it was like a big circus family. Everybody knew everybody. We knew the stars, we knew the smaller actors, and there wasn't quite the caste system as there is now, because it was too young a business. . . .
—Eddie Sutherland, 1958

We were all young. The air in California was like wine. Our business was also young and growing like nothing else ever seen before.
—Keaton, 1960

When Buster left New York for California, along with Arbuckle and the rest of the Comique Corporation's staff, Natalie Talmadge was with them on their long train trip across the country. She went along to keep a job she had begun to like more and more ever since she had met Buster. Buster's parents had quickly obtained a large apartment for the entire family in Long Beach the moment Buster told them about the move to California. He had never lived all by himself and had no intention of starting now; his family ties were as strong as ever. The apartment was sufficiently large so that Myra and Joe offered Natalie a room, and they gave every sign of liking their pretty young boarder from Brooklyn.

The fact that Natalie lived with Buster's family was not particularly novel, for life in the Hollywood of this time often had a vaudeville or circus touch to it. Since a great many of the people who had flocked to Hollywood came from the stage, it was not at all strange that the old tradition of theatrical boardinghouses should flourish there. Such living arrangements were nothing new to Buster, but some found the communal living patterns repellent. Chaplin asserted his total independence of this way of life by choosing to live at the YMCA in downtown Los Angeles.

British-born Eddie Sutherland, Chaplin's co-director on *A Woman of Paris* and *The Gold Rush,* was fascinated by the essentially "open" or classless society that prevailed in the early years of Hollywood. It was a society in which distinctions of earning power still had little or no impact. As Buster claimed,

> It was a common thing for a prop man in our studio to say "Good morning, Joe," when the boss of the studio came walking past. We didn't need to have to put policemen on the gates to stop each other from going to the other one's studio. I'm liable to go to Mr. Schenck's house and there'd be the assistant cameraman, invited to the party. . . .

The Comique Corporation began work at the Horkheimer brothers' new studios in Long Beach. These facilities, renamed in April 1918 the Comique Film Corporation Studio, were located at Sixth and Alamitos streets in Long Beach. Natalie went on with her duties as the general factotum of the Arbuckle company and was given the title of Secretary & Treasurer. She also continued to appear in bit parts as the occasion arose, among them the firm's first West Coast production, *A Country Hero.* Chaplin turned up one day to give his blessing to the return of Arbuckle to California. Buster and Chaplin had their picture taken together to mark the occasion.

As Eddie Sutherland remarked, picture making was truly a very young business in the Hollywood of 1915; it dated back less than a decade. The very first films were made in 1909 by a struggling British firm called Nestor Films. It was another four years before Cecil B. De Mille began shooting his first feature film there, the famous *Squaw Man,* on December 29, 1913. De Mille's two partners in New York, Jesse Lasky and Samuel Goldwyn, had planned to have *The Squaw Man* shot in Arizona, but a totally unexpected snowstorm there changed everything. De Mille sent Jesse Lasky a wire:

FLAGSTAFF NO GOOD FOR OUR PURPOSE. HAVE PRO-CEEDED TO CALIFORNIA. WANT AUTHORITY TO RENT

BARN IN PLACE CALLED HOLLYWOOD FOR $75 A
MONTH. REGARDS TO SAM. CECIL.

Their answer was a cautious one:

AUTHORIZE YOU TO RENT BARN BUT ON MONTH TO
MONTH BASIS. DON'T MAKE ANY LONG COMMITMENT.
REGARDS. JESSE AND SAM.

Until this time, the area around Hollywood had been largely occupied by small farms and orange groves; it was truly rustic. De
Mille shot his famous first feature film, *The Squaw Man,* in the
barn located at the corner of Selma Avenue and Vine Street,
now in the center of downtown Hollywood. (The barn owner's
sole request when he rented his premises to De Mille was that he
be allowed to go on stabling his carriages and horses there during the shooting.) A year later, at the end of 1914, the same barn
was accommodating five directors, five cameramen, and a stock
company numbering eighty actors, all of them employed by the
Famous Players-Lasky company. That same year Griffith's *The
Birth of a Nation* appeared, the film that quickly made Hollywood
the film center of the world.

Another barn that became famous was the one purchased by
Mack Sennett at Edendale as the home for his Keystone Studios.
Chaplin remembered the place as ". . . a dilapidated affair with
a green fence around it, one hundred and fifty feet square. The
entrance to it was up a garden path through an old bungalow—
the whole place looked just as anomalous as Edendale itself." He
spoke of the farmlike atmosphere of the place.

> The studio had evidently been a farm. Mabel Normand's dressing
> room was situated in an old bungalow and adjoining it was an-
> other room where the ladies of the stock company dressed. Across
> from the bungalow was what had evidently been a barn, the main
> dressing-room for minor members of the stock company and the
> Keystone prize fighters. I was allotted the star dressing-room used
> by Mack Sennett, Ford Sterling and Roscoe Arbuckle. It was an-
> other barn-like structure which might have been the harness-
> room. . . .

The rusticity of Hollywood was short-lived, though, for by 1920 films had become the fifth largest industry in the United States; by the beginning of 1918, 70 percent of all the films made in the world were being produced in southern California, almost all of them in and around Los Angeles. There were facilities for making pictures in Culver City, Burbank, Ventura, Glendale, Malibu, Edendale, and Santa Monica, as well as in Hollywood itself. Cars were still very expensive in 1918, but high-speed electric trolley cars served the whole area. One could whiz at full speed from one town to another in these trolleys, a real delight that everyone looked forward to.

There was sheer excitement at being part of the film life of Hollywood. The region's incomparable climate, the unbelievable freshness of the very air itself, gave one the feeling of living in a paradise on earth. And most important of all, everything was *new;* anything could happen. It was surely a place in which to be young, in which to have a never-ending good time, and that is what Buster and his friends at Comique did.

The whole area of Hollywood was not very far from what had only recently been a wilderness. At about the same time that Buster first arrived in Long Beach, Douglas Fairbanks bought a house that had originally been built as a shooting lodge. It was located in what Chaplin called "the center of what was then the scrubby, barren hills of Beverly. The alkali and the sage brush gave off an odorous, sour tang that made the throat dry and the nostrils smart." Chaplin recalled that

> in those days Beverly Hills looked like an abandoned real estate development. Sidewalks ran along and disappeared into open fields and lamp-posts with white globes adorned empty streets; most of the globes were missing, shot off by passing revellers from roadhouses.

Fairbanks often invited Chaplin to spend weekends with him in this lonely retreat of his in Beverly Hills. Chaplin accepted, but the place made him uneasy: "At night from my bedroom I would listen to the coyotes howling, packs of them invading the garbage cans. Their howls were eerie, like the pealing of little bells."

Buster loved everything about California, as did his parents. Buster's entry into movies had been a blow of sorts to Joe Keaton, for he hated them as much as ever. He began to change his mind about them only when Buster got him some small parts in the first two-reelers the Comique Corporation made in Long Beach. Arbuckle utilized Joe's famous "high kick" to full advantage in *A Country Hero*, in which Joe easily manages to kick the entire cast of the film into a huge trough. He was glad to be back at work again, even for these short spells, telling people who knew his aversion to films that "movie acting is all right if Buster's directing me!"

But at home Joe drank heavily and became violently abusive to the whole family. Louise Keaton feels that Joe had established a policy of "taking it out on Buster," who often became the chief target for his attacks, both verbal and physical. He could never accept the fact that Buster had grown up and was no longer a child; in fact, he continued to call him "Bus," or "Bussy." Buster's younger brother, Harry (Jingles), was never as adroit as Buster in dodging Joe's onslaughts, for Buster was a past master at ducking.

The constant wrangling and bickering between Joe and Myra continued. These endless arguments were especially painful to Buster, who hated and dreaded quarreling of any sort all his life and did anything he could to avoid it. In later years, he faced any oncoming argument by muttering, half-audibly, "No debates, no debates. . . ." In these early growing-up years, Buster acted as a surrogate parent for both Louise and Harry Keaton. He felt responsible for them; their concerns were his concerns. For Louise, then and later, he represented the world outside the family, the world of adventure and fun. In fact, Buster was agonizingly shy and withdrawn. At social gatherings he seemed cut off from most of the people around him, and he was terrified of crowds. He developed a lifelong habit of deciding within seconds if someone was interesting or not. Women always found him attractive but would say to Louise, "He's hard to know, isn't he?"

There was an unworldly quality about Buster that never changed from first to last. He had a strange affinity with animals of all sorts, an eerie ability to get along amazingly well with them. At the zoo, lions and tigers would take one look at Buster's unsmiling face and come to him immediately. Birds would settle on his head and shoulders in complete trust. He often seemed to communicate far more easily with animals than with people. It was not chance that made Buster choose a cow as the true heroine of his *Go West*.

He made people uneasy with his long silences. Much of the time he seemed mysteriously preoccupied or, as Louise said, "You never knew what he was thinking about! Never, never!" A possible explanation is that he was brooding about what he called his "writin'," or the mapping out of his elaborate physical routines for one of his films.

Natalie Talmadge took the fights at Buster's home in her stride, for fierce family spirits were nothing new to her. The members of her own family were all as intensely concerned with themselves as the Keatons. Natalie became attached to Myra at this time, a friendship that lasted for decades. The Keatons thought that, for the first time, Buster had a "serious girl friend," as opposed to some of the other girls he had known. One of the "nonserious" girls was the reputedly lovely Helen McGuinnes of Long Beach. Buster was fond of her for a short time and regarded her as truly beautiful. He felt a kind of awe about female beauty and thought Lillian Russell the most attractive woman he had ever seen. He also regarded Natalie as beautiful, but she disagreed with him about this; she had only to point to what the world thought of her two famous sisters. The strength of Buster's feeling for Natalie at this time is not clear. They saw a lot of each other, but little seems to have come of it all—at least for the time being—for Buster spent a great many of his evenings with Arbuckle and the rest of Arbuckle's many friends in Hollywood.

[2]

Didn't need a script, knew in my mind what we were goin' to do because with our way of workin' there was always the unexpected happened. Well, any time something unexpected happened and we liked it we were liable to spend days shooting in and around that.

—Keaton, 1958

Within the first few months of their arrival in Long Beach the Comique Corporation turned out a series of extraordinarily fine two-reelers in Arbuckle's typically energetic style. Buster's position in the company rose rapidly as his suggestions for these films were eagerly accepted by Arbuckle. His rate of pay increased from $75 per week to $125, and by the time the shooting of *The Bell Boy* and *Moonshine* was finished, he was getting $250. Until Buster's arrival at Comique in New York, Al St. John, Arbuckle's nephew, had been the company's number-two man, but Buster rapidly overtook him not only by virtue of his superior acrobatic skills but also by his amazingly rich contributions to the gags that began appearing in these films.

The basic working schedule for the company involved turning out a new two-reel picture every seven or eight weeks, with little free time between them. Arbuckle and Buster often discovered that a particular theme or locale was not turning out as well as they had hoped, and changes in concept had to be made while the film was still in production. This explains why some of these early films seem to start off by being one kind of picture and quite suddenly change direction in the middle. There was no such thing as a script; three or four sentences scrawled on the back of an envelope was often the closest they ever got to putting it down on paper.

The California landscape was perfect for making pictures. There were incomparable beaches: Malibu and Balboa, Hermosa and Redondo, mile after mile of absolutely lovely oceanfront all up and down the Pacific. One of the minor pleasures of watching many of these early comedies shot outdoors in California at this time is the sheer joy of seeing these completely unspoiled beaches. Many of the early films also used the high bluffs and cliffs along the ocean to achieve breathtaking rescues from cars dangling over their edges.

However, there was a limit to how often the beaches could be used, and Buster and Arbuckle tended to search out less familiar backgrounds. *Moonshine* (1918), for example, was shot at Mad Dog Gulch in San Gabriel Canyon. Arbuckle and Buster play the parts of a U.S. Internal Revenue agent and his loyal assistant, attempting to capture the members of a large, unruly southern family of moonshiners. The film contains at least two notable moments that show the development of Buster as both actor and filmmaker. The first is the unexpected meeting in the woods between Buster and one of the gang, who is armed with a shotgun. Buster raises his arms high in quick surrender but almost immediately begins to scratch himself vigorously under the armpits. He continues the scratching and takes on other simian qualities at an ever-quickening pace: his astonished captor is transfixed with horror. Buster proceeds to become a total ape and scampers away madly for the nearest tall tree, gibbering all the while; he finally disappears at the very top of the tree from the eyes of his speechless enemy. As a piece of pure pantomime it is unsurpassed; it is also an early and extraordinary example of what Buster could do with his body.

In *Moonshine* Buster also revealed his developing talents in the field of trick effects with the camera. At one point he opens the door of a large touring car and graciously allows his staff of fellow Internal Revenue agents to emerge from the car. Fifty-four men issue forth, one right after the other. The sight of this apparently never-ending stream of agents sent the audiences of the day into convulsions. The trick was accomplished by the not overly complicated method of masking one-half of the camera lens, shooting, rewinding the film to the starting point, and then masking the other portion. Buster also utilized a car that had been carefully prepared in advance in order to display the necessary jiggling quality that would convince the audience that what they were seeing was real. Moviegoers of 1918 loved these tricks—all done for the first time—and clamored for more of them, but Buster's interests soon turned to performing genuine feats on screen rather than faking them with the camera.

The almost total freedom granted them by Schenck often involved Arbuckle and Buster in spending large amounts of the company's money. They might demolish half a dozen cars in head-on collisions for a detail lasting only a moment. However, audiences were duly impressed by the extravagance, and the Arbuckle films increased in popularity day by day. His output was dependable, and exhibitors were now advertising his comedies above the feature films on their marquees and in the newspapers.

In Europe, six thousand miles away from the making of these Arbuckle comedies, the war had entered its fifth year. Buster came very close to missing it, for though he had volunteered for service he had been turned down by the army because of his flat feet and lack of a trigger finger, the one that he may have lost in the clothes wringer. He was nevertheless drafted into the army in June 1918. A large farewell banquet for him was given at Seal Beach by Paramount, at which Arbuckle gave a mock-heroic address to the new inductee. The army sent Buster to Camp Kearny near San Diego, where he was assigned to Company E of the 140th Infantry Division, then known as the Sunshine Division. Myra and Joe gave up the apartment in Long Beach and returned to Lake Muskegon, where they stayed until the end of the war. Joe worked briefly in a nearby armaments factory.

Buster always saw his army days as a complete farce, for he was issued military uniforms that never fit him properly, and size-eight shoes for his size-six feet. His military training period was quite brief, and he was shipped east for embarkation to France within a matter of just a few weeks after his induction. His final camp in America before sailing was Camp Upton on Long Island, where he managed to see Natalie, who had also come east to rejoin her family in New York.

The 140th Infantry had little use for Buster in any capacity except to supply entertainment for the troops, a task that occupied nearly all the time he spent in France. He was assigned to a troupe that had been assembled by the division headquarters by simply selecting, as he put it, "twenty-two men who could do something." This group became known as "The Sunshine Players." Their task was to travel all over the area in which the division's troops were billeted and entertain them as best they could. The troops needed all the entertainment they could get, for they were suffering terribly from boredom, especially after the end of hostilities in November 1918. Buster became renowned throughout the entire division for his Snake Dance, as well as for a series of outrageous parodies of some of the more famous performers of the day, whom he had studied from the wings as a child. His performances were always accompanied by a full display of acrobatic skills. A pretty clear idea of what he did for the troops can be seen in his 1930 sound film *Doughboys*, in which he reenacted some of the high spots. Buster always believed that his gifts as an all-around entertainer kept him in France longer than if he had been just another soldier.

Toward the end of his army chores, while still stationed in the Amiens area, Buster became almost totally deaf due to a painfully prolonged ear infection. This plagued him unmercifully, and he later claimed that it had nearly cost him his life one dark and rainy night when he failed to hear a sentry's challenge. Not hearing a thing, Buster proceeded ahead in the downpour and came to a dead stop only when the sentry fired a warning shot in the air.

His pantomimic gifts had practical results when he provided himself and his friends with scarce foodstuffs from the proprietors of the local French stores. He was able to convey the notion of a terrible, anguished hunger with such telling effect that he invariably returned to the billet with wine, bread, and all the other pleasant things they desired so much. But what he really craved was a discharge.

The army did not release him until the end of March in 1919, but this may well have been due to his relatively late induction into the service, rather than to his entertaining abilities. Upon his return to the States he was sent to the Johns Hopkins Hospital in Baltimore for the cursed ear infection and remained there for several days under observation. Nothing significant was found, and the condition quickly cleared up. He began to await his discharge with great anticipation. One day, while out on pass from the hospital, he took a long walk around Baltimore and found himself directly in front of Keith's Theater, in which he had played many times with his family. He went in on impulse and was soon reunited with the house manager, the theater crew, and all the performers, who gave him a rousing backstage welcome. He was really at home again in his own world.

The army authorities had mistakenly assumed that Buster's home was in Lake Muskegon in Michigan, and he was sent to Camp Custer for his discharge. It was not until the very end of April 1919 that he finally returned to work in California, where he found the Arbuckle Company in new quarters on Allesandro Street, adjacent to the Mack Sennett studios in Edendale. He was returning to his old pre-army salary of $250 per week, although he claimed on many occasions that he had been offered $1,000 a week by both William Fox and Jack Warner. His appearances in the last films he had made in the spring of 1918 had made him sufficiently well known to justify such demands for his services. But money never made the slightest difference in what Buster wanted to do, and now he wanted to remain with the two men who had introduced him to filmmaking: Arbuckle and Schenck.

Buster's loyalty to his two friends, as well as theirs to him, was unshakable. To convey his feelings about Joe Schenck at this time in his life, Buster liked to tell about a visit to Schenck's office in New York, just prior to his discharge from the army. He described Schenck's concern at seeing a somewhat dilapidated and undernourished-looking Buster Keaton standing before him. Without any questions Schenck opened his wallet and gave Buster its entire contents: a man in need was a man in need. As for Roscoe Arbuckle, Buster was later to show his gratitude to his teacher in a manner that neither of the two friends could have predicted in 1919.

---
[3]

> An audience will laugh at things happening to
> you, and they certainly wouldn't laugh if it hap-
> pened to them.
>
> —Keaton, 1960

For a time Buster roomed at the home of Viola Dana and her
sister, Shirley Mason, also an actress; both girls had been acting
in films since their early teens in Brooklyn. The sisters had been
born there with the name of Flugrath and had changed it immediately upon their arrival in Hollywood. Their mother, Mrs. Flugrath, ran a theatrical-style boardinghouse. Viola was starring in
comic roles at Metro Pictures, and a number of publicity pictures
of Viola and Buster appeared in the fan magazines of the time,
with accompanying hints that they were more than just good
friends. Buster dutifully took her out, but he was much more interested in Alice Lake, an extremely pretty young actress who
had appeared with him in a number of the Arbuckle shorts. He
had more sexual interest in Alice than in Viola, or so he told his
agent, Ben Pearson. For at least a year, Alice and Viola were the
two women in his life. Natalie Talmadge was still in New York,
working with her two sisters.

It was as if he had never been away; Buster started work right
away in the films *Back Stage* and *The Hayseed,* very much the same
kind of films he had been making before he left for France.
About this time Buster and Arbuckle began to create reputations
for themselves as practical jokers. They had developed a little
circle of actor friends who, like them, delighted in concocting
these jokes, among them John Gilbert, Norman Kerry, and Lew
Cody. A favorite meeting place for the group was the Watts Tav-
ern in Vernon, one of the best-known drinking places of the entire era. It was only now that Buster began to drink at all, for it is
quite likely that Joe's example had served as a dreadful warning
to avoid booze. Bill Cox, one of Keaton's closest friends of his
last years, claims that Buster had once told him that he had not

had anything to drink until he was well into his mid-twenties. But Arbuckle and his friends were all heavy drinkers, most of them dying of it eventually; and if Buster wanted to belong to the group, he was bound to have to overcome any qualms he might have felt.

Together, the group began to concoct some elaborate schemes. Perhaps the most famous was the joke they played on Arbuckle's new employer after 1919, the diminutive Adolph Zukor of Paramount. Zukor was invited to an intimate supper party given by Arbuckle for some of his close friends in Hollywood. The place was Arbuckle's awesomely expensive house, the former residence of Miss Theda Bara. In order for the complex plot to work, all of Arbuckle's guests had to be perfectly aware of what was scheduled to happen that evening. Among the guests were four young ladies then appearing in films: Anna Q. Nilsson, Bebe Daniels, and Buster's friends Alice Lake and Viola Dana. No one seems to remember the names of the male guests, with the exception of Sid Grauman, the founder of the Chinese Theater on Hollywood Boulevard that bore his name for many years.

Buster's part in the joke required him to pose for the entire evening as an incredibly inept and clumsy butler who wreaks havoc on both the guests and their dinner. Since Buster had yet to appear in a feature-length film, it was thought that Zukor would not recognize him, but to make sure, the lights were dimmed slightly. Arbuckle's part in the farce was to appear as the stunned and outraged host who screams aloud about the cursed stupidity of a butler who starts the evening off by serving the shrimp hors d'oeuvres to the men before the women: "You stupid numbskull, don't you *know* better than to serve the men first?" Writhing with acute chagrin, Buster abruptly removed the troublesome shrimps, some visibly half-eaten, from the men and gave them to the women.

There was a serious problem with the soup. After carefully laying out the soup plates, Buster suddenly disappeared into the kitchen. A short silence was followed by the unmistakable sound of a hideous crash, itself followed by lesser bangings and thuds: Buster had actually thrown everything in sight into the kitchen sink. He then doused himself liberally with water and returned to the dining table, unmistakably soaked. He began to remove the soup plates without a word of explanation. Zukor began to wonder what he'd gotten himself into. The other guests continued to munch gloomily on the last of the shrimp, listening to Roscoe denouncing his idiot of a butler, and debating with increasing fury the whole problem of what to do about servants in Los Angeles. He began to talk about selling his new house, leaving Los Angeles, and abandoning the picture business forever—all, of course, for the benefit of Zukor, who swallowed every word of it. The personal happiness of his stars meant a lot to Zukor, and here, obviously, was one on the brink of leaving him. Arbuckle continued his ranting and raving, while an increasingly worried Zukor picked at the last of the hors d'oeuvres.

The beautiful Miss Daniels, sitting to Arbuckle's right, asked Buster if she might have some of the fresh ice water he had suddenly appeared with at her side. As if transfixed by Circe herself, Buster stared down helplessly into her eyes while he slowly poured the entire contents of the pitcher into Arbuckle's lap. Screaming "Idiot, Idiot, *Idiot!*" Arbuckle seized Buster around the neck and attempted to drag him out of sight into the kitchen. He was forcibly restrained by the men at the table, and a cringing Buster retreated into the kitchen. Conversation was uneasily resumed, and the long wait for the food continued, with Zukor totally shaken by the way the evening was turning out.

It was at last time for the turkey. This final item was planned with the assistance of Arbuckle's physical trainer, who was also in on the joke. Buster emerged triumphantly from the swinging doors of the kitchen bearing a twenty-four-pound turkey on a huge silver platter. As he took his first step into the dining room, he dropped his service napkin. He bent over to retrieve it while maintaining a steady grasp on the platter. At the instant he started to bend over, the trainer, right on cue, pushed open the swinging doors of the kitchen, knocking Buster and the turkey to the floor. There then followed a curious kind of ballet, with Buster and the trainer attempting to get the slippery turkey back on the platter. This took some time because of the great ease with which it always seemed to elude their grasp, slipping out of their hands and back on the floor again. Arbuckle and his guests watched all this in a sort of hushed bemusement, as if they were witnessing a first-rate pantomime performance, save for Zukor, who had begun to doubt his senses.

After a mighty effort, the turkey was finally restored to its platter. A gravy-bespattered Buster began to clean up the battered bird with the now filthy napkin that had been the turkey's downfall. This sight was apparently too much for Arbuckle. As if with the strength of a madman, he threw off the arms of those who sought to restrain him and managed to drag his craven servant out of sight into the kitchen. Zukor and the guests then heard what sounded like screams for mercy. After a series of sundry crashes and screams, the guests were entertained by the sight of Arbuckle chasing Buster around and around the house. Upon his return, Arbuckle finally permitted himself to be calmed down and assured the group that a "standby" turkey was already in the oven and that the rest of dinner would be served by the cook in an hour or so.

After circling the block a few times, Buster reentered the house by the back door and calmly changed his clothes in one of Arbuckle's many upstairs bedrooms. Two hours later, after the serving of the second turkey, Buster picked up the phone to call his host downstairs. He graciously accepted the impromptu invitation to come right over for dessert and coffee. He dutifully appeared at the front door and was soon introduced to Zukor, who clearly did not recognize him as the curious butler who had vanished in the night. Only when Sid Grauman pointedly observed Buster's strange resemblance to the departed one did Zukor catch on to what had been arranged for him that night.

Whether true or not, this story contains a great deal that is at the very heart of what continues to fascinate us about Hollywood's past. It demonstrates that Hollywood was a place where a singular form of innocence prevailed. The air was indeed like wine in 1919 when Arbuckle and Buster could devote such loving care to the preparation of Zukor's supreme supper party.

These pranks gradually became a tradition. On another famous occasion, Sid Grauman made front-page headlines by managing to steal the legendary "million-dollar rug"—so named because of all the great financial wheelings and dealings that had taken place among the moguls standing upon it—from the lobby of the Ambassador Hotel in downtown Los Angeles in broad daylight. Grauman had his thieves pose as men from a rug-cleaning firm. Weeks later, he invited the hotel manager to attend one of his shows at his luxurious new theater. The show included live vaudeville acts, and the first thing the manager saw on Grauman's lavish stage was all fifty feet of his immense Oriental rug covered with swirling dancers. Grauman returned the rug to the hotel, and the feat was justly celebrated. For a while, anyway, he acquired the title of chief Hollywood prankster.

Buster and Roscoe (as Keaton always called him) usually aimed their sights high in their practical joking. Not long after the Zukor dinner it was the turn of Marcus Loew, the founder of what became MGM. As Buster told the story, it involved his pretending to be Roscoe's goggled and mustached chauffeur. The occasion for the deception arose when Loew, on one of his rare visits to Hollywood from New York, ran into Arbuckle as he was leaving Metro. Arbuckle offered him a ride back to his hotel in Los Angeles. Loew accepted gladly, and with Buster at the wheel, the car took off on an incredibly high-speed tour of the entire area around Hollywood. The main point of the exercise was for Buster to stall the car at the exact point on the trolley tracks where it could safely remain while the express trolleys whizzed by it on both sides.

The pranksters had carefully checked out the length of Arbuckle's car and knew to an inch exactly where it could be stalled—for maximum safety and terror. Loew was even more frightened of getting out of the car than of staying in it as the trolleys screamed past. Arbuckle occupied the time by abusing his stupid lout of a chauffeur for choosing *this place* of all places to stall the car. Eventually, Buster started it up again and drove to Los Angeles by every crooked, bumpy road he could find, at a full sixty miles per hour. Loew was completely shaken up by the mad drive, and Arbuckle kept offering his profuse apologies for his idiot of a chauffeur. When they finally got to his hotel, Loew and Arbuckle relaxed a bit over a drink in Loew's room. There was a knock at the door, and Buster, minus goggles and mustache, entered the room with a broad, knowing smile.

Still another target of a Keaton-Arbuckle hoax was the famous actress Miss Pauline Frederick. As was common practice among many of the newly arrived, prosperous inhabitants of Beverly Hills, Miss Frederick had invested heavily in a huge, showpiece lawn in front of her mansion. Arbuckle and Buster decided to pay the lawn their proper respects. Disguised in the uniforms of the Los Angeles Power and Light Company, they drove up at dawn in an old pickup truck with their friend Lew Cody. They emerged carrying picks, shovels, and all sorts of surveying instruments, and set up their equipment in a coolly professional manner.

The surprised servants came rushing out of the house to be told that there was a serious gas leak from the main that ran directly under the beautiful lawn. It must be checked at all costs. At this point, Arbuckle and Keaton went through the ritual performance of spitting on their hands and appeared to be ready for a day of steady digging. The heated protests of the servants counted as nothing, for Cody told them with considerable dignity that the entire neighborhood was in grave danger: "Would you risk the public safety for a greensward?" Miss Frederick, finally roused from her slumbers by the screaming on the lawn, came on down to see what could be causing it. She recognized the famous trio immediately, bringing the game to a pleasant end. After only a few of these pranks, Buster acquired a notoriety for them, which may have been one of the reasons why his future mother-in-law, Peg Talmadge, did not trust him very much.

The artfully elaborate and painstaking care that Arbuckle and Keaton took in preparing their hoaxes indicates that while this may have been play, a kind of counterfeiting, it was also work as well. The same energies that hatched these serpentine plots made the films; work *was* play, as it was never to be again.

In December 1919 the collaboration of Arbuckle and Buster was brought to a sudden and unexpected end. Joe Schenck and Adolph Zukor had finally made up their minds about something, and this decision was to change a lot in Buster's life.

Joseph M. Schenck in the mid-twenties. *Museum of Modern Art / Film Stills Archive*

4
A WEDDING AND A TRAGEDY

[1]

Schenck . . . looked for all the world like a Buddha
with a perpetual hangover. But his looks were deceptive. . . .
———Frank Capra, 1970

Mr. Schenck . . . is the fine old type referred to as
"a sturdy oak." . . . Norma always calls him Daddy.
———Peg Talmadge, 1924

Buster had found a second father in Joe Schenck, a man only
eight years his senior but one whom he could trust both in family
affairs and in the handling of his career. In many ways, his relationship with Joe Schenck was the most important one in his
whole life. Buster desperately needed someone like Joe, for he
found in him what both he and his real father totally lacked: a
solid business sense. Both of Buster's great rivals, Chaplin and
Lloyd, were born businessmen, but Buster was always totally in-
capable of handling his own finances. As an adult, Buster saw
much of the world the way a child might; the direct unabashed
vision of his best films is the vision of a marvelous child. He had
a unique creative sensibility and a personality that went along
with it. This involved a total dependence upon a father figure
like Joe Schenck and a wife like Natalie Talmadge.

The main facts of Joe Schenck's career are well known, but his
private life has remained obscure. Film historians have tended to
denigrate him as a dull, profit-seeking figure, a shadow in the
background of the exciting people he had working for him at
one time or another: Gloria Swanson, the Talmadge sisters,
D. W. Griffith, Rudolph Valentino, Darryl F. Zanuck, John Ford,

and Marilyn Monroe. In Ken Russell's *Valentino* he is simply an anti-Semitic caricature. Yet "Honest Joe," as Chaplin called him, had a livelier side: Adolph Zukor always believed that it was Joe Schenck who helped Sid Grauman steal that famous rug from the lobby of the Ambassador Hotel, and Louise Brooks vividly recalls him dancing a sensational rhumba with Sonja Henie, his ice-skating star, at Arrowhead at the end of the thirties.

Unlike all the other major film producers, Joe Schenck was relatively tall and was nearly always in the company of beautiful women. He appreciated jokes and liked telling them: he told newspaper reporters in 1934 that his marriage of eighteen years to Norma Talmadge had failed because he hadn't sent her any flowers for a long time. He had a ruling passion for blue and gray; all his private offices from the beginning to the end were decorated in these colors. He was a yachtsman, and it was on his boat that Chaplin first met Paulette Goddard. In 1941 Schenck elected to stand trial as the bagman on behalf of the entire film industry during the William Bioff labor extortion scandal. Schenck served a jail sentence of four months and five days until he was pardoned by Harry Truman in 1946. At the beginning of the fifties he advised Marilyn Monroe, with some success, on how to advance her career at Twentieth Century–Fox. For many years he was the most trusted man in Hollywood.

Born in the Volga town of Rybinsk in czarist Russia in 1887, Joseph Schenck came to the Lower East Side of New York as a child of six with his brother Nicholas and his sister Annie. The two Schenck brothers, William Fox, Adolph Zukor, and Samuel Goldwyn were all Jewish immigrants who rose from poverty to riches by an immense capacity for hard work and a genius for long-term planning. In their early days in New York Joe Schenck was at first a pharmacist, Zukor a furrier, and Goldwyn a glove salesman. Traditionally lumped together as "the Moguls," these five men were often identified by their enemies as "the pants pressers" or "the pushcart operators"; all of them spoke with strong accents, which they never lost in all their years in America. They were gamblers, often carrying their passion for speculation into their work as film producers. These five men were vital to the creation of the American film industry.

The turning point in the lives of the Schenck brothers was the start of their relationship with Marcus Loew in 1907. Until then, the two brothers had confined their interest in entertainment to operating two amusement parks in the New York City area, Paradise Park in upper Washington Heights and a much more famous one, Palisades Park in New Jersey, which they continued to run successfully until the mid-thirties. Loew had achieved great success in running a chain of vaudeville theaters in and around the city, and he hired Nicholas to manage these theaters for him while Joe was given the job of hiring the talent and, somewhat later, of booking the films that had suddenly loomed so large on the entertainment horizon. It was through this type of work that Joe first met Norma Talmadge, whose film career led him into producing his first really successful pictures.

Schenck's decision of 1919, the one that was to mean so much to Buster, was when he elected to sell or really rent Arbuckle's services to Adolph Zukor of Paramount so that Arbuckle could begin making expensive feature films technically superior to those turned out by Comique. Schenck had actually farmed Arbuckle out to Paramount, so that both the Comique Corporation and Arbuckle profited handsomely from the deal. In his recent biography of Arbuckle, David Yallop claims that Paramount agreed to pay Arbuckle the sum of $3 million spread over a three-year period. This is, however, a considerably inflated figure, even by 1920 standards. The deal that Schenck actually set up was one in which Arbuckle was paid by both Comique and Paramount at the same time. His contract with Schenck guaranteed him $1,500 a week, and the Paramount arrangement gave him an additional $3,000 a week. The combined earnings from these two contracts was just under a quarter of a million a year, and he was also to receive 25 percent of Comique's profits.

With the departure of Arbuckle from Comique it was a foregone conclusion that Joe Schenck would offer Buster the chance to replace him as the chief star and creative force of the company. There were many advantages for Buster, including a salary increase and a quarter of the firm's profits. It was the chance of his life.

And the minute Schenck did that, he turned the company over to me and then went and bought me a studio. Fact, he bought me Chaplin's old studio, and named it the Keaton Studio. And all he did as producer, he says, "You're to make eight two-reelers a year we're going to release through the new outfit that Marcus Loew has just bought, called Metro.

The new Comique was installed at 1066 Lillian Way in Hollywood, and there Buster was free to do pretty much as he liked. "So Schenck never knew when I was shooting, or what I was shooting. I just set out to make those eight pictures a year. Well, I did that. . . ."

He made eight masterpieces, but before he could begin them, Schenck made a separate deal for Buster to appear as Bertie the Lamb, the leading role in the film that was released at the end of 1920 as *The Saphead*. This was based on a new version of an old play by Bronson Howard called "The Henrietta," which had starred Douglas Fairbanks in a 1913 Broadway revival. Fairbanks's own film commitments made it impossible for him to appear in the film, and after Metro had bought the play, Fairbanks had a discussion with its producer, John Golden. This is how Buster reports it:

> "Metro's going to make 'The Henrietta,' and William H. Crane's going to play his own part."
> He said, "Who's going to play my part?"
> "We don't know."
> Fairbanks said, "I know who to get."
> "Who?"
> "Keaton."
> He said, "Well, after all, Keaton's never had anything on but misfit clothes and slap shoes all his life, but dress him up and he'll play Bertie the Lamb for you."
> So I did.

The Saphead has only recently reemerged for public viewing; for decades it was thought to be lost. It is an intriguing film on several counts, for besides being the very first of Buster's feature films, it marks the birth in film of the languid, spoiled, and wealthy character that Buster played in a number of his own feature films in the twenties, among them Rollo Treadway in *The*

Navigator and Alfred Butler in *Battling Butler*. Rollo, Alfred, and Bertie all start off as apparent dimwits and then undergo that total transformation of character that is a basic feature of all of Buster's major films.

In *The Saphead*, directed by Herbert Blache, Buster is cast as a rich, completely vapid young man who is thought to be the idiot of the family. His father is known as the "Wolf of Wall Street," while Bertie, unable to cope with anything, is called "the Lamb." The crux of the film is when Bertie proves that he's not a weakling at all by saving his father's brokerage interests on the very floor of the Stock Exchange. Buster's appearance in this sequence, dressed in formal morning coat, as he attempts to buy up all the available shares in the Henrietta gold mine, is remarkable. He has only one thing to "say"—the constantly repeated phrase *"I'll take it! I'll take it!"* as he is carried around the floor of the Stock Exchange by his friends.

The Saphead demonstrated that Keaton was without doubt a comic actor of considerable charm, but the film itself is merely a showcase for these acting talents: it does not approach the quality of the spectacular two-reel films that he began to make in the summer of 1920.

The Saphead, 1920. *National Film Archive / Stills Library*

[2]

At this point it is necessary that you see a bullfight. . . . There are two sorts of guide books; those that are read before and those that are to be read after and the ones that are to be read after the fact are bound to be incomprehensible to a certain extent before; if the fact is of enough importance in itself. So with any book on mountain ski-ing, sexual intercourse, wing shooting, or any other thing which it is impossible to make come true on paper, or at least impossible to attempt to make more than one version of at a time on paper, it being always an individual experience, there comes a place in the guide book where you must say do not come back until you have ski-ed, had sexual intercourse, shot quail or grouse, or been to the bullfight so that you will know what we are talking about.

—Ernest Hemingway,
Death in the Afternoon

Keaton's films are perhaps the most carefully constructed in the history of the industry. They are also in many ways among the most deeply personal of all films, reflecting a consistent view of the world through the unwavering eyes of a unique sensibility. The details have been worked out with an astonishing imaginative power and a logical precision that is unsurpassed. The films can be seen again and again, with each viewing offering new delights. It is sometimes hard to reconcile their essentially ordered nature with the spontaneity with which they were made.

Buster started off with a complete triumph in his first two-reeler, *One Week*, released by Metro in September 1920. He had made one earlier film, *The High Sign*, but chose to hold back its release for a full year because *One Week* was so much better. It was described by a trade journal as "likely to produce the laugh heard round the world."

In *One Week* Buster attempts to assemble the elements of a "you-too-can-build-your-own-house" package he has been given as a wedding present. A great deal of the film depicts the actual construction of the monstrous house that Buster laboriously puts together by carefully following the plans, totally unaware that the numbers of the various parts have been switched by his arch-enemy, the former suitor of the girl he has married. When completed, the door of the house is on the second floor. The house is a surrealistic wonder, and it was the presence of such elements in Keaton's films that was responsible for the early and enthusiastic European interest in his work from Luis Buñuel, Garcia Lorca, and Samuel Beckett.

After an exciting night of gala housewarming, which takes place in a howling storm that causes the new house to revolve like a carousel, Buster discovers that he has built it on the wrong building lot. After superhuman efforts, he and his bride finally manage to tow the house by car across town toward the correct location. En route, they get it stuck on a railway track, and see to their horror that a fast express is approaching. The young couple close their eyes to avoid witnessing the destruction of the new home. A sudden and miraculous surprise: the approaching train was actually on a parallel track. They have been spared, and their house is safe. Fierce, uncontainable joy. Then, with no warning whatever this time, another and completely unexpected train crashes into the house, reducing it to kindling wood.

One Week produced considerable excitement on its release; one trade paper called it the "comedy sensation of the year." It can be taken as a fair example of the work Buster turned out during the following three years. The best of these short films have a terrible and inexorable logic to them, especially in the way Buster contends with the potentially hostile objects all around us: boats, houses, trains, and women. The films are certainly more than just the simple two-reel comedies they purport to be. James Agee once said about Harold Lloyd's films, "If great comedy must involve something beyond laughter, Lloyd was not a great comedian." This may or may not be true, but a great many of Buster's best films do indeed involve a lot beyond laughter, often creating what Agee called "a disturbing tension and grandeur to the foolishness, for those who sensed it, there was in his comedy, a freezing whisper not of pathos but of melancholia."

All eight of Buster's two-reelers for release by Metro bear the names of Keaton and Eddie Cline as the co-directors. What Cline contributed to these films is a question that comes up with regard not only to Cline but to all those other directors whose names appeared in the credits of Keaton's films of the twenties. The answer is, not very much, although Cline's later screen credits might make one hesitate, for he directed *Million Dollar Legs* in 1932 and the last three of W. C. Fields's films in the early forties. Cline had worked with Mack Sennett from about 1912 onward and was probably the man who introduced bathing beauties into the Sennett films. (This came about when the American government asked the film industry for help in persuading people to cut down their consumption of meat in favor of fish during the war. Having no idea of what he could possibly do to get this message across, Cline took his entire company to the beach one day, procured suits for the girls, and started shooting. The consumption of meat did not go down, but the bathing beauties became a tradition in Sennett's films.)

Cline's middle name was Francis, and Buster and he regularly addressed each other in mock formality as Master Francis. Buster found him easy to get along with, but Eddie Sutherland found him much too easy-going to be a comedy director.

> Eddie never had a drink in his life. . . . He was too kind-hearted to be a great man. He wouldn't fight with people, he'd agree with them, and you can't be a comedy director, or really a director, without a little ferocity. . . .

Buster had no appetite for ferocity at any time in his life; Cline was the perfect director for him.

The collaboration of Buster and Cline produced a total of sixteen two-reel pictures between the end of 1920 and the spring of 1923. There were an additional three films, two of them directed by Mal St. Clair and one by Buster alone; the last eleven films were all released by Associated–First National, with whom Joe Schenck had arranged even better rental terms than he had with Metro. The two St. Clair films bear no stylistic differences from those of Cline, which indicates that both directors functioned as Buster's assistants and were easily interchangeable.

Trade ad for *The Scarecrow. New York Public Library*

Trade ad for *Neighbors. New York Public Library*

The first film for First National, *The Playhouse,* is one of the strangest of Buster's short films. It features a traditional minstrel show in which he plays not only all the minstrels but the entire theater staff and the audience as well. While he was shooting this obliquely autobiographical film, he may have remembered a jingle from his childhood: *"Little Buster Keaton is a whole show within himself; he's a regular theater."* It is a trick film in that the illusion of an endless series of Keatons is achieved by a wide variety of multiple-exposure techniques. There was a decisive reason for making the film at this time, for he had broken his leg while shooting *The Electric House.* In *The Playhouse* he could dispense with the exhibition of his athletic prowess.

It is a superbly rich film, startling in its free use of images and in its bizarre, dreamlike evocation of the terrors of childhood. There is one particularly curious scene, which takes place in a shabby hotel bedroom reminiscent of Buster's days in vaudeville. Buster is roughly awakened by a huge, brutal-looking "detective." As Buster starts to leave the bedroom, pushed and shoved toward the door by the detective, it suddenly becomes apparent that there *is* no bedroom, that these walls are simply flats, and that Buster is now stumbling around backstage in a theater. From sleep he has reverted to his real world—the theater.

Natalie Talmadge Keaton, 1924. *National Film Archive / Stills Library*

Buster, Myra, and Joe in Hollywood, 1922. *Margaret Herrick Library of the Academy of Motion Picture Arts and Sciences*

[3]

Natalie's letters and telegrams from Buster became more and more frequent. . . . He wired Natalie that he would meet her in New York and that she
had better be prepared to give an answer to an important question! He then hied himself straightaway
for the east. . . . Constance teasingly persisted in
declaring it, "a mail-order romance. . . ."
—Peg Talmadge, 1924

The engagement of Natalie Talmadge and Buster Keaton was
announced in the pages of *Variety* in February 1921. There
were several unusual items in the story. There was to be no engagement ring; no letters had passed between the engaged couple for some time; they had not actually seen each other for two
years. On the twenty-fifth of March, *Variety* ran a story with this
headline: TALMADGE ENGAGEMENT BROKEN. Besides
demonstrating that the name Talmadge was still of greater interest than Keaton, the story also hints at some mystery underlying
the broken engagement, which has never been explained.

Peg Talmadge, the mother of the Talmadge girls, is generally thought to be the main source of many of Lorelei Lee's witty remarks about men and money in her friend Anita Loos's *Gentlemen Prefer Blondes*. Anxious as she was for her daughters' welfare, she was very conscious that while both Norma and Constance had made successful marriages by 1921, Natalie was still without a suitable husband. There is a fairy-tale quality to much in Peg's ghostwritten story of her daughters' drive to fame and success, *The Talmadge Sisters*. She displays an uncertain tone about the suitability of Buster for her middle daughter, whom she liked to call her "home girl": "He looks at strangers out of his straight brown eyes in an almost disconcerting fashion." She went on to observe, somewhat primly, that Buster was not really a great reader.

In spite of her disclaimer, several members of Buster's family, as well as some of his best friends, are convinced that it was Peg, possibly in league with Schenck, who arranged the marriage. The love letters mentioned above were probably the products of her imagination. Buster was good looking, talented, and clearly on the way up in the movies. Natalie was not really an ugly duckling, but she lacked the glow and sparkle of her two talented sisters: why shouldn't their Just-So girl marry Buster Keaton? Buster usually did what he was asked to do, and he certainly liked Natalie. He even claimed later that he loved her. As for Natalie, it is difficult to tell how she felt about Buster, for she was as private as he was, revealing little about herself at any time and always looking to her mother and sisters for guidance.

The on-and-off engagement was definitely on by April, and Natalie and Buster were married on the thirty-first of May 1921 at the Schencks' country home in Bayside, Long Island. The bridesmaid was Anita Loos and the best man Ward Crane, who later played the part of the villain in *Sherlock, Jr.* Constance was the maid of honor. It was a festive occasion with roses everywhere. Peg was deeply moved by the loss of her daughter: "But in the main, it was a very happy event. . . . with the sunshine streaming down on bright faces and bright flowers, and she departed amidst a perfect bombardment of rice, old shoes, kisses, hugs, admonitions, and congratulations."

The wedding of Natalie and Buster, Bayside, New York, 1921. *National Film Archive / Stills Library*

There was no honeymoon, for Buster had to finish a picture back in California, so he and Natalie set out at once for the West Coast. Peg claims they traveled across the country in a car supplied by Joe Schenck, but Buster remembered it clearly as a train trip that took five days. Upon their arrival in Los Angeles a "modest house" was obtained, and Buster resumed work on *The Playhouse.*

Natalie soon discovered that the man she had married was an extremely dependent person, requiring someone to help him get places on time and even to get dressed. Buster's dependence had started with Myra's devoted attention to these matters, and it never left him. In his richer years he used the services of his manservant, Caruthers, for these functions.

About this time Buster became friendly with William Collier, Jr., known professionally as Buster Collier. He joined Keaton's closest circle of friends, which now included Lex Neal, an old friend from his boyhood at Lake Muskegon, as well as Norman Kerry, Arbuckle, and Lew Cody. Collier, the son of the famous stage actor William Collier, was nearly ten years younger than Buster and just beginning his own screen career. He recalls some of the stranger aspects of Buster's marriage by contrasting the vibrant Buster with the completely passive Natalie, quietly doing her needlepoint work day after day and nearly every evening, "a real quiet girl." She did like to go on frequent shopping expeditions, often going out to buy brand-new facial compacts for all the female visitors back at the house. She totally lacked her two sisters' great social gifts, especially Constance's electric warmth that charmed nearly everyone; she had none of Norma's strong sensuality. There were some publicity shots taken of Buster and

Buster and Natalie, 1922. *National Film Archive / Stills Library*

Natalie shortly after the marriage, showing Natalie valiantly trying to act the part of Buster's bright-eyed, fun-loving wife, but
they have a pathetic, unconvincing air about them. She simply
lacked the energy to keep up with him.

The Buster Keaton that Collier remembers best from the early
twenties onward was a man in the joyful possession of a superb
body, a first-rate athlete, intensely physical and energetic. He
didn't seem to need sleep then, and he was always ready for
something new, something different. Louise Brooks, who was
briefly married to Eddie Sutherland, also knew the Keatons in
the late twenties. She is the legendary American actress from
Kansas who went to Berlin in 1928 to star in the G. W. Pabst
films *Pandora's Box* and *Diary of a Lost Girl*. Both she and Anita
Loos described Natalie as dull and unsociable and Buster as a man
with a huge appetite for life. He loved to hunt and fish, and he
loved making films more than anything else in the world.

Buster and Natalie, 1922. *National Film Archive / Stills Library*

Louise Brooks and Eddie Sutherland at the time of their marriage in 1926. *Museum of Modern Art / Film Stills Archive*

At the beginning of his marriage to Natalie there seemed to be no complaints on Buster's part as to the sexual side of their new life together. In spite of his shyness he had always had an active sex life. His casual affairs had started when he was a teen-ager, in the later days of "The Three Keatons." There were many willing girls in the backstage world of vaudeville, and Buster found them agreeable and enthusiastic. He was unsure of himself only if there was a doubt in his mind about the girl's feeling for him; once convinced that she liked him, all went well. Interestingly, he was especially attracted to girls who appeared in "sister acts" and enjoyed bestowing his attentions on both sisters at the same time. Joe Keaton had noticed this predilection, and the moment a sister act was announced as appearing on the bill with them, he would embark upon some heavy jokes about the depraved taste of his older son.

Baseball was another of Buster's major passions. Harold Goodwin, the actor who appears as the villain in both *College* and *The Cameraman*, a close friend of Keaton's for forty years, recalls that Buster gave a sort of exam for actors applying for work at the Keaton Studio. The exam consisted of only two questions: "Can you act?" and "Can you play baseball?" The passing score for a job was 50 percent, and nearly everyone passed. The Keaton Production Company, Inc., was in fact an ever-ready baseball team, prepared to start a game on a moment's notice. That moment would often come whenever a production problem arose that seemed to defy immediate solution. Buster would officially declare that a game was in order. If someone had an inspiration halfway through it the shooting would resume.

Buster took enormous trouble with his productions to make sure that nothing was ever faked if it was possible to do it "straight." This would often involve him in considerable physical danger: all his films of the twenties contain scenes in which he risks his life in order to obtain a specific effect. Painstaking efforts were required to get things done in the right way, Keaton's way, even if it took all afternoon, the next morning, and maybe the next day. Perfection was the goal. Needless to say, this was, and remains, the most expensive way to make pictures. But with his new brother-in-law's paternalistic policy in full operation, combined with the high rental fees from the exhibitors of his films, Buster continued to enjoy his freedom to the utmost.

[4]

There was nothing he could do, or anybody else could do. It was very unfortunate for him, because he had a great future, and of course his future ruined. . . .

—Adolph Zukor, 1958

Shortly after completing his last Paramount picture, *Fast Freight,* Roscoe Arbuckle drove up with two friends to spend the long Labor Day weekend of 1921 in San Francisco. He had just begun still another film, ominously entitled *The Melancholy Spirit,* before this weekend that proved to be fatal.

What happened on that Labor Day Monday is now well known. A great number of people went in and out of Arbuckle's two-bedroom suite at the St. Francis Hotel, then as now the city's leading hotel. There was a continuous party, with a great deal of drinking at a time when drinking had been a crime for less than two years. Virginia Rappe, a pretty but unsuccessful Hollywood bit player, came to Arbuckle's room almost by chance. An acquaintance of the man who had driven Arbuckle up from Los Angeles noticed her in the lobby of the hotel. He invited her to renew her slight acquaintance with Roscoe, and she joined the party on the twelfth floor. The party continued all that Monday. On the following Friday, the ninth of September, Virginia Rappe was dead in a private nursing home, and Arbuckle was quickly indicted for rape and murder.

Very few people who knew Arbuckle ever thought, then or now, that he had anything whatever to do with her death. It has become obvious that the Arbuckle case was a manufactured scandal, aided and abetted by the press and the judicial system then prevailing in San Francisco. There are many who think that Arbuckle's biggest single mistake in the conduct of his defense was in bringing in an attorney from Los Angeles, a move that merely increased the hostility toward him in the Bay City. The whole affair became one of the major scandals of the decade. Buster believed that he had once heard William Randolph Hearst say that the Roscoe Arbuckle story had sold many more of his newspapers than the sinking of the *Lusitania*.

There was an eerie Beauty and the Beast quality about the case from the very beginning and endless speculation about the image of a three-hundred-pound "funny man" violating an innocent blond young girl. Many impassioned groups were determined that Arbuckle would pay the full price for his crime. Others, convinced of his innocence, were deeply disturbed that this genial man, the idol of their children, could even be thought guilty of such a crime.

The actual facts of the case were clear enough. Virginia Rappe was no Lucrece, for she had already had several abortions by the time she was sixteen. She had quickly established the reputation in Hollywood of being easily available. She was also known for stripping off all her clothes at parties and then screaming uncontrollably, and this is what she did in full view of a number of witnesses that fatal afternoon in Arbuckle's suite at the St. Francis Hotel. The autopsy showed no signs of rape, but it did show that she had been suffering from a ruptured bladder; the immediate cause of her death was peritonitis.

Over the course of the years since 1921 a persistent story has circulated about the nature of Virginia Rappe's death. It depicts Arbuckle as the prototype of Faulkner's Popeye, the impotent gangster in his *Sanctuary,* who achieved the violation of Temple Drake with the aid of a corncob. In the various versions of the Arbuckle case it is always either a Coke or champagne bottle that he utilized to achieve his "rape." Arbuckle's biographer, David Yallop, quotes Arbuckle's first wife, Minta Durfee, as claiming that her husband was sexually impotent as early as 1917. If this was true, and if it was at all common knowledge among Arbuckle's circle of friends, it is not difficult to see how the "Coke bottle rape" rumor, as a plausible explanation of the ruptured bladder, might have originated.

In 1958, thirty-six years after the three Arbuckle trials, Adolph Zukor, then eighty-one, attempted to tell Joan and Bob Franklin in his own understated way some of his feelings about Arbuckle and the case against him:

I knew Arbuckle personally very well. . . . *He wasn't anything like chasing women or making dates with girls—he wasn't physically or mentally equipped for that.** He was a big, heavy, easy-going, 300-pound comedian. He loved life, he loved parties, he loved people to come to his place. In my judgement, whatever happened I don't know, except that whatever happened was an accident.

Zukor also spoke of the heartbreak of Arbuckle's lost career: "The public dismissed him." In 1922 Zukor, Schenck, and Arbuckle faced an extremely hostile climate of opinion, a climate they felt they couldn't beat. There were many civic groups who demanded that Arbuckle's films be banned from the screen forever. Other groups pleaded for the rehabilitation of an innocent man. Buster once recalled the terrible scene that greeted Arbuckle at the old Santa Fe Railway station in Los Angeles, where he encountered

a heat-frenzied mob of 1,500 men and women who seemed to want only to get close enough to tear him to pieces. And they yelled at the fat man they had loved so much a few weeks before, "Murderer!" "Big, fat slob!" "Beast!" and "Degenerate bastard!" . . . Roscoe never got over that experience.

Buster remembered to the end of his life the dreadful period of the three trials, which dragged on month after month. He had wanted to testify in behalf of his friend but was talked out of it by Arbuckle's lawyer, who thought it might damage the case if prominent Hollywood stars testified. Arbuckle suffered hung juries on the first two trials and was finally acquitted on the third. Many felt that Hollywood money and power had bought the verdict.

The uproar produced in America by the Arbuckle scandal led ultimately to the creation of the Hays Office, the film industry's self-regulating censorship board, as well as the restricting production code for film industry practices, which remained in full force until the beginning of the 1950s. The Arbuckle scandal, coupled with the Wallace Reid drug affair and the unsolved murder of William Desmond Taylor, created an atmosphere of

*Emphasis added.

fear in Hollywood, for the entire film community felt itself under attack just as much as Arbuckle did. This was not collective paranoia, for millions of Americans were convinced that Hollywood and its films were pernicious influences on the moral tone of American life, that films had become the showcases for all the outward signs of what was coming to be called the Jazz Age: drinking, dancing, and worst of all, sexual freedom. In effect, when Arbuckle was "dismissed" from the screen, as Zukor put it, the film industry was offering him up as a living sacrifice to appease these angry millions who could find their perfect scapegoat in this hard-drinking, fun-loving fat man. The film industry hoped that by preventing Arbuckle from appearing in any more films and by creating the new Hays Office that would carefully scrutinize everything appearing on the screen, outside censorship of films, either by the federal government or on a state-by-state basis, could be avoided. In these endeavors the film industry was successful.

Arbuckle's career was smashed just as Zukor had said it was: "There was nothing he could do, or anybody else could do." The public's outcry prevented the production of any more Arbuckle films, so Schenck replaced him with Buster as the sole star of the Comique Film Corporation. On March 2, 1922, the corporation changed its name to Buster Keaton Productions, Inc., for the very name of Comique was to be forgotten along with Arbuckle.

The combined efforts of both Buster and Joe Schenck gave Arbuckle a hold on life when he most needed it. Buster had been horrified by this total eclipse of his old friend's career, and he and Schenck now took steps to provide Arbuckle with financial support for the rest of his life. In the spring of 1922, after the third of Arbuckle's trials, Schenck drew up a document that relieved Buster Keaton Productions of the responsibility of paying Arbuckle the $1,500 per week due him under his Comique contract of 1920. Arbuckle in turn gave Buster's new firm a general release from that contract, but reserved to himself the "Additional Compensation" called for in it—a much lesser sum, but generous under the circumstances. What it amounted to was that 35 percent of all the future profits on Buster's films was to be paid to Arbuckle. Buster's work was to be the chief source of income for Arbuckle, a financial responsibility that the share-holders who owned Buster's production company (the Schenck brothers and the Loew family) honored until Arbuckle's sudden death in June 1933.

Money helped, but it was work that Arbuckle needed more than anything to restore his self-esteem and to forget the out-raged screams that day at the Santa Fe station. In 1923 Schenck created a corporation called Reel Comedies Incorporated, which was set up for the sole purpose of letting Arbuckle pseudony-mously produce and direct a series of two-reel comedies. Under this contract Arbuckle received $20,000 for each film, out of which he had to pay all his production expenses, in addition to his own salary of $1,000 a week. The firm was capitalized at $200,000, with six Hollywood production firms contributing $33,000 apiece. The firms were Buster's (the Schenck brothers), Metro Pictures, Paramount (Zukor), Samuel Goldwyn, Universal Pictures (Carl Laemmle), and Educational Pictures, the firm that would distribute the films and, ironically, the same firm that would hire Keaton in his darkest days of the thirties.

The existence of this firm has gone unnoticed until now, but it shows that the entire American film industry didn't turn its back on Arbuckle in 1922. He got the help he needed and, for the next few years, turned out his two-reelers under the name of William B. Goodrich. He always hoped that the industry would one day allow him to use his own name again, but that did not happen until 1932. Roscoe Arbuckle's old friends Buster Keaton and Joe Schenck saved his life when no one else either could or would. The old debt arising from the chance meeting with Bust-er in the street that rainy day in March was amply repaid.

It has often been remarked that Hollywood was never the same again after the Arbuckle scandal. A nervous feeling of cir-cumspection followed immediately and lastingly in the wake of "The Day the Laughter Stopped," a phrase of Buster's that has stuck.

5
ON HIS OWN

If someone had thrown their arms around him
and hugged him and kissed him, he'd have been the
happiest man in the world . . . what he wanted,
what he really needed was affection.
—Buster Collier, 1977

When Buster took Natalie Talmadge as his wife, he also took
on the entire Talmadge family. In the first few months of the
marriage Peg Talmadge spent a great deal of her time with
Natalie and Buster, and when Natalie's first pregnancy was announced, at the end of 1921, Norma and Constance persuaded
Joe Schenck to move their production companies from New
York to Hollywood so that they could be close to their sister.
Schenck obliged them, and both sisters' films were henceforth
made in Hollywood. He also obtained a job for the girls' father,
Fred Talmadge, as a doorman at the Schenck studio. Schenck
himself continued to spend most of his time in the East, for the
financing of filmmaking was still in New York.

Buster soon found himself living in a new house filled with
Talmadges. The house, on Westmoreland Place, was enormous—large enough to contain a formal ballroom on the third
floor and for Constance to be able to practice riding her new
bicycle up and down the corridors. Constance was now married
to John Pialoglu, and her mere presence in the house guaran-
teed an atmosphere of fun and excitement. Constance and Buster had always gotten along wonderfully, and some of their
friends wondered why he hadn't married her instead of Natalie.

The house quickly became a gathering place for all the friends of the Talmadges, and people came and went at all times of the day and night. At first Buster's family, for whom he had bought a house of their own in Hollywood, were also frequent visitors, but as the Talmadges took over they came less and less often, for this was clearly a house for the Talmadges.

The Keatons' first child, James, was born in June 1922, and the second, Robert, followed in February 1924. If Buster had hoped to call his first-born Joseph VII, in the Keaton family tradition, it would probably have been in vain, for right from the start Peg and her two daughters took a special interest in the two boys, an interest that never wavered all their lives. Since neither Norma nor Constance, in their combined total of seven marriages, ever had any children of their own, their extraordinary and continuing interest in the two Keaton boys is not as puzzling as it might at first seem.

The Talmadges were a united family who combined their common love for success and excitement with a thorough-going practicality in most areas of their life. Peg would often say that her daughters' happiness could be ascribed to the fact that she had forbidden them to marry actors. Buster recalled being puzzled at this observation, only to be told, with a wise smile, *"You're not an actor at all, you're a comedian!"*

When Buster's sister, Louise, was still in her late teens, she began working as Norma Talmadge's stand-in, especially for her dress fittings (in fact, she went on doing so until nearly the end of Norma's career). Louise got to know this oldest and most practical of all the Talmadge girls quite well, a lot better than Constance, of whom she always remained in awe. She remembers talking endlessly with Norma about Buster's marital problems; she discussed them with Natalie as well, but never with her brother, who would have found the subject unbearable.

While Norma and Constance envied Natalie for having the courage to bear children, the possibility that she might have more than two horrified them; to them, it was so "obviously and completely animalistic." Natalie's sisters were scarcely puritans— both of them were leading extremely active sex lives—but they had always balked at having children. Norma's refusal sprang from her fear that it would hurt her career, which always came first, but for Constance the problem was one of fear. The subject of childbirth was a peculiarly sensitive issue to them, so much so that they decided to intervene in Natalie's sex life with Buster. Shortly after the birth of Bobby Keaton, both Norma and Constance insisted that Natalie refrain from any more of this "animalistic behavior." She appears to have given in without a fight, and it was not long before the Keatons were sleeping in separate bedrooms, a policy that was rigidly enforced by Natalie herself.

When Buster spoke in later years of his banishment from Natalie's bed, he was cheerfully straightforward about it: "Having got two boys our first three years, frankly, it looked as if my work was done. I was ruled ineligible. Lost my amateur standing. *They* said I was a pro. I was moved into my own bedroom." He also said, though, that he went in desperation to Peg to appeal the family decision, but to no avail. He warned her that he had no intention of giving up his sex life because of the family's edict. This declaration probably caused no surprise to anyone in the Talmadge family, for they surely couldn't have expected him to become celibate.

Natalie's turning away from Buster sexually was inexcusable, and the marriage should have come to an end in 1924. It didn't, and she attempted the increasingly impossible task of keeping the marriage going simply because she wished to hold the family together. On the other hand, there can be little doubt that Natalie suffered a great deal in her marriage to Buster; most women would have found the situation intolerable.

For Buster, the end of sexual relations with Natalie must have been devastating. Whatever real intimacy he had been able to achieve with her was now a thing of the past. His mother and sister always believed that Buster never stopped loving Natalie. But this was something that Buster would never talk about with anyone, not even his closest friends, for he found it impossible to communicate his deepest feelings with any of the people he ever knew. Words seemed to be totally inadequate to express his feelings of anguish and pain, and he kept his mouth shut about them. Buster Collier thinks that Keaton craved affection all his life and never really received it.

Buster began to fill his nonworking hours with diversions. Because Buster was intense about everything he did, he devoted as much energy to these diversions as to the film work that already consumed so much of his time. The first and most enduring of these pastimes was bridge, a game that became a passion. He had become a convert to the game in 1922 as a result of a particularly shaming encounter with Hiram Abrams, then the president of United Artists, on a train bound for New York while he was in the company of Nicholas Schenck. In those days the long trip from coast to coast was made bearable by drinking, talking, and endless games of bridge. Abrams and his wife offered to teach Schenck and Buster how to play. Buster showed such a marked lack of ability with the cards that Abrams became mercilessly abusive, and Buster finally left his compartment in disgust. The defeat immediately became a challenge, and a challenge to Buster meant hard work; this is exactly what he did. He read everything he could on the subject and played with anyone who cared to join him. His progress was spectacular, and within a year or so he became a master. It became an obsession—he would play for days on end.

The Schenck brothers, Adolph Zukor, and a number of other prominent film figures soon became aware of Buster's phenomenal abilities with cards. They began to match him against other players who were out for games with high stakes, "murderous games," as Collier calls them. The games would last for many hours and often involved thousands of dollars. Bridge games like these were fine for people with lots of time and money on their hands, but not for a hard-working filmmaker.

Collier recalls Buster's self-imposed work and play schedule as physically impossible for anyone without his incredible strength and boundless energy. He would arise at six or so and arrive at the studio for the day's work, which might involve part or all of a baseball game, with a long and talkative lunch with his working crew in the middle of the day. The shooting of the picture in progress would proceed only when Buster was exactly ready to shoot it. If it didn't turn out the way he wanted it, he would do it again and again. This sort of working day went on until six or so, and after a brief dinner at home he would seek out the bridge game scheduled for that evening. It might start at nine and con-

The Electric House. Rudi Blesh

tinue past midnight. Buster drank very little during these long and taxing games, for it would have been impossible to drink and play the way he did. But when the game was finished, it was time for a few relaxing drinks, a few "quick belts" as he called them. He would go to bed at one or two and wake again after four or five hours of sleep, ready to start another day just like the previous one.

During this period he made a virtually unbroken series of classic masterpieces: *The Boat, The Paleface, Cops, My Wife's Relations, Daydreams,* and *The Balloonatic.* All of them were successful at the

box office, but they were strongly personal films and not to everyone's taste. Right from the beginning there were those who found Buster's comedies disturbing rather than funny. Many thought his films so personal as to be strangely unsettling or, at best, puzzling. This is the main reason why Buster never rose to the level of universal acceptance achieved by Chaplin and Lloyd. This personal factor in his work is one of the main reasons why his films seem so peculiarly modern and why his work has not become significantly dated. Today Buster's films are seen by some as paradigms of the human condition, as existential films that deal with Heidegger's *Dasein,* his notion of what it's like "being there" in the world. *One Week* can be interpreted in this way, as can *Cops,* one of Keaton's greatest achievements.

The opening shot in *Cops* shows Buster's face framed by what seem to be prison bars; the camera pulls back to reveal that they are actually the iron gates of the mansion in which his girl lives. The prison bars are illusory, but they clearly foreshadow what is to come. The proud girl spurns him, demanding that he go out and succeed in the business world. Buster immediately turns to find ways to improve his lot. There follows a rapid series of events, in all of which Buster's good intentions produce precisely the opposite effect of what was intended. By helping a disguised detective to his feet, Buster winds up with the contents of his wallet. He buys a horse and wagon from a bystander who had no intention of selling them. A con man sells Buster a load of furniture that is lying on the street, telling him that he is helping a family being dispossessed, but the furniture turns out to belong to a policeman's family about to move into their new home. Nothing is what it seems to be.

Buster is next seen as a dealer in used furniture, driving his ancient horse and wagon through the city streets. He inadvertently winds up in the middle of the annual Policemen's Day Parade which is marching its way through town. An anarchist suddenly hurls a bomb at the main reviewing stand; it lands on the seat next to Buster, who lights his cigarette with it. He discards the sizzling bomb by throwing it in the direction of the reviewing stand, where it explodes. Every cop in the city then goes in pursuit of Buster.

Cops, 1922. *Museum of Modern Art / Film Stills Archive*

The great chase through the city streets begins—a chase of enormous inventiveness on Keaton's part, as he eludes these hundreds of arms grasping at him in fury. Finally cornered, he takes refuge on a plank perched on a high fence; he converts the plank into a catapult that hurls him down on the body of the man whose money he'd stolen earlier. Escaping his pursuers at close quarters, he begins to run again. At one moment in the chase the camera, in a long shot, shows a strangely deserted street; in an instant the tiny figure of Buster comes around the corner, the cops right behind him. His knees are raised high for running, while his arms are like pistons as he charges directly at the camera. It is as memorable an image as that of Harold Lloyd desperately clutching the hands of the clock in *Safety Last.* We see Buster finally enter a large building and disappear; the camera shows us that it is the city police station. There is a fade-out, followed immediately by a shot in which one of the uniformed cops is backing slowly out of the front door of the station. He turns, and we see that it is Buster. He has the keys to the station in his hand. He locks the door and throws the keys into a trash bin. He is triumphant—he has outwitted all the policemen in the city. At that moment his beloved passes by in the street, and he greets her happily. She rejects him with even greater contempt than at the beginning and stomps off in a rage. Buster recovers the keys from the trash bin and allows himself to be yanked back into the station house to meet the annihilation that surely awaits him there. The final shot of the picture is that of a tombstone, clearly his, with his familiar porkpie hat perched on top of it.

Cops was popular, but did not please everybody. Some found Keaton's mixture of elements entirely too ambiguous, too disturbing, and not what they had paid their money to see. But with Schenck backing him all the way, Buster was permitted to go on making these remarkable pictures; other producers might have looked unfavorably upon films that so resolutely defied popular taste. Buster totally rejected any serious explanations of what he was doing in these films. They were simply made to make you laugh, he always said, denying any idea of "serious intentions."

Keaton's unique imagination produced a world suffused with extraordinary pessimism, combined with a genuine delight in the comic possibilities of that same world. His incomparable comic gloom is nowhere better seen than in his 1921 two-reeler *The Boat.* In this picture Buster is the father of two small boys who wear little porkpie hats just like their father's; the mother is patient and wears middy blouses. The film depicts the adventures of this little family with their small pleasure craft, *Damfino.* It begins with the boat being dragged from Buster's basement, where it has been assembled piece by piece. With Buster at the wheel of his car, the attached towing rope stiffens tautly until the boat slowly begins to lurch forward. The *Damfino* advances impressively as Buster's entire house is leveled to the ground; the boat has ripped its way through the foundations of the house. The launching of the boat is equally doomed, for Buster backs his car off the pier and into the water; the christening bottle

The Boat, 1921. Museum of Modern Art / Film Stills Archive

does not break as it should but instead leaves a noticeable dent in the hull.

The launching produces one of Keaton's greatest images: Buster standing in the bow as the *Damfino* slides slowly down into the water, the bow slowly engulfed by the water, and then all the rest of the boat down to the stern. The boat continues straight to the bottom with Buster standing firmly in place, absolutely immovable. When the *Damfino* has finally disappeared in the swirling water, all that is left is Buster's porkpie hat floating away. As the boat sinks before your eyes, it is impossible to avoid Buster's terrible logic: *This boat was meant to be sunk, and now it is sinking.*

In 1921 there were many who laughed and laughed and came back to see it more than once. There were also those who might have been heard muttering at the end of the film, *"But did he really have to sink it?"* It confused some people, for with Chaplin and Lloyd you knew where you were—it was funny or it wasn't.

But with Keaton things were never so sure. A tombstone at the end of a *comedy?*

Buster's films were relatively expensive to make, but he rarely took money into consideration when making them. He did not believe in economies or shortcuts, and Joe Schenck observed more than once, "If there is a costly way to make a movie, he'll find it!" Throughout his life Buster displayed a complete inability to handle money. He did not trust himself with it, for he was more than likely to give it away or lend it to those who asked for it. He hardly ever cared to have more than five dollars in his pocket, and any purchases he made were usually charged; he never managed a checkbook in his life. This inability to deal with money proved to be a major stumbling block in Buster's career at the beginning of the sound era, when his freedom to spend it was suddenly and shockingly checked.

Buster's problems with money cannot be ascribed to his lack of a formal education. Chaplin had little if any more schooling than Buster, yet he demonstrated a "wheeler-dealer" business sense that rivaled both Schenck's and Zukor's, as Joe Schenck found out to his dismay in his days as a partner of Chaplin's at United Artists. As a virtual pro at bridge, Buster had no trouble keeping score. His feelings about money must have stemmed from deeper sources, for he really was completely indifferent to it, always relying on those closest to him to keep him informed, in a general sort of way, how things stood. His best films owe their most expensive components (the ship in *The Navigator* and the railway engine in *The General*) to a filmmaker who had a complete disdain for haggling over what they might cost, for Buster wanted them and he got them.

Natalie must have worried about their financial position, for only a year and a half after their marriage it was arranged legally that all of Buster's earnings from the Buster Keaton Productions firm would be paid directly to her. This agreement was signed by Buster on the thirtieth of October 1922. It was a remarkable thing for him to do, for he was now bound to give his wife all the money he would make in the next five years. It seems an unduly severe measure, but the Talmadges wanted to "make it all legal."

Buster was perfectly aware that her family had cause to fear that his generosity to all and sundry would leave their daughter in poverty and, besides, it was one less thing to worry about. He was more interested in concentrating on his work, where he was confident and at times aggressive. He could be violently abusive when he became aware that one of his employees was deliberately shirking the job he was paid to do or when someone violated his trust. With his working crew at the studio there was never any doubt who was boss.

The only evidence of what Buster may have thought about the clannishness of the Talmadge family can be seen in his film called, aptly enough, *My Wife's Relations*. Produced just a year or so after the marriage, the film is a wild caricature of home life in which he depicts himself as a piece of human refuse found in the street and taken home to live with the members of a particularly vulgar Irish family. He is harassed and victimized by everybody in the house, but he eventually emerges victorious over all of them. Buster's treatment as a child is recalled here as well as his position with the Talmadges. The film gives us a glimpse of what he thought of both families, for, after all, he was only a comedian.

---

[2]

This had such a nice theme that it just kept growing—and we let it grow. It grew into a five-reel picture.

—Harold Lloyd, 1969

Once we started into features, we had to stop doing impossible things. . . . We had to make an audience believe our story.

—Keaton, 1958

Keaton's work became much more complex after 1923 because of his relatively sudden changeover to feature films. Although

Mack Sennett had made his famous *Tillie's Punctured Romance* as a feature as early as 1914, this was considered a one-time experiment and was not repeated, despite the film's great success. Chaplin's *The Kid* had also led the way at the beginning of 1921, but he did not make another feature until *The Gold Rush* in 1925. The switch from short films to features was difficult even in the area of dramatic films, for there was a great deal of opposition to them from many of the leading studio heads. But Adolph Zukor fought hard for them:

> I felt sure that moving pictures would survive and last forever if we would give them the pictures the people want. I urged the longer pictures on Mr. Laemmle, on Mr. Aitken, but at that time I couldn't get them to see my way. . . .

Harold Lloyd was the first American filmmaker to abandon the old two-reel comedy format on a regular basis, although he did so almost by accident. During the course of filming his *Sailor Made Man* in 1921 he found that his crew had shot what amounted to four reels of material and some of it "was too good to delete." With some misgivings, the picture was released in its four-reel form and proved to be reasonably successful. The same thing happened again with *Grandma's Boy,* during the shooting of which he had told his crew, "Let's play it out." Here the greater length resulted in a very successful picture, but it was only with *Dr. Jack* in 1922 that Lloyd regularly began making what he called "real features."

The great success of these Lloyd features, as well as some of the Fairbanks comedies, was not lost on Keaton and Schenck, and Buster was given the go-ahead to start making his first feature, in the spring of 1923. It was *The Three Ages,* the structure of which was suggested by Griffith's *Intolerance,* with its four instances of bigotry in the world's history. In Keaton's film two young men are in competition for the same girl in different epochs: the Stone Age, ancient Rome, and Prohibition America. In each age Buster is the boy and Wallace Beery his boorish antagonist. Thirty years later Buster frankly admitted that *The Three Ages* is essentially three two-reelers spliced together to give the illusion of being a full-length feature. It is the weakest of his longer films and is really a warm-up exercise for the next film. The most memorable image in it is perhaps where Buster, after being cast into the lion's den, discovers that lions really *do* like to have their paws rubbed.

The first of Keaton's great films of the twenties was *Our Hospitality*, most of which was shot on location up and around Lake Tahoe and along the banks of the Truckee River in the Sierra Nevada mountains. This film was a tremendous leap forward for Buster, demonstrating here a total mastery of the feature film form. Like *The General, Our Hospitality* is a period piece, a "historical" film set in the American South in 1831. The idea for the film came from one of Keaton's gag writers, the fat and jolly Jean Havez, who had suggested a Hatfield and McCoy story about the most famous of the feuding families of the old South, the kind of family that Twain included in *Huckleberry Finn* as the Grangerfords and Shepherdsons. Buster changed the names to Canfield and McKay as a whimsical precaution in case there were any vengeful survivors of the original clans. The story line is simple: Buster plays the part of young Willie McKay, who has come down South to claim his inheritance in the town of Rockville; he pictures in his mind a columned antebellum mansion. Before leaving New York he is told by his aunt that he is the last of the McKays and about the feud that has killed his father and all the other McKays. Thoughtfully, he begins his long train journey to the South.

Buster always loved to talk about Willie's wonderful journey and the railroad he constructed for the trip:

> I used a story of a feud in the South, and placed the period in 1831 to take advantage of the first railway train that had been built. That's when they took the stagecoaches and put flanged wheels on 'em. And they had those silly lookin' engines—one called the Stephenson "Rocket" and one called the "De Witt Clinton." And they're naturally narrow-gauge, and they weren't so fussy about layin' railroad track . . . if it was a little unlevel, they just ignored it. They laid it over fallen trees, over rocks. . . . So I got quite a few laughs ridin' that railroad.

Keaton chose the Stephenson Rocket because it looked funnier, and he had it precisely duplicated for the film, later giving it to the Smithsonian in Washington. The long trip southward on the Rocket is an extended sequence with a wonderful dreamlike, idyllic quality to it that has few parallels in film. Phillip Rahv once wrote about William Faulkner that, in his superb stories about the American Indians who owned black slaves in the early South, he had been able to imagine the unimaginable. We get the same feeling from *Our Hospitality* as the tiny train, toylike and yet real, wanders through the deep forest of the Shenandoah Valley.

The title and much of the humor in the film arise from the highly vaunted tradition of Southern hospitality:

Our Hospitality, 1923. *National Film Archive / Stills Library*

But when . . . I got down South to claim my father's estate, I ran into the family who had run us out of the state in the first place. And the old man of the outfit wouldn't let his sons or anybody shoot me while I was a guest in the house 'cause the girl had invited me for dinner. Well, I'd overheard it and found out. As long as I stayed in the house I was safe. . . .

A good deal of the film is devoted to the host's efforts to get Willie out of his house so that his sons can kill him without violating their famous hospitality. Eventually Willie leaves the house in disguise and makes for the nearby river. He is pursued by the girl's two brothers, as well as by the girl (played by Natalie), who fears for his safety. When they arrive at the river, Natalie falls in.

Our Hospitality, 1923. *National Film Archive / Stills Library*

Buster's pictures nearly always conclude with a spectacular sequence. In *Our Hospitality* it is the rescue of Natalie, the "fair young stranger," from the Niagara-like waterfall just as she is about to be swept to her death far below. Springing from a ledge to the left of the falls, Buster uses his body as a pendulum as he swings across the face of the falls in a giant arc to catch her in his arms. The scene is a spectacular display of Keaton's agility, but it was not achieved painlessly:

> A couple of times I swung out underneath there and dropped upside down when I caught her. I had to go down to the doctor right there and then. They pumped out my ears and nostrils and drained me, because when a full volume of water like that comes down and hits you and you're upside down—then you really get it.

He also got it in the raging tumult of the foaming rapids of the Truckee River. Before the rescue scene it was necessary for Buster to be secured to a sixteen-foot log by a thin, invisible security line. Without warning the wire suddenly snapped, throwing both the log and Buster into the rapids. Only by a supreme effort did he avoid being battered to death by the heaving log. He finally pulled himself to safety by reaching upward toward some overhanging branches as he spun past the banks of the river. A good deal of this can be seen in the film, for Keaton's cameramen were always told to keep shooting until he told them to stop. This was no exception, and on this occasion they came close to shooting a drowning. As was the custom in the silent era, two cameras were used, placed side by side. This allowed for a duplicate negative for producing positive prints in Europe and it also ensured that if one camera malfunctioned, the scene would not be lost—especially important in the case of big, expensive scenes involving a great many people.

During the shooting of *Our Hospitality*, high in the California mountains, a photograph was taken of Buster having an early morning shave in his car. It is clear from this picture, as well as from virtually all the existing "casual" pictures of him, that he was extremely sensitive about having his photograph taken. He would invariably adopt the appropriate nonsmiling expression for the photographer, the one described by Louise Brooks as his "on" expression.

Our Hospitality was very much of a Keaton family picture: Buster cast his father as the rambunctious engineer of the Rocket, his one-year-old son Jimmy as himself at that age, and Natalie as the girl with whom Willie McKay shared a railway carriage on the Rocket's trip down South. This was her last appearance in a film, for she was pregnant with their second child during the shooting and chose this occasion to retire for good.

On location for *Our Hospitality*, Lake Tahoe, Oregon, 1923. *Rudi Blesh*

Our Hospitality was a big box-office success. Metro promoted the picture heavily, taking a full four-page ad in *Moving Picture World*. Its main rival in the industry, *Exhibitors Herald*, claimed that "nothing so novel or funny has ever been pictured. Success is assured." Not everyone, however, was pleased with either *The Three Ages* or *Our Hospitality*, for *Moving Picture World* stated flatly that "Buster is going to wear out and lose out. We played his *Three Ages* and this one and neither were anything to write home about. There were a few laughs but they could have been put in one reel. Better go back to two-reelers, Buster, you fit them." His reaction to criticism of this type, or any type, was mostly indifference: "I'd been reading house notices since I was born, and was used to that. This critic likes you and this don't, so that's that."

[3]

I don't feel qualified to talk about my work.
                                        —Keaton, 1964

Films are not made out of the minds of screen-writers.
                                        —Werner Herzog, 1977

Keaton always refused to think of himself as an artist. For him, the word smacked of pretentiousness and "book culture." He was uncertain about what could properly be considered art, though he felt it had some connection with the printed word:

> I never realized that I was doing anything but trying to make people laugh. . . . I never took extravagant praise seriously because neither I, my director, nor my gag men were writers in any literary sense. The writers most often on my staff were Clyde Bruckman, Joe Mitchell, and Jean Havez. They never wrote anything but gags, vaudeville sketches, and songs. I don't think any of them ever had his name on a book, a short story, or even an article for a fan magazine. . . . They were not word guys at all.

Buster's writing and directing crew in 1922: Buster, Joseph Mitchell, Eddie Cline, Clyde Bruckman (seated), unknown, Jean Havez. *National Film Archive / Stills Library*

"Artist" was a word that could only be applied to published writers of books, most certainly not to the gag men he kept on his payroll for several years.

Buster had managed without gag writers when he and Eddie Cline were making his superb series of two-reelers in 1920–23. But when Schenck and Buster decided to go ahead with features, they found it necessary to have some sort of writing talent around at least to lay down a kind of basic framework for the "story" in the film. As Buster said, he

> learned in a hurry that we couldn't make a feature-length picture the way we had done the two-reelers; we couldn't use impossible gags like the kind of things that happen to cartoon characters. We had to eliminate all these things because we had to tell a logical story that an audience would accept. . . .

Clyde Bruckman was the writer with the longest professional association with Buster, from 1923 until the early fifties. He decried not only his own contributions to Keaton's films, but also those of the other gag men:

> I can tell you—and so could Jean Havez if he were alive—that those wonderful stories were ninety percent Buster's. I was often ashamed to take the money, much less the credit . . . we were all overpaid from the strict point of view.

Bruckman was probably leaning overboard here in order to give Buster the maximum credit, for he said this in 1956, at a time when Buster was largely a forgotten man.

There is no doubt that Clyde Bruckman's contributions to Buster's films were considerable. He collaborated on the stories for the first five features and shared the directing and writing credit on what is commonly regarded as Buster's masterpiece, *The General*. His services were very much in demand, for he directed Harold Lloyd's first three sound films, in addition to directing W. C. Fields in his *Fatal Glass of Beer* and *The Man on the Flying Trapeze*.

This is an impressive list of credits for a man who has always seemed on the dim and shadowy side. People who knew him well, like Harold Goodwin and Ben Pearson, seem agreed on two things about him: he was not very funny, and he drank too much. He was very much a chameleon, always capable of adapting himself to the particular kind of talent he found himself working for. There is no continuing sense of Bruckman *personally* as he worked first for one man and then another. But all of Buster's films *do* contain the ongoing presense of Keaton himself. While his films, like all films, are works of collaboration, the Keaton element is stronger than anything else: *his* is the presence that makes them unique.

Bruckman also made large claims for Keaton as an actor: "You wouldn't believe a comedian could be so serious. He showed them all how to underact. He could tell his story by lifting an eyebrow. He could tell it by *not* lifting an eyebrow." He also spoke of Buster's complete mastery of direction: "Most of the direction was his, as Eddie Cline will tell you. Keaton could have graduated into a top director—of any kind of picture, short or long, high or low, sad or funny, or both. . . ."

In short, Bruckman viewed his friend Keaton as a total film maker, as much one as D. W. Griffith, Sergei Eisenstein, Orson Welles, or Ingmar Bergman. This was the largest claim of all, but it is demonstrably true. In the short time span of only seven years Keaton made a half dozen or so films that have, above all others, resisted the erosions of time and taste.

Until the advent of sound in 1928 and 1929 it was standard practice for some Hollywood stars regularly to turn out highly personal pictures in which nearly every aspect of the finished product was directly controlled by its maker. The films of Pickford, Fairbanks, and Chaplin are all examples of this system, and Keaton had the same arrangement for a time. Directors' names would appear on the credits of their pictures, but the credits were often given out of sheer kindness, for the real work of the director was performed by the stars. Actors were primarily actors, but they were also the total creators of their films. They were even film cutters, as Eddie Sutherland liked to point out:

> A director used to cut his own pictures. Back in the days of Sennett, everybody would be cutting them, you did it yourself. When I was Chaplin's assistant, I used to go into the cutting room. I let Charlie do the final cutting on it, but I did the first one. All the silent pictures I used to cut with my own hands.

Sutherland's language here makes the pictures sound like hand-crafted objects, and in many respects this is what they were. Obtaining the services of the necessary craftsmen was often difficult and costly. Chaplin and Lloyd maintained full production staffs all year round for their films at a cost of several hundred thousand dollars a year. This was an economic luxury, for it left these expensive technical crews with little to do for months, in Chaplin's case often years, at a time. The makers of films like *The Gold Rush, The Freshman,* and *The Thief of Baghdad* could afford such luxuries, and if they chose not to, they found their production crews deserting them. There was considerable rivalry for the services of these writers, directors, and cameramen. Keaton hired the writer Jean Havez away from Lloyd after he had written *Grandma's Boy* for him, along with *Dr. Jack* and *Safety Last*. It went both ways, for Buster lost his best cameraman, Elgin Lessley, in 1925 to Harry Langdon, only regaining him for *The Cameraman* in 1928. Lloyd estimated that his writers had cost him seven and eight hundred dollars a week each, with four and five of them on the payroll at once. Some of the fixed costs could be reduced by lending out the technical people to other studios, but this couldn't be done with the writers or directors. In addition to his staff of writers, Buster built up a first-rate technical staff, without which he could never have come up with some of the dazzling effects seen in his major films. By the beginning of 1924 he was head of a production team whose technical proficiency was second to none.

Buster's next picture, *Sherlock, Jr.,* could probably *only* have been made under the team system, for it required all sorts of technical expertise. He got this from Fred Gabouri, who could seemingly supply anything Keaton required in the way of props; he came through with the wildest and most outlandish of Buster's requests.

It is a film in which Keaton delights in playing with many of his discoveries about the camera; the real subject of the film is film itself, or illusion. The story concerns a young film projectionist who, after being falsely accused of having stolen a watch belonging to his girl friend's father, falls asleep up in his booth at the theater. Down below, a film called *Hearts and Pearls* (or *The Lounge Lizard's Lost Love*—A Veronal Production) can be seen on the screen. As he sleeps, another Keaton, a ghostly transparent one, begins to scrutinize the screen below him. It appears that the people in this film are the very same ones he has just had so much trouble with: his girl, her father, and the real thief, his treacherous rival. There the resemblance stops, for the people in this film are rich and elegantly dressed. Their problem is how to recover the necklace, which has been stolen from the father's safe. The "dream" Keaton leaves his booth and comes down into the auditorium to enter the screen and join the action, but this proves to be a difficult task. He is violently rejected by this "other" reality in a series of abrupt film cuts that hurl him into a lion's den, a snowbank, and a formal garden. At last he succeeds in entering the door of the mansion, now properly and fully *in* the film, and he is suitably attired as a splendidly tuxedoed Sherlock Holmes.

A great deal has been written about *Sherlock, Jr.* as a delightful investigation into the nature of film reality. It is an endlessly innovative film utilizing a wide variety of the visual tricks that Buster remembered from his vaudeville days. The most dazzling of his virtuoso techniques is seen in the sequence involving Buster's escape from a room in which he is being held prisoner by thugs. In order for the viewer to see everything there *is* to see—there is no trick photography here—Keaton built the set for the room without a fourth wall. At the beginning of the scene, just as he enters the room, Buster leaves a hoop in the window sill. When he makes his move to break away from his captors, he takes a flying dive through the air, his body passing through the hoop. After he has hit the ground, the viewer sees that the hoop concealed a voluminous woman's dress and that Buster is now wearing it as he walks up the alleyway before the startled gaze of the thug guarding it.

Some of the tricks in *Sherlock, Jr.* were motivated in part by Buster's interest in the illusion of film, they were also clearly intended to be revealed for what they were: tricks. He wanted there to be no doubt that the marvelous displays of physical agility were his and his alone. His body was that of a highly trained athlete, and he took immense pleasure in placing that body under as much stress as it would take.

The element of real physical danger became so great that Buster's production crew would occasionally try to talk him out of performing certain stunts. Keaton soon acquired a considerable reputation in the industry for his willingness to take enormous risks. The danger was not always apparent, as in the train sequence in *Sherlock, Jr.*, when Keaton runs along the tops of a number of freight cars until he reaches the very last one. He then grabs the waterspout on a water tower along the track, and the spout immediately starts to descend under his weight. As he comes down with it, the waterspout deluges him with water; this was the intended gag, but Buster had not counted on the terrific strength of the flood, which smashed him down to the ground. It was extremely painful, but he was up and on with his work in a moment. For months after, he suffered a series of blinding headaches; he had actually broken his neck, as a physical examination a decade later confirmed. Buster loved to talk about these hazards:

> So my scene was where the cops were chasing me that I came to this thing and I took advantage of the lid of a skylight, and I laid it over the edge of the roof to use as a spring board and backed up, hit it and tried to make it to the other side which was probably about eighteen feet, something like that. Well, I misjudged the spring of that board and I didn't make it and I hit flat up against that other set and fell to the net, but I hit hard enough that it jammed my knees a little bit, and my hips and elbows, 'cause I hit flush, flat that I had to go home and stay in bed for about three days. . . . So the boys the next day went into the projecting room and saw the scene anyhow 'cause they had it printed to look at it. Well, they got a thrill out of it so they came back and told me about it. It's a miss. Says, "Well if it looks that good let's see if we can't pick it up this way. The best thing to do is to put an awning on a window, just a little, small awning, just enought to break my fall, 'cause on the screen you could see that I fell about, oh I guess about sixteen feet, something like. I must have passed two stories. So now we go in and drop into something just to slow me up, to break my fall, and I can swing from that onto a rainspout and when I get a hold of it, it breaks and lets me, sways me out away from the building hanging on to it and for a finish it collapses enough that it hinges and throws me down through a window a couple of floors below. . . .

Buster's firm belief in tempting fate has been echoed in a recent remark by the German director Werner Herzog. "Disasters can be positive. The momentum of disaster lets you build up to a beautiful scene."

[4]

"It was called the *Buford* . . . and we found that you could have this boat for twenty-five thousand dollars."
"You could buy it for that?"
"Buy it! Now, it's an ocean liner about five hundred feet long. A passenger ship. Well, we got our start. . . ."

—Keaton, 1964

It was *The Navigator,* the first of his pictures to achieve wide popularity, that established Keaton as a major force in American films. He thought of it as his best film, second only to *The General.* The idea for *The Navigator* was conceived when Buster heard that the S.S. *Buford* was bound for the wreckers. He bought it the moment he found he could; there would have been no *Navigator* if there had not been an actual S.S. *Buford.* It was Buster's technical man, Fred Gabourie, who first discovered that the old liner was about to be junked and immediately informed Keaton, who jumped at the chance to have an ocean-going ship as the main prop for a film:

> Well, we went to work right then and there and says, "Now, what could we do with an ocean liner?" Says, "Well, we can make a dead ship out of it. No lights aboard. No water running. Just afloat." Well, we set out to figure out how to do that and to write a story about it. . . .

The story they put together centers around young Rollo Treadway, as wealthy and spoiled as Bertie the Lamb. He finds himself on an abandoned ship that has been left deliberately adrift to sink. His estranged sweetheart is the only other person on board. She "never saw a kitchen in her life, doesn't know how to boil a cup of tea." Neither Rollo nor the girl suspects each other's presence on board, "adrift in the Pacific Ocean on a dead ship. Well, that's *The Navigator*. . . ."

When James Agee published his famous essay "Comedy's Greatest Era" in *Life* in 1949, it marked the real beginning of the enormous revival of interest in Keaton's work. Agee has often been taken to task for his "inaccuracies" in describing some of the greatest moments in film history, but his enthusiasm frequently transcends more careful observations. In attempting to show what was really at the heart of silent comedy in Keaton, he chose the scene in *The Navigator* where Rollo and his girl begin looking for one another, after each has discovered that someone else is on board this ghostly liner:

Buster as Rollo Treadway in *The Navigator*, 1924. *Maryann Chach*

He drops a lighted cigarette. A girl finds it. She calls out and he hears her; each then tries to find the other. First each walks purposefully down the long, vacant starboard deck, the girl, then Keaton, turning the corner just in time not to see each other. Next time around each of them is trotting briskly, very much in earnest; going at the same pace, they miss each other just the same. Next time around, each of them is going like a bat out of hell. Again they miss. Then the camera withdraws to a point of vantage at the stern, leans its chin in its hand and just watches the whole intricate superstructure of the ship as the protagonists stroll, steal and scuttle from level to level, up, down, and sidewise, always managing to miss each other by hair's breadths. It is an enchantingly neat and elaborate bit of timing.

The Navigator, 1924. National Film Archive / Stills Library

Agee goes on to describe how Keaton managed to bring the two together:

> The girl, thoroughly winded, sits down for a breather, indoors on a plank which workmen have left across sawhorses. Keaton pauses on an upper deck, equally winded and puzzled. What follows happens in a couple of seconds at most: air suction whips his silk topper backward down a ventilator; grabbing frantically for it, he backs against the lip of the ventilator, jackknifes and falls in backward. Instantly the camera cuts back to the girl. A topper falls through the ceiling and lands tidily, right side up, on the plank beside her. Before she can look more than startled, its owner follows, head between his knees, crushes the topper, breaks the plank with the point of his spine and proceeds to the floor.

Without a pause, Rollo asks the girl the same question he'd asked her in San Francisco: *"Will you marry me?"* Her unhesitating answer is still the same: "Certainly not!"

This sequence is an absolute visual joy as well as a triumph of editing; it astonishes and delights viewers today as much as in the autumn of 1924. The second part of *The Navigator* is taken up with a series of now classic routines involving the preparation of breakfast for two in a kitchen designed to prepare food for five hundred, an encounter with a folding chair that does nothing *but* fold, and a conclusion in which Keaton and the girl encounter cannibals on a cannibal isle. Buster derived nearly all these routines from the physical construction of the ship and the things he found on it, a method of filmmaking that he found extremely rewarding.

Advance screenings of the film convinced Metro that it would score a triumph at the box office. They began a huge promotional effort, emphasizing the services of John Held, Jr., the artist most commonly associated with the flappers of Fitzgerald's Jazz Age. All the trade papers ran full-page ads featuring Held's brilliant nautical cartoon of Buster in gold ink. The Capital Theater, the showcase for Metro attractions and the largest film house in New York, did extremely well with the picture, with many Standing Room Only performances. The film went into a second week's run, an event that occurred there only three or four times a year.

This success was a great victory for Buster, for he had shown

Joe Schenck that he could turn out his own films in his own way and produce a smash hit in the theaters, the kind of success that Schenck understood best. If Schenck had been having doubts about a man who wanted to buy up old ocean liners, *The Navigator* was the surest sign that Keaton did indeed know what he was doing.

Buster told a number of his interviewers in the late fifties that his feature films usually grossed between $1 million and $1.5 million. He was greatly exaggerating, as the actual gross earnings on the first four Metro features distributed by Metro attest:

The Three Ages	$448,606
Our Hospitality	537,844
Sherlock, Jr.	448,337
The Navigator	680,406

It may be that by the late fifties these Metro grosses seemed so small by the prevailing standards of the day that he simply doubled them. The doubling is surprising for, in spite of his uncertain grasp of financial affairs, he was generally reliable about matters of fact. Another explanation is that the doubling was done by Charles Samuels, the author of Buster's "as told to" biography, *My Wonderful World of Slapstick*.

On the basis of the advance success of *The Navigator*, Schenck gave Buster a new contract in September 1924. This seems to be the earliest of Keaton's contracts that has survived. It is a standard artist's contract of eight pages, written in businesslike English, with only one slight departure, in paragraph seven, which contains the special clause: *"The artist specifically agrees that his services are of a special, unique, unusual, extraordinary and intellectual nature and of great and special value to the producer. . . .*

Under the terms of the contract Keaton was to be paid the sum of $27,000 per completed film; it called for at least two films per year. If Buster did produce a third film, he was to be paid $40,000 for it: Joe Schenck was offering a bonus for increased productivity. The usual 25-percent profit sharing was still in full effect, and his weekly salary was $1,000. This was the first time he was actually paid this amount, despite prior claims. All the costs of production were to be borne by the producing firm, Buster Keaton Productions, Inc. The contract was to go into effect with the film currently in production, *Seven Chances*, and was to cover a total of six films. The additional five would be *Go West*, *Battling Butler*, and the three pictures Schenck released through his own United Artists: *The General, College,* and *Steamboat Bill Jr.* In essence it was a three-year contract.

Amazingly enough, Buster owned no shares in the production firm that bore his name. He felt that if he acquired shares, he would be obliged to worry about how the firm was doing, and he was confident that Joe Schenck would always take care of his best interests. Both Chaplin and Lloyd owned their own production companies, and this was a factor of great significance in their careers.

The main shareholders in Buster Keaton Productions, Inc., a firm that remained a viable concern until 1940, included three members of the Schenck family: Joe, Nicholas, and the latter's wife, Pansy, who owned a total of $39\frac{1}{3}$ shares out of 100 among them. The two sons of Marcus Loew owned 14, while the composer Irving Berlin had 12. The only other shareholder of size was the North American Realty Corporation with $12\frac{2}{3}$. The remaining 22 shares were scattered among a group of family friends and executives of the firm, such as Lou Anger, the studio manager, and Leopold Friedman, the secretary. Although placed in formal dissolution in 1940, it was not until 1971 that the assets of the firm—the rights to Buster's films—were finally sold to Raymond Rohauer.

By the fall of 1924 Buster's marriage to Natalie was "in name only." She continued to occupy herself with the two children and was very much concerned with houses, desiring one that was commensurate with Buster's ever-increasing popularity. There were many other women in his life, but keeping up the facade of the marriage made things difficult at times. As for Natalie's feelings, or even knowledge about Buster's interest in other women, there is no reliable evidence, although Louise Brooks seems to think that Natalie wasn't particularly concerned about it, at least in this early stage of his extramarital affairs.

When Buster and Natalie came to New York for the opening of his *Seven Chances* in April 1925, there was a gag photograph of them taken standing on the rooftop of the Biltmore Hotel. The photo bore, in part, the following caption: *"Natalie Talmadge, his wife, is urging him to be careful."*

Buster and Natalie on the roof of the Biltmore Hotel, April 1925. *Museum of Modern Art / Film Stills Archive*

6
A MAN OF PROPERTY

[1]

Buster's whole life then was a movie. . . . His
house was a set, the swimming pool was a set, the
barbecue pit was a set.
—Louise Brooks, 1977

In 1925 Buster and Natalie had a monumental house built for
them in Beverly Hills, similar to the other showplace homes then
being built, the Greenacres of Harold Lloyd and, grandest of
them all, the Pickfair of Mary Pickford and Douglas Fairbanks.
Buster's place wasn't quite as grand as those, but it did stand on
a lawn covering three and a half acres. If you were a star of the
first order in 1925, a house along these lines was customary, and
Natalie saw no reason to regard herself and Buster as exceptions. In later years Buster always claimed that the idea for a
house of this size was entirely Natalie's. He also claimed that he
had secretly bought her a much less grand one that she rejected as entirely too small for the kind of entertaining she had
in mind. She was one of the three Talmadge girls and wanted to
live like one.

The house at 1004 Hartford Way quickly became known
throughout Hollywood as Keaton's Italian Villa. Buster later estimated that it had cost $200,000 to build and another $100,000
to furnish. These figures may be inflated, but there is no doubt
that the house was expensive by the standards of the time. It was
certainly ample for the needs of the Keaton family:

. . . a two-story mansion with five bedrooms, two additional bedrooms for the servants, and a three-room apartment over the
garage for the gardener and his wife, who worked as our upstairs
maid. This made six servants with a cook, butler, chauffeur, and
governess.

The Italian Villa, 1928. *Museum of Modern Art / Film Stills Archive*

Jimmy and Bobby Keaton and their Little Italian Villa, 1928. *Rudi Blesh*

Despite his initial opposition to living in such a large house, Buster took to it with gusto. He had a great fondness for mechanical gadgets of every possible variety, and at the Italian Villa he had room to indulge himself freely. He installed a trout stream that meandered its way through the grounds, and an elaborate playhouse, an exact scale replica of the main house, was constructed for the two boys, Bobby and Jimmy. The grandiose steps running down to the swimming pool were justly admired, and in Buster's 1931 MGM film *Parlor, Bedroom and Bath,* shot in part at the Keaton home, they can still be seen as they originally were.

Natalie and Buster did a lot of entertaining at their new mansion, especially over the weekend, when they had barbecue parties for all their friends, with Buster presiding as chief cook. He had always had a strong interest in good food, and now his cooking became the talk of Hollywood. Some fifty or sixty guests would show up for Keaton's specialties, Chinese spareribs and huge English mutton chops. His friends from that time, Gilbert Roland and Buster Collier, can still remember the smell of those spectacular mutton chops half a mile away from the house.

The superb cuisine and festive ambiance of the Italian Villa attracted many regular visitors to the Keaton home, including all the members of the Talmadge clan, who liked to meet their many friends there. Peg liked to sit by the swimming pool with a long cool drink in her hand, shrewdly observing all the lovely and talented people who came to admire her wonderful daughters. Constance and Norma spent more time at Buster's than at their own homes and played with Buster's two little boys for hours on end.

Buster's family came to the new house much less frequently than the Talmadges, although Natalie remained on very good terms with both Myra and Louise. About this time Myra and Joe decided to separate, and Joe took up permanent residence at the Continental Hotel in downtown Los Angeles. There he quickly formed a relationship with a woman who practiced Christian Science. Joe stopped his drinking and never drank again for the rest of his life. There were no outward signs of bitterness at the separation; Myra and Joe had found they simply couldn't live together with any real peace. Joe and his "Christian Science Lady," as she was called by the Keaton children, were regularly invited to dinner at Myra's house on the children's birthdays and on holidays. Myra continued to live with her two younger children, Louise and Harry, in the house that Buster had bought her. Buster kept his father working in these years by using him to play the girl's father in *Sherlock, Jr.* and a barber who appears briefly in *Go West.*

Buster regarded his new home as a giant toy. Long before the two boys could possibly have been interested, Buster built an extremely complicated set of electric trains with which he himself played endlessly. This fascination with electric trains continued for the rest of his life. He also indulged to the full his love of practical jokes, and he had various items of furniture "arranged" so they would produce unexpected sounds if sat upon by the unwary. He constructed an especially strong drapery on which he could swing himself effortlessly down into the living room in acrobatic stunts similar to those performed by his friend Fairbanks in *The Black Pirate.*

There are those who think of Buster's infatuation with mechanical toys and games as indicative of a "childlike" mind. This quality, coupled with his total ingenuousness about money and people, has confirmed an image of Keaton as a gifted simpleton—a judgment that is far from accurate. If there was anything childlike about his love of mechanical things, it would be necessary to add, "but what an extraordinary child!" The astoundingly acute analytic powers found in Buster's films of this time flow directly from his very serious passion for comprehending the way in which things really work. The man who liked to build things is the same man who made *The Playhouse, Sherlock, Jr.,* and *The General.* He always said that he would have liked to have been a civil engineer if he had not been raised in the theater.

Buster held many card games at the Italian Villa. He found a perfect bridge partner in the well-known German-born stage and screen actor Louis Wolheim, who had created a sensation in 1924 with his Broadway performance in *What Price Glory?* A former professor of mathematics, Wolheim possessed a strong talent for cards and could maintain just as rigid a poker face as Buster. The two soon became famous as the "Deadly Pair" who were willing to take on anyone's challenge. This came on a number of occasions from Sam Goldwyn, who played badly and was always a bad loser.

Buster's mansion was also his stage—a place where he could show off his graceful acrobatic stunts, practice and test in front of his friends the bits of comic business he might later use in a film. The house was an ideal place in which to perform in front of an audience. Louise Brooks maintains, "One impression I stick to—Buster was always 'on.' I can see how this would be a great trial to even such a vacuous lump as Natalie." He was always on the go, "always composing and visualizing, inventing scenes. . . ." Keaton shared with Chaplin and George Gershwin this "let's-try-it-out-on-the-guests" way of solving their current technical problems.

At the age of thirty, Buster seemed to the people who knew him then to be reasonably happy. Though he was not a superstar, each of his recent films had made more than the last, and it looked as if he might soon become one. His marital problems were still unsolved, though, and he may well have remained in love with Natalie despite his many infidelities and her coolness and apparent apathy. Both Gilbert Roland and Collier recall the Keaton of 1925 as a friend of great personal warmth and unforgettable sweetness. He was fiercely enthusiastic about nearly everything, and he was doing the kind of thing he loved best of all: making films for his own pleasure under circumstances that have been enjoyed by few filmmakers, then or now. And yet along with this smiling image of success and happiness was the darker, enigmatic side of Keaton, the side that keeps showing up in so many of his films and that Samuel Beckett found so intriguing that he had Keaton in mind when he wrote *Waiting for Godot.* This is the Keaton none of his friends ever reached, the private Keaton that remained cut off from the world, unable or unwilling to communicate with his friends. Alcohol helped. He had apparently mastered his earlier fears about drinking and could now outdrink almost everyone he met. Accompanying this steadily growing capacity for alcohol was a striking ability to appear sober no matter how much liquor he had actually consumed.

[2]

I think Joe Schenck was the first old turtle Darwin
saw when the *Beagle* anchored off the Galapagos—
certainly not a cuddly "father figure" for Keaton.
Anyhow Buster, like Peter Pan, didn't want a father.
He had his magic world of film production and his
house rigged like a Douglas Fairbanks set—or Peter
Pan's ship.

—Louise Brooks, 1977

The work of the great silent comedians received very little critical attention at the time of their triumphs in the 1920s, for comedy was thought to be of suspect value. This lack of serious criticism may well have been a great blessing, for it prevented the
terrible self-consciousness that overtook Chaplin in the thirties.
Edmund Wilson was among the few critics to pay any attention
to Lloyd, Chaplin, and Keaton in the twenties. At the time of the
opening of *The Gold Rush* in the late summer of 1925, Wilson
wrote a long piece for *The New Republic* in which, after express-
ing the greatest admiration for the film, he went on to predict
that Chaplin's personal comedies would soon be supplanted by
the new "gag" comedies being turned out by Keaton and Lloyd
with the aid of their highly paid writing staffs. A few months
later, in a review of Keaton's *Go West,* Wilson was surprised to
find that he had been wrong, for Keaton and Lloyd had suddenly taken to imitating Chaplin. Wilson found the pathos in
both Keaton's *Go West* and Lloyd's *The Freshman* to arise from
what he thought must surely be the determined effort of both to
capture the huge and profitable *Gold Rush* audience. In *Go
West* and *The Freshman* the great number of gags had been replaced by what he called "straight drama." Wilson went on to say
that Keaton and Lloyd "or their producers have tried to follow
Chaplin's example of allowing their comic characters to become
partly credible as human beings: they have gone in for wist-
fulness and pathos."

Wilson's idea about the pathos in *The Freshman* probably arose
from the scene where the brokenhearted Harold breaks down

and cries, with his head in the lap of his girl. Correctly observing that Lloyd's talents as an actor were not really up to this kind of role, Wilson noted that Buster was far more capable, saying, "But Buster is an able pantomimist: his sullen and sensitive face commands a certain sympathy. We are, therefore, not entirely unresponsive to his newest picture *Go West*. Here he figures as a friendless boy on a remote Western ranch, who conceives an attachment for a cow."

Wilson's views about what motivated Keaton and Lloyd to develop in the direction they did are interesting, although Lloyd's debt to Chaplin at the time of *The Freshman* is less evident than Keaton's in *Go West*. Wilson's ideas bring up the fundamental question of just how free Keaton was in what is generally known as his "independent" period. Wilson was careful to add the words "or their producers" when he spoke of what had motivated this change of direction. In the case of Lloyd there is no problem, for he was his own producer. Buster's producer was Joe Schenck, who was quite responsive to what he thought were current trends. But, although Buster had a good deal of freedom, he still had to receive Joe's approval of a project before any money was spent.

In addition, several of these projects originated with Joe and his associates rather than with Buster—a problem that neither Chaplin nor Lloyd encountered. After *Go West*, Buster's next two films, *Seven Chances* and *Battling Butler,* were both properties that had been bought for Buster without consulting him and were presented to him as faits accomplis.

There were other problems with Joe Schenck: he gave Buster poor actresses to play the heroines in all his films of the twenties. Schenck had good reason to believe that Buster's girls in these pictures were just passive bystanders, girls who get stuffed into sacks, or who get thrown into the water to be rescued from drowning. He saw no sense in paying expensive, competent young actresses to play these simple roles. It wasn't that Schenck was cheap, for he had been willing to pay $25,000 to buy the S.S. *Buford* for *The Navigator*. *That* he could see, but not a dime more than the bare minimum for actresses. This may explain the lackluster quality of the girls in *Seven Chances* and *Go West*.

Although, as Louise Brooks has observed, Schenck was scarcely a "cuddly father figure" for Buster, he nevertheless performed some fatherly functions, especially in his role of the paymaster. In the mid-twenties, Buster's pictures were costing Schenck and his fellow investors about $200,000 per film as the actual negative cost. The additional costs of making prints, publicity and promotion expenses, plus advertising, brought the total cost up to $350,000 and $400,000. The gross receipts were between $500,000 and $750,000, leaving a net profit of anywhere from $100,000 to $400,000. These were not huge profits, nor were they in the million-dollar class that Buster later claimed they were.

Certainly Joe Schenck's relationship with Buster as his brother-in-law had much to do with the relative freedom he gave him to make these films, for it was startling that he entrusted relatively large sums of money to the hands of someone who had absolutely no interest in money. As the twenties advanced, it must have become clear to Joe and his brother Nicholas of MGM that Buster was not in the million-dollar class with Chaplin and Lloyd and never would be, that he was somehow a "special case."

By Buster's own reports, he accepted Schenck very much as a dutiful son would: if that father said NO, YOU CAN'T DO IT! Buster might argue, but Joe's decision would be final, and there were no lasting bad feelings between them. Besides being genuinely fond of his card-playing young star, Schenck had a tremendous admiration for talent, and there was no doubt that Keaton had it. The box-office grosses didn't adequately reflect it, but at least they showed *some* profit. And Schenck kept hoping that Buster would eventually break into the bigger grosses, so he continued to buy story properties for him that he considered to be more commercial than Buster's own projects.

As a ferociously enthusiastic cardplayer himself, Schenck admired Buster's ability to make fools of most of the big players in and around Hollywood at the time; he loved to match Buster against rival producers like Sam Goldwyn. Joe spent a lot of time at the Keaton home, often finding Norma there with one of her lovers, along with Constance and Peg. He too was a victim of Buster's endless practical jokes: he was the lucky recipient of a number of high-grade exploding cigars, which he nevertheless continued to accept whenever they were offered to him.

In the last months of 1924 Buster began shooting *Seven Chances*, a film that he later placed far down on his list of personal favorites. At least one major reason for his low opinion of it was the fact that Schenck had bought the film rights to the 1916 play by Roi Cooper Megrue without telling him about it in advance: "That was bought by someone and sold to Joe Schenck without us knowing it. . . . He just went to the preview. . . . And he buys this thing for me and it's no good for me at all. . . ."

The play is about young Jimmy Shannon, who finds out one day that, if he can find a bride by seven o'clock that evening, he will inherit a million dollars. Jimmy knows seven girls to whom he can propose before seven o'clock—there is no end to the sevens. Buster asked his three writers to turn this into a Keaton film, but no one at the Keaton Studio was happy with the results. As Buster said later: "I had a bad picture and we knew it too. And there was nothing we could seem to do about it."

A chance effect provided an escape from the sure failure they all felt:

> I had a short sequence in there where I was running away from a batch of women, man had advertised for a bride. Didn't say what age or anything, just said, "Bride wanted at the church by three o'clock or something and these women, all shapes, and forms had showed up with home made bridal out-fits on, lace curtains, gingham table cloths for veils and this chase was on. . . . And I led them off into the open country and was coming down the side of the hill and there was some boulder rocks on that hill and I hit one accidentally, sliding down that hill on my feet most of the time and jarred this one rock loose and it actually hit two other rocks and I looked behind me in the scene and here come three boulder rocks about the size of bowling alley balls coming at me, bouncing down the hill with me and I actually had to scram to get away from them. . . .

This scene was shown to one preview audience, and then another; both audiences began to laugh uncontrollably at the sight of Keaton being pursued by all those little rocks. He took the hint and promptly went back with his crew and . . .

. . . built fifteen hundred rocks, starting from grapefruit size up to one that was eight feet in diameter and spotted one of those big barren mountains with these rocks and then I went up there and got started. . . . Some of them, for instance, the big one weighed four hundred pounds. . . . You could get hit with it all right. Well I got in the middle of the rock chase and it saved the picture for me and that was an accident. . . . It was just an out and out accident.

The wild chase down the side of the mountain with Keaton dodging and ducking the boulders is one of the most electrifying of all the chases in his films. Another odd and disquieting scene takes place just prior to the great chase. Totally exhausted by his exertions in proposing to nearly every woman he has met during the day, Buster has turned up at the church, where he hopes to meet one who will be his willing bride. His friends have placed an ad in the paper setting forth his desperate need. It is now nearly three o'clock, and he falls asleep in the first aisle of the silent, empty church, stretched out full-length in the pew. Suddenly one of his prospective brides turns up, all properly veiled, followed in a moment by another, and then another, in an ever-quickening tempo. The church is soon filled with hundreds of these would-be brides. Buster awakens slowly to discover, with mounting horror, that he is the groom they have all come to meet. The scene is grandly, magnificently bizarre, and

its surrealist overtones were noted with great interest by Lorca and Buñuel in Spain.*

Buster could have told Joe Schenck YOU WERE WRONG, SEE, WRONG, for *Seven Chances* was not as successful as *The Navigator;* it grossed $598,288 or nearly $100,000 less than its predecessor. One good reason may have been the formidable competition that year from Keaton's main rivals, Chaplin and Lloyd, with both *The Gold Rush* and *The Freshman.* Many reviewers had noted the strong resemblance of the *kind* of character that Buster portrayed in *Seven Chances* to the type of "go-getter" young man that was Harold Lloyd's specialty, even down to his wearing a straw hat in the picture. Joe Schenck was undoubtedly aware that such comparisons would be made, but he thought that they would have beneficial effects at the box office. He knew all too well that Lloyd's films outgrossed Buster's by a wide margin and believed that Buster's appearance in "Lloyd material" could only help him. If this was the plan, it didn't work, for in the long run there *was* no resemblance; Buster took over this material and made it his own, despite all his grumbling.

At the time of the New York opening of *Seven Chances* in March 1925, the newspapers carried accounts of an interview that Buster had given the press. At this "interview," a press release which purported to contain Keaton's ideas about the future of film comedy was distributed. It is, however, obvious that Buster didn't write a word of it; it is surely the product of Schenck's publicity department. The press release stresses the idea that Buster would continue to make his pictures along legitimate dramatic lines, with a reduction in the number of gags. This story may have attracted Edmund Wilson's attention to the way Keaton might be heading. Wilson may also have read that Keaton's team of writers, Bruckman, Mitchell, and Havez, were all going their separate ways, probably for financial reasons. Bruckman was hired to work for Lloyd on his *For Heaven's Sake,* not returning to Buster until the summer of 1926, while Mitchell joined Paramount to write for Raymond Griffith. But a "real writer" was going to replace them.

Shortly after the press conference in New York, Buster an-

See Appendix.

nounced that he had hired Robert E. Sherwood, the drama and film critic, to write an original "screen story" for him. The gags for the forthcoming production would be supplied by Lex Neal, Buster's old summertime friend from Lake Muskegon. In 1925 Sherwood, the future Pulitzer Prize dramatist and speech writer for Franklin D. Roosevelt, was working as an editor for what is now known as "the old *Life*" to distinguish it from Henry Luce's pictorial *Life* of the thirties. In the 1920s *Life* was a national humor weekly for which Sherwood reviewed plays and films. He displayed enthusiasm for Buster's work as early as 1920 when he reviewed *The Saphead,* singling it out for high praise. Sherwood was widely read as a critic and was very much a tastemaker in the cultural life of the twenties.

The decision to hire Sherwood seems to have been an attempt to give the Keaton productions a touch of class. Chaplin was the only one of the silent comedians who got any serious critical attention at the time. Schenck and his associates, particularly John W. Considine, Jr., knew that this attention paid off at the box office, for there were still many people who rejected the movies as "trashy." If Sherwood admired Keaton that much, why not have him write an original screenplay for Buster? Sherwood's name on a Keaton film would give it the added prestige of a well-known literary name. Zukor and Sam Goldwyn had been the trailblazers in this practice of hiring famous writers during the twenties.

Sherwood's plot for Keaton concerned the fate of a young couple who find themselves trapped at the top of a sixty-story building under construction in New York. Buster was to play a character associated with the firm responsible for the building. To impress his girl he takes her up to see the view at twilight from the top of the building, a wilderness of bare steel beams, eerie catwalks, and wooden platforms. The couple discover that the elevator has stopped working for the night and they must accommodate themselves to spending the night aloft. Besides resembling the basic dramatic situation of Keaton's own *Navigator,* there is a strong suggestion of Harold Lloyd here as well, for his famous *Safety Last* of 1923 was still very much in people's minds, including Sherwood's.

Nothing ever came of Sherwood's idea for the film, for neither he nor Lex Neal could devise a sufficiently interesting way to get the couple down from the building. Thirty years later, Buster was sitting with his third wife, Eleanor, in the lobby of the Savoy Hotel in London when the tall and distinguished figure of Sherwood glided by. Without breaking stride, Sherwood addressed Keaton out of the side of his mouth: *"Don't worry, Buster, I'll get you down from there yet!"*

Despite all Schenck's costly efforts, Buster never became a superstar. Chaplin was clearly in first place, with Lloyd just behind him and Keaton running a very poor third. In fact, Lloyd was always in first place in dollar earnings because of his regular output of two films per year compared with Chaplin's one every three or four years: *The Kid* in 1921, *The Gold Rush* in 1925, *The Circus* in 1928, and *City Lights* not until 1931. Buster made just as many films as Lloyd but never reached anywhere near as wide an audience, somehow remaining a bit special in the eyes of many exhibitors. He never emerged as a public personality, for Buster never gave the kinds of interviews that fan magazines and newspapers of the twenties liked to print. Stars were asked their views on such subjects as companionate marriage, the Scopes trial in Tennessee, flappers, Prohibition, Wall Street, and the future of the cinema. Buster had not much to say about any of these subjects, for his favorite things to talk about were baseball and the technical aspects of filmmaking. He simply wasn't good copy. He remained a very private person, striking many of his interviewers as remote and detached.

Buster also made enemies because he could not or would not remember people's names; he simply had no use for them. Ben Pearson, Keaton's agent for fifteen years, recalls Buster emerging arm in arm with Noel Coward from an elevator of the Sherry Netherland Hotel in New York in 1958. After a few final words, Pearson observed the two men shaking hands affably, Coward proceeding on to the street outside. Buster's first words on greeting Pearson were that he "hadn't seen that fella in thirty years. What's his name?" The last time that Buster had encountered Coward was in 1925, when he had served him a giant mutton chop at the Italian Villa in Beverly Hills. People's names stuck with Buster only if they were very close friends indeed. He worked professionally with some people for years without ever getting their names straight, and he couldn't see why some of them managed to get so upset about it.

Daily life at Buster's Italian Villa was relaxed, in spite of Buster's stunts. Louise Brooks recalls it as a peaceful place:

> The Talmadge women were the most natural, comfortable people I ever knew. Connie may have suffered briefly with English Royalty fever but she remained naturally delightful; Natalie was a very comfortable lump; Norma, curled up in a chair, was very comfortably bored (even with Gilbert Roland). And Peg—old Buddha—was kept comfortable, as she surveyed the scene, by her attentive daughters. . . . The teaching of old Buddha was sound. Get money, and then get comfortable. . . .

Constance had divorced her second husband and was about to marry her third. Norma, after eight years of marriage to Joe Schenck, had embarked on a long relationship with Gilbert Roland, which Joe had taken in his stride. Harold Goodwin recalls the first meeting of Roland and Schenck.

> Buster started to barbecue and who showed up but Joe Schenck. I was a newcomer to this kind of situation and I thought maybe there would be some fireworks but everything went smoothly. Schenck treated Gilbert like a long lost son.

Norma's marriage to Joe remained "in name only" until their divorce in 1934, whereas her younger sister Natalie seemed content to go on living with a man she had not slept with now for nearly three years.

[3]

Beneath his lack of emotion he was also uninsistently sardonic; deep below that . . . for those who sensed it, there was in his comedy a freezing whisper not of pathos but of melancholia.

—James Agee, 1949

I used to daydream an awful lot in pictures; I could get carried away and visualize all the fairylands in the world. Dream sequences. . . . Perhaps that's why Agee says that. I guess it was just my natural way of workin'. . . .

—Buster Keaton, 1958

As Friendless in *Go West*, 1925. *Museum of Modern Art / Film Stills Archive*

More than any of his other feature films, *Go West*, Buster's second 1925 release, has a "freezing whisper of melancholia." The central character, Friendless, is surely the most pathetic of all Keaton heroes. He is without human ties, completely on his own in the world, the kind of person that Samuel Beckett has spent most of his life writing about. In making this film Buster may have had in mind a phrase he liked to repeat—"Comedy is a serious business"—for it is filled with much of what Agee called Keaton's "disturbing tension" and "dreamlike beauty."

After some preliminary mishaps on freight trains, Friendless arrives at his destination, a rather somber ranch in Arizona. He is given employment by the owner and quickly shows his ineptness at everything he touches. There is one exception, for he soon finds his only true friend, the cow Brown Eyes, whose love he stirs by removing a stone from her hoof. Like Androcles and the lion, Friendless has by this single gesture endeared himself to Brown Eyes forever. Friendless is so far removed from the life around him that he seems scarcely human; he is truly alone. As Keaton correctly surmised, his alienation works wonders to establish Friendless as someone we *do* care about.

As the critic Daniel Moews has indicated, all the Keaton films contain an elaborate system of symmetrical effects or balances. In *Go West*, Brown Eyes is scorned by the large herd of cattle of which she is nominally a part: she is just as much an outcast in the bovine world as Friendless is in his. When at long last Brown Eyes licks Friendless's hand and he proceeds to return the caresses of his beloved, a sense of genuine affection is conveyed. It has somewhat the same emotional intensity as Chaplin's final close-up in *City Lights* when he reveals his true identity to the girl whose sight he has restored. Some critics have suggested that *Go West* is an extended ironic commentary on Chaplin's sentimentality. But perhaps Keaton really wanted to see how far he could go with pathos and still succeed in making a superbly comic film.

Go West is an experiment in mixing things up constantly to startle the audience. We don't know what to expect and we can't anticipate our response. There is a curious sequence in which Friendless, desperate for money to buy Brown Eyes so that she will not have to be shipped off to the slaughterhouse, plays poker with three of his fellow ranch hands. The ranch foreman starts dealing himself aces from the bottom of the deck, and when Friendless protests, the foreman pulls a gun, repeating the famous line from Owen Wister's *The Virginian* as he does so: "When you say that—SMILE!" But of course Friendless/Keaton *can't* smile, so with the aid of his fingers, he forces his facial muscles into a dreadful mockery of one. Keaton got this idea from the famous motif in Griffith's *Broken Blossoms* in which Lillian Gish, in the midst of several hysterical episodes with her brutal father, performs the same feat.

The filming of *Go West* was expensive and took a lot longer than had been expected, for the entire picture was shot on location.

> We shot *Go West* about 60 miles out of Kingman, Arizona. We were really out in open country . . . four cameramen . . . electrician—generally takes about three men with him . . . technical man—takes a couple of dozen carpenters with him. . . . Then we house 'em up there, see—we take tents and everything else and a portable kitchen.

Things went wrong, for the heat of the Arizona desert nearly melted the emulsion on the film. The cameras had to be covered with small canvas shrouds filled with ice. Brown Eyes went into heat halfway through the shooting, and since there was no possibility of finding a substitute, Buster and his company had to wait around until she got over it, which took nearly two weeks. Besides the members of his large technical crew, Buster took Natalie and the two boys along for company in the desert.

The climax of the film was to have included the wildest cattle stampede that Buster could devise:

> I actually turned 'em loose here in Los Angeles in the Santa Fe depot in the freight yards, and brought 'em up Seventh Street to Broadway. . . . And we put cowboys off every side street to stop people in automobiles from comin' into it. . . . I brought 300 head of steers up that street. . . . I saw a costume place, and I saw a Devil's suit. . . . 'Cause I was tryin' to lead 'em towards the slaughter house. I put that suit on and I thought I'd get a funny chase sequence. . . . But as I moved, they stopped too. They piled up on each other. They didn't mind a stampede at all. . . .

Buster obtained some extraordinary scenes with hundreds of cattle milling about in barber shops, police stations, grocery stores, and even a china shop. His own verdict on the film was strangely negative: "Some parts I liked, but as a picture, in general, I didn't care for it." At the box office *Go West* did almost exactly as well as *Seven Chances,* grossing just under $600,000.

The last of Buster's features made for Joe Schenck to be released by MGM was *Battling Butler* of 1926. This film was based on the Broadway play that had starred the popular British song-and-dance man Jack Buchanan. Buster was not consulted about the purchase, but on this occasion he bore no grudge against Joe for buying it, for it became the most successful of all the silent films he made.

The film recalls both *The Saphead* and *The Navigator,* for Alfred Butler is another spoiled weakling who undergoes a transformation to strength and power through the love of the heroine. In order to woo the girl, Alfred is forced to pretend that he is really the famous boxer Battling Butler. Through a series of complications the real and quite nasty Battling Butler discovers the deception, while Alfred discovers that he must enter the ring against Butler's next opponent, the Alabama Murderer. The play had concluded with a cop-out situation in which the real Battling Butler takes on the Alabama Murderer himself in the ring, thus sparing Alfred a beating. This may have worked on Broadway, but Buster and his four writers knew it wouldn't work in a film.

> We knew better than to do that to a motion picture audience. We couldn't promise 'em for seven reels that I was goin' to fight in the ring and then not fight. So we staged a fight in the dressing room with the guy . . . and myself. And it worked out swell.

It did, for Buster and the writers came up with an entirely new ending in which the real Butler comes to Alfred's dressing room after the fight with the idea of beating him to a pulp in the presence of his terrified girl friend. The timid Alfred is forced to defend himself against the onslaught but is helpless in the hands of the boxer. Suddenly Alfred looks over at his girl and is transformed into a maniacally aggressive fighter, smashing Butler to the floor again and again, until he is finally pulled away from his now helpless enemy. The transformation of Alfred Butler from a likable but spineless weakling into a raging fury is quite magical and, strangely enough, quite convincing, for Buster staged the fight so that it truly looks as if he has gone berserk.

Both Schenck and MGM were convinced that in *Battling Butler* they had another hit equal to *The Navigator,* and they began to promote it heavily months before its release. They again hired John Held, Jr., for the ad campaign, and his cartoon of Buster appeared in all the popular magazines of the time. Their hopes were fulfilled, for the film earned a two-week engagement at the Capital Theater in New York City, the principal show spot for Loew's major attractions. Within a year after its release in August 1926 the picture had grossed nearly three-quarters of a million dollars, more than any of Keaton's previous films.

Two years earlier, at the time of the triumphal opening of *The Navigator* in late 1924, Joe Schenck had rewarded Keaton with a new contract. This time the reward was to be of much greater consequence to him—he allowed Buster to go ahead with the production that became the most expensive of all his films, as well as the one that lost the most money. It was his masterpiece, *The General.*

7

THE MASTERPIECE
THAT FAILED

[1]

Well, the moment you give me a locomotive and things like that to play with, as a rule I find some way to get laughs out of it.

—Keaton, 1965

It means that we're goin' to have a lot of film with no laughs in it. But we won't worry about it. . . .

—Clyde Bruckman, 1926

My job is to figure the costs. . . . I'm a business man.

—Joseph M. Schenck, 1941

In early 1925 Schenck gave a private dinner party at the Hotel Roosevelt on Hollywood Boulevard to celebrate his acquisition of Rudolph Valentino. A photograph (page 136) taken there shows Joe to be a very happy man, for he has under contract, or is in partnership with, nearly all the major acting talents of the silent film era: Pickford and Fairbanks, Chaplin and Keaton, Valentino and William S. Hart, and the Talmadge sisters. As Schenck faces the camera, his smile is that of a proud and happy ringmaster.

Buster might never have been able to make *The General* had it not been for Schenck's recently formed connection with United Artists, the distributing organization created for the independently produced films of D. W. Griffith, Chaplin, Douglas Fairbanks, and Mary Pickford. All four had been equally anxious to avoid the high financial toll exacted by releasing organizations like Zukor's Paramount and Associated–First National, which had been consuming large portions of the grosses of their films. They had decided to bypass Zukor and all the rest of his compet-

Joe Schenck's dinner party: Natalie Talmadge Keaton, William S. Hart, Norma, B. P. Schulberg, Douglas Fairbanks, Peg Talmadge, unknown, Buster, unknown, Mary Pickford, Charles Chaplin, Charlotte Pickford, Joe Schenck, Natasha Rambova, unknown, Rudolph Valentino, Constance Talmadge, John Considine, unknown, unknown. *Louise Keaton*

itors and created in 1919 what they called "the Company Built by the Stars."

Right from the start the chief obstacle to the success of the firm was lack of product. These four stars (Griffith was just as much a star as his partners in the mind of the public) had created a worldwide distribution organization to take care of just their own output. But because of prior contractual commitments to Associated–First National, Chaplin, for one, was unable to supply his partners with a film until *A Woman of Paris* in 1923, a film which made no money whatsoever; it was not until 1925 that he gave his friends a triumph with *The Gold Rush*. Despite their annual grosses of as much as $13 million, the firm continued to operate at a loss for six of its first eight years. When there *were* profits they were pitifully small: $68,000 in 1923 and $86,000 in 1926; but the losses ran as high as $470,000 in one year.

Besides the burden of the financial losses, Pickford, Fairbanks, and Chaplin were distressed to find out that their fourth partner, D. W. Griffith, had signed a director's contract in early 1924 with Zukor at Paramount. He had been forced to do so because of the huge losses he had sustained in running his studio in Mamaroneck, New York. Griffith's defection meant even less product for the firm to handle, leaving only Pickford and Fairbanks to supply it regularly with pictures. Someone was badly needed to rescue United Artists from its plight, and the obvious choice was Joe Schenck, the president of Buster Keaton Productions. The three partners felt that no other man in the industry could turn up producing talent as well as he could. They also felt that he was the best man around to work with the "difficult" producers, such as Sam Goldwyn. The partners had made their first overtures to Joe Schenck as far back as 1920, but he refused, knowing that their main reason then was to secure the release of his wife Norma's films. By 1924 things had gotten far worse for United Artists and they offered Joe a full partnership, a challenge which he readily accepted.

Within a few months Joe had signed up Valentino for his last two films, *The Eagle* and *The Son of the Sheik*. He soon added Gloria Swanson and her independent productions to the United Artists' fold. Joe was convinced that the twenty-two-year-old Howard Hughes was one of the younger producing talents who could make profitable films; he became one of United Artists' regular producers. Joe persuaded his doubtful partners that it would be good business to take on Sam Goldwyn, first merely as a releasing producer like Hughes, but later as a full partner. No matter what they thought of Goldwyn personally, he did produce films that made money.

The first president of United Artists, Hiram Abrams, died suddenly in early 1926 and Joe Schenck was elected to take his place. One of his first decisions was that the firm would distribute the next Keaton film, despite his prior arrangements with his brother Nicholas and MGM. Joe's decision to give Buster the additional funds to make *The General* was undoubtedly influenced by the production "company" he was now keeping: Chaplin, Pickford, and Fairbanks, all of whom budgeted their pictures on a lavish scale.

The General is now commonly regarded as Keaton's master-piece and as one of the two or three indisputably great silent film comedies. All categories aside, there are many who consider it to be among the greatest films ever made. There is currently available a *Film Guide to The General,* and the film is studied at many American universities. When the American Film Institute polled its members in 1977 on the fifty best American films of all time, the resulting list slighted the silent era but did include *The General.* Only four other silent films were included: Griffith's *The Birth of a Nation* and *Intolerance* and Chaplin's *The Gold Rush* and *City Lights.*

The present high critical standing of *The General* is relatively new: except for sporadic screenings at the Museum of Modern Art in New York City and at a few other archival collections in the 1940s and 1950s, it was not widely viewed for many years; it was not anywhere near as familiar as *The Gold Rush* and *The Freshman.* Before attaining its current status as a classic, Keaton's most ambitious film had to go through a long period of almost total rejection.

Buster always freely credited Clyde Bruckman with the idea of filming William A. Pittenger's Civil War narrative of 1863, *Daring and Suffering: A History of the Great Railway Adventure.* (After 1893 the title of the book became *The Great Locomotive Chase.*) All the bare bones of Keaton's story were in Pittenger's book, which concerned the true adventures of a handful of Union spies disguised as Southern civilians. They had as their leader James J. Andrews, a man of considerable courage with a gift for wily enterprise. He and his followers had seized a Confederate locomotive and a few cars of rolling stock near Atlanta, Georgia. Their initial purpose was to head north with the stolen train in the direction of Chattanooga, Tennessee, destroying all communication lines along the right of way; their ultimate aim was to get the train safely behind the Northern lines. Buster later summed up their plan in his usual terse style: "As soon as they stole that engine, they wanted to pull out of there, to disconnect the telegraph and burn bridges and destroy enough track to cripple the Southern army supply route." The stolen Confederate train was immediately pursued by its angry engineer, who,

The General, 1926. National Film Archive / Stills Library

with the help of the Southern troops, finally recaptured his beloved locomotive. The spies were captured, and a number of them eventually died on the scaffold.

Buster's amazing zeal for absolute historical accuracy, for "getting things right," was his central concern in the making of the picture. "I took that page of history and I stuck to it in all detail. I staged it exactly the way it happened." There was, however, one significant change: Pittenger's book saw the whole affair from the Union's point of view, but Keaton changed it to that of the Confederacy. He later said, "You can always make villains out of the Northerners, but you cannot make a villain out of the South."

No pains were spared to make the film as authentic as they possibly could—"until it hurts," as Buster said. He even attempted to use the actual stolen locomotive that had been enshrined in the Chattanooga railroad station since the end of the Civil War. This proved to be impossible, for the Tennesseeans of 1926 refused permission, uneasy at the notion of a comic film about the Civil War.

As with all his previous features, Buster was responsible for nearly every aspect of *The General.* "Now this was my own story, my own continuity, I directed it, I cut it and titled it. So actually it was a pet." He still loved to talk about its production a full forty years after he had completed it.

> I went to the original location, from Atlanta, Georgia, up to Chattanooga, and the scenery didn't look very good. In fact, it looked terrible. The railroad tracks I couldn't use at all, because the Civil War trains were narrow-gauge. I had to have narrow-gauge, so I went to Oregon. And in Oregon, the whole state is honey-combed with narrow-gauge railways for all the lumber mills. So we got the rolling equipment, wheels and trucks, and we built the freight train and our passenger train, and we remodeled three locomotives. Luckily, the engines working on these lumber camps were all so doggone old that it was an easy job. . . . At that time they didn't pay much attention to numbers on engines—they named them all. That's why the main engine was called "The General" and the one I chased it with was "Texas." . . .

Buster's chief technical man, Fred Gabourie, had discovered that the area around Cottage Grove, Oregon, was a feasible substitute for Georgia and Tennessee, and it was there that *The General* was shot in June and July of 1926. It required seventeen railway carloads of equipment—all of it shipped up from Los Angeles. Five hundred men were hired as extras to play the Union and Confederate soldiers in the picture, all members of the Oregon National Guard. "And we managed to locate about 125 horses. . . . I housed the men for a week in tourist cars given to us by the Union Pacific . . . and put 'em in blue uniforms and bring 'em goin' from right to left, and take 'em out, put 'em in gray uniforms, bring 'em goin' from left to right. . . . And fought the war. . . ."

Many of Keaton's critics have commented on the stunningly convincing look of *The General,* often comparing it with the Civil

Buster and his production crew for *The General*, Cottage Grove, Oregon, June 1926. *Margaret Herrick Library of the Academy of Motion Picture Arts and Sciences*

The General, 1926. *Museum of Modern Art / Film Stills Archive*

War photographs of Mathew Brady. In the fifty years since it was made, *The General* has become a piece of American folklore. The critic Elliott Rubinstein has made the claim that *The General* for many of us *is* the Civil War, for few films have ever come as close to rendering the physical look of a period in history.

The story is almost solely devoted to the recovery by Johnnie Gray (Buster) of his stolen locomotive. In a brief prologue we are shown that young Johnnie has two loves in his life: his girl, Annabelle, and his beloved *General*. While paying a formal courting visit to her home, Johnnie receives the news of the firing on Fort Sumter. Annabelle expects that Johnnie, along with her brother, will enlist for the Southern cause. Johnnie tries to oblige her but is turned down for service because he is valued more as a railway engineer, although he is not told why he has been rejected. Annabelle angrily spurns Johnnie as a coward, and their engagement is broken. At this point the Great Locomotive Chase begins; the Union spies seize Johnnie's *General* and Annabelle as well.

Nearly all the rest of the film is concerned with Johnnie's fierce, impassioned, and even inspired efforts to recover his beloved train. He commandeers a handcar and starts pumping away after *The General*. After coming to a missing piece of track, the handcar falls into the river. Johnnie then seizes a bicycle with a huge front wheel, which does not take him very far. On foot, he finally reaches his destination, a Southern troop encampment, where he is given a locomotive, *The Texas*, with which to pursue *The General*.

The death of *The Texas; The General*, 1926. *Museum of Modern Art / Film Stills Archive*

The death of *The Texas; The General,* 1926. *National Film Archive / Stills Library*

The film is a masterpiece of improvisation; at no other time in his career did Buster manage to accomplish such a miraculous blend of story and gag. What at first may seem to be a straightforward "chase" picture is gradually revealed to be an intricately related structure in which all the parts fit together with a very precise logic. As with most of Keaton's silent films, there is an almost perfect symmetry to *The General:* most of the events in the pursuit of *The General* by Buster in *The Texas* have their counterpart on the return trip southward where everything is reversed. Now Johnnie is in *The General* being pursued by *The Texas,* and he revenges himself on his enemies by doing to them what they had done going the other way.

The climax of the picture occurs when Johnnie lures the pursuing *Texas* to a log bridge over the Rock River and sets the bridge afire before proceeding on his way with *The General* and Annabelle. A fiercely proud Union general gives the command to the train's engineer to proceed across the burning bridge, for he is convinced that it will hold up under the crossing. It doesn't, and the train plunges into the river below with a huge splash of scalding steam. It's quite clear that it is a real locomotive collapsing into a real river, and the stunned expression on the Union general's face is one of the greatest moments in film. This single take of the train going to its death reputedly cost Joe Schenck about $42,000, probably the most expensive single take in films until that time. It has the smashing effect of a blow.

The General was first shown publicly in Los Angeles on December 22, 1926, but it was not put into general release until the following February. The early version was somewhat longer than the one that is shown today, for it contained some scenes with Snitz Edwards, the little actor who had appeared with Buster in *Seven Chances* and *Battling Butler*. There exist some tantalizing stills showing Buster attired in a stovepipe hat, talking to his friend, but by February, Edward's part in the picture had been completely eliminated, reducing the running time to about 82 minutes.

The New York reviews of the picture were terrible. There were then eleven major papers in New York reviewing films, and of these eight were completely hostile, two were cautiously favorable, and only the reviewer in the Brooklyn *Daily Eagle* recognized it as a work of genius. Keaton's principal backer as a critic, Robert E. Sherwood, objected to the film on the basic principle that a comedy cannot contain scenes of killing, and he deemed *The General* a failure for this lapse in judgment.

The regular *New York Times* critic, Mordaunt Hall, perhaps the man with the greatest track record in film history for being wrong, felt that "it is by no means as good as Mr. Keaton's previous efforts." The *Herald-Tribune* found it "long and tedious—the least funny thing Buster Keaton has ever done." The *Daily Telegraph* was quite blunt, describing it as "a pretty trite and stodgy piece of screenfare, a rehash, pretentiously garnered of any old two-reel chase comedy. . . . The audience received 'The General' with polite attention, occasionally a laugh, and occasionally a yawn . . . disappointing." The *Daily Mirror* found it "slow, very slow . . . ," with its reviewer advising Keaton to "pull yourself together, Buster. That's all." Despite his high praise for the film in the *Daily Eagle* Martin Dickstein indicated that the picture would not please everyone and that it was for the select few: "Probably lots of people . . . will not think it funny at all. . . . I give you 'The General,' a comedy for the exclusive enjoyment of the matured senses. . . . Buster Keaton has made a financial *faux pas,* perhaps. . . ."

Buster never cared to admit the critics' rejection of his favorite film. He usually didn't pay much attention to what reviewers thought of his films, but with *The General* the hostile press was difficult to ignore. The domestic gross was only $474,264, over $300,000 less than his previous film, *Battling Butler*. *The General* had been an expensive film to make: its negative cost was $415,232. For a film even to begin to make a profit it had to at least double the negative cost, and the picture emerged as a complete financial disaster for Schenck and United Artists.

The most likely reason that the film failed so badly at the time with both the critics and the wider public is the sheer richness it offers—it was just too good. A great many things happen with great rapidity in *The General,* so many things that the audiences of 1927 may have found it too difficult to follow and told their friends to stay away from it, which they did.

The total failure of his most ambitious film must have hurt Buster badly, but he never spoke about it. He always *had* to keep his pain to himself, concealed from everybody, even his closest friends. He had learned to hide his emotions as a child in vaudeville, and now at thirty-one he couldn't change. Buster Collier recalls it was *impossible* for his friend to express any sort of pain at any time.

Aside from the emotional hurt, the failure of *The General* inevitably threatened to some extent the creative freedom that Buster had so far enjoyed in making his films. The liberty to experiment, to take pains, to be wholly original, is always facilitated by financial success. Buster never admitted that *The General,* his pet of pets, had actually lost money, but Schenck must have told him the truth in no uncertain terms and no doubt told him that his next film had to be based on surefire material and cost a lot less than *The General.* Schenck was determined that there be no more expensive fiascos. The result was Buster's *College* of 1927, the Keaton feature film that most superficially resembles the work of Harold Lloyd. Lloyd's *The Freshman* had been one of the most popular films of 1925, with the critics and especially at the box office. Schenck's decision to have Buster undertake a picture about a bumbling, would-be athlete at college was certainly a comedown from the heights of *The General.* Buster couldn't have felt very happy, but he was not giving the orders.

[2]

He could never say he was hurt. . . . It was those
hangovers that began to do him in. . . . Oh boy,
those hangovers!

—Buster Collier, 1977

He seemed unable to deal with people in the real
world. That is when, I suspect, booze ceased to be a
creative release and became his solution to wretched
reality.

—Louise Brooks, 1977

By about 1925 drinking was a central part of Buster's life. He
had become an alcoholic and exhibited many of the classic symp-
toms of that disease, such as increasing capacity and denial that
he had a problem. From a purely medical point of view alcoholism is today generally regarded as a disease of unknown or-
igins for which there is no known cure. It is tempting to put
forward Buster's painful childhood on the stage, the physical
abuse he received from his father, or his father's own alcoholism
as possible causes, but medical opinion today considers such explanations inadequate. Alcoholism is sufficiently autonomous as
a disease for its ravages against the victim to proceed steadily
onward with or without the presence of any of these apparent
explanations. Once the addiction has taken hold, the drinking
becomes an end in itself, a way of life.

Buster's increasing use of alcohol actually coincided for a short
time with the period of his greatest creativity, just as it did with
many of his famous contemporaries such as Hart Crane, F. Scott
Fitzgerald, and William Faulkner. Although there were sober
days in the lives of the creators of *The Bridge*, *The Great Gatsby*,
and *The Sound and the Fury*, there is no doubt that their alcoholism was well advanced when they wrote these books. Buster's case was very different from the writers', for he was above
all a physical artist who always required his body to be in absolutely first-rate condition. For a number of years he ac-

complished daily the miracle of drinking late into the night and turning up at his studio the next morning in apparently great shape. He was young and resilient—in fact, he never really thought he would grow old. But as time passed, his powers of recovery from the increasingly bad hangovers began to wane.

Some of his friends began to worry about the drinking, but their concern was of no avail, for it was almost impossible to argue with Buster about anything. He had definite opinions about things, and drinking was no exception. He was confident he could control it and did not require the concern or the advice of his friends. He certainly wasn't going to stop drinking. Besides, nearly all his friends and everybody at the Italian Villa— Norma, Constance, and Natalie—drank. A life of abstinence was unthinkable.

In Collier's opinion Buster's heavy drinking arose in part from his boredom with Natalie. As time went on, they had less and less to say to each other. He became aware that the Talmadge family looked down on him not only as a mere comedian, but as a mere buffoon, lacking class or distinction, or even education: *he was a common man.*

Buster retaliated by having affairs with many of the women who wanted him, for there were many girls in Hollywood who were eager to go to bed with the gracefully shy Buster Keaton. Most of them were from the fringes of Hollywood life, but some of them, including Alice Lake and Mae Busch, had appeared in a number of films.

Beginning with *College* and continuing on with *Steamboat Bill, Jr.,* Buster's pictures bore other people's names on the directing credits, and he found himself working with people he didn't much admire. He had few kind words to say about the nominal director of *College,* James Horne: ". . . absolutely useless to me. Harry Brand, my business manager, got me to use him. He hadn't done many pictures and no important ones. Incidentals, quickies. I don't know why we had him, because I practically did *College.*" He made similar comments about the man who received the writing credits for both *College* and *Steamboat Bill, Jr.,* Carl Harbaugh: "He wasn't a good gag man, he wasn't a good title writer, he wasn't a good story constructionist. But I had to put up someone's name and he was on salary."

Schenck was paying that salary, just as he was paying everyone else's, including Buster's. From now on he kept a close check on Buster's activities, especially those involving money. He had both Harry Brand and John Considine report back to him on all such matters. This may sound like spying, but Schenck was still spending most of his time in New York. He needed eyes and ears in California.

Even more important than the directing credits were the words "Supervised by Harry Brand," which also appeared in the opening credits of *College*. Louis, or Lou, Anger, Buster's studio manager ever since the early days on East Forty-eighth Street, was drafted by Schenck to head the United Artists Theater Circuit. His replacement was Harry Brand, who had been running Buster's publicity department. As studio manager his main job was to watch the film's budget and to report any deviations from it to Schenck. This was his job, and Buster did not resent him nearly as much as he did Considine. Considine was a company man with a vengeance. Collier recalls that he was referred to openly as "Schenck's fink." (He also incurred the wrath of F. Scott Fitzgerald at about this time by turning down the script Fitzgerald had written for Constance Talmadge.)

College is the weakest of all of Buster's feature films, excepting *The Three Ages*. It lacks a strong form and the episodes follow one another in a sluggish fashion, unlike the precise rhythm of *The Navigator* and *The General*. Harold Goodwin, who portrayed the villain in the film, recalls playing a lot of baseball during the shooting of the picture. Buster demonstrated endless patience to get what he wanted. Goodwin remembers him trying to bounce a football off his skull several hundred times before finally admitting that it *couldn't* be done. For the first time in Buster's career, a California athlete, Lee Barnes, was hired to do the pole-vaulting sequence in the picture. Buster simply wasn't up to the task, but the faking depressed him.

The shooting of *College* was completed in May 1927 and the film opened to generally favorable reviews in September. The trade press was enthusiastic, for they felt that here was a Keaton

Buster, Natalie, Constance, and Buster Collier, 1927. *Museum of Modern Art / Film Stills Archive* film that the exhibitors could easily sell to their audiences. But, in the end, *College* had less box-office appeal than *The General*. It earned only $423,000 in the domestic market, about $50,000 less than its great predecessor. Schenck's only comfort was that *College* had cost only $289,277, about $150,000 less than *The General;* there was at least *some* hope for a profit, even if a small one. Both Keaton and Schenck may well have been mystified at the comparative failure of *College,* but it can be partly attributed to United Artists, who did not promote the Keaton films as ably or forcefully as MGM had. When *Battling Butler* was released in 1925, MGM had taken a four-page color ad in the pages of a trade paper, *Moving Picture World.* Both *College* and *The General* were announced by a single page in the same journal; at no point was an artist of the caliber of John Held, Jr., ever used by United Artists for promotional purposes. In addition to their poor job of publicity, United Artists continually ran into open hostility from many of the exhibitors, largely because these exhibitors felt they were being forced to pay far too much for the films and that there was no way to make any money on them. Actually, the exhibitors simply couldn't afford *not* to book the films of Chaplin, William S. Hart, the Talmadge sisters, Pickford, and Fairbanks: Schenck was perfectly aware he was offer-

Buster with Bobby and Jimmy, 1929. *Rudi Blesh*

ing the film trade the very best, and he made them pay for it. The fantastic popularity of Chaplin in the twenties withstood this exhibitor pressure against paying Schenck's price, but in the case of the less popular Keaton the exhibitors had the option of not booking his films at all. This may explain the appallingly low grosses.

Day-to-day life at the Keaton home went on pretty much as it had for some time: the Sunday barbecues, the card games, the practical jokes, his two growing boys, the gadgets. A publicity photograph showing "Sunday afternoon at the Keatons' " depicts Buster and Natalie, accompanied by her sister Constance and their close friend Buster Collier. Buster is "on" as usual for the cameraman, but there seems to be a new expression of true anguish on his face—almost as though he had some sense that he was losing his creative independence, or at least what he had been able to obtain of it.

Buster began to brood about money: he felt that he was not being paid what he deserved. His September 1924 contract with Schenck was still in effect at the same rate of pay. Buster often had long discussions with Collier about the investments he would like to make, all of which required a great deal more than the $1,000 per week he was still receiving. In the late summer of 1927, one of the last of the real boom years, stocks went up and up and the sky was very much the limit. Before the year came to an end, Keaton would be earning three times as much as he had at the beginning of 1927, but under radically changed circumstances.

Buster in his bedroom, 1929. *Pierre Sauvage*

[3]

We try all the time to make successes. A success is a picture accepted by the public as fine entertainment. A big box office return on a picture is the only way we can find out whether or not the public accepts it. . . .

—Joseph M. Schenck, 1932

I personally think that when the producer came in, as theoretically the artistic head of production, the pictures started to deteriorate. . . .

—Eddie Sutherland, 1957

We loaned [Keaton] out, just like we did with Arbuckle. It was too much of a risk making these pictures ourselves . . . better to have Metro risk them.

—Leopold Friedman, 1977

The successive failures of both *The General* and *College* were probably not uppermost in Schenck's mind in the fall of 1927, for he had considerably bigger things to worry about. The biggest of them all was the onset of sound, which began with the wildly successful premiere of Warner Brothers' *The Jazz Singer* in September. In some ways the advent of sound came at the worst possible time, for the industry was in a period of violent retrenchment due to steadily falling box-office receipts and soaring production costs. The result was a state of terror in the entire industry. The uncertainty of what lay ahead in the sound era filled a great many people in films with considerable anxiety.

All during the late summer and fall of 1927 the New York and Hollywood trade papers were filled with rumors of what was happening or what might happen. There were various proposals of salary cuts, ranging from 10 percent to 25 percent right across the board. The general feeling of panic was considerably augmented by a mysterious trek to the West Coast by the reigning industry figures in New York: Zukor and Sidney Kent from Paramount, William Fox and Winfield Sheehan from Fox, and

Nicholas Schenck from Loew's (MGM). (Nicholas had recently taken over the direction of Loew's, Inc. after the death of Marcus Loew in September.) The conclave met over a period of two weeks in Hollywood, with Carl Laemmle of Universal and the Warner brothers joining their visitors from the East. One of the main items on their agenda was how to obtain funds for the wiring of theaters throughout the country. Hundreds of millions of dollars would be required, and the heads of the industry knew that financing of this size could only be obtained from the Wall Street investment houses. For an independent filmmaker like Joe Schenck, as well as his partners at United Artists, Wall Street was a sensitive subject, for Eastern bankers were notoriously opposed to independent film production on the grounds of its being expensive and risky. Joe Schenck was aware that the days of the large-scale independents like himself might be numbered.

These meetings were held in November, but Hollywood was a place of great tension as early as July 15, the date that Buster began shooting his last picture for United Artists' distribution, *Steamboat Bill, Jr.* The picture was originally budgeted at $300,000, but the panic prevailing in the industry caused a reduction in the budget to $200,000 by September. The film finally wound up costing more than $400,000, after Buster had succeeded in convincing Joe that a picture about a Mississippi River flood stood a good chance of repeating the success of *The Navigator.* The flood idea was fine, but reality intervened with the actual Mississippi River floods of 1927, the worst in the history of the United States. In the circumstances, Schenck and his associates felt that a comedy based on the flood would fail with the public, and a cyclone was hastily substituted.

Most of the film was shot on location in and around the state capitol at Sacramento, California, along the banks of the Sacramento River. The heroine of *Steamboat Bill, Jr.,* Marion Byron, recalls the more strenuous parts of the shooting, especially the scenes involving her immersion in the river. Marion was only sixteen when *Steamboat* was shot and was not a very good swimmer, so Buster's sister, Louise, was used as a double for all her underwater scenes—the women were nearly identical in height and weight. The strong tide of the Sacramento was powerful enough to make shooting difficult, and the rescue scene in which Buster saves Marion from drowning required a great many retakes.

Louise recalls the lengthy diving sequence into the extremely cold water of the river, from which she and Buster would emerge half-frozen after several of these unsuccessful takes. Buster had instructed his man Caruthers to stand by with a bottle of the best procurable French brandy. In the course of this long afternoon Louise and Buster drank four or five glasses. Louise finally thought she had had about enough, but Buster told her to keep quiet, as he wished the supply to keep coming without interruption.

Steamboat Bill, Jr. can be described as a "Tempest"-like review of many of Buster's favorite themes. The story, devised by Carl Harbaugh, takes place on the last of the Mississippi River steamboats. Buster and his girl (Marian Byron) figure as the children of two old and long-embattled rival riverboat captains. Buster's father (Ernest Torrence) is the proud owner of an ancient, battered craft, the *Stonewall Jackson,* while the girl's wealthy father commands the sleek new *King.* Steamboat Bill, as Buster's huge father is known, is deeply disappointed that his son is of diminutive stature, plays the ukelele, and sports both a beret and a mustache. There is a superb scene at the beginning of the film in which Buster tries on a series of ever more unsuitable hats for his angry father's inspection in a men's apparel store, including his familiar porkpie hat, which he whips off before his father can see it.

The most extraordinary part of *Steamboat* is the cyclone sequence at the very end. It begins with Buster in a hospital bed after he has been hit on the head. The fury of the storm tears down the walls around him, and his bed begins a strange journey through the streets of the devastated village. The air is filled with flying tree trunks and all the debris created by the torrential winds. His bed finally brings him to a partially wrecked theater, which he proceeds to examine. There follows a series of images unmistakably drawn from Buster's own childhood. He encounters an evilly threatening jack-in-the-box, a stage floor with hidden trapdoors, a mysterious ventriloquist's dummy that peers back at him with a frightening stare. There is a dreamlike, nightmarish quality to the entire sequence.

One of Buster's most celebrated stunts occurs in *Steamboat Bill*. Standing in stunned disbelief in the empty street, staring at the ravages of the cyclone roaring around him, Buster is not aware that the entire façade of the house behind him is about to fall on him. It does, but he is saved by the fact that a tall window frame at the top of the house passes safely over his body, leaving him perfectly unharmed. In order to accomplish this feat without trickery, it was necessary for extremely accurate measurements to be taken of both Buster and the window above him; a mistake of an inch or so would have proved fatal, for the façade weighed over a ton. There is a story that one of the cameramen found the suspense so intolerable he looked away at the last moment, but everything went off exactly as planned, with the window and the façade just managing to clear Buster's body.

Steamboat Bill was completed by the early fall of 1927, but it was not released until May 1928. It then proved to be the worst disaster at the box office of all of Buster's United Artists releases, earning a domestic gross of only $358,839. The negative cost alone had been $404,282, and the final loss on this film probably exceeded a quarter of a million dollars. But the losses on *Steamboat* were by no means the worst for United Artists, for the films made at this time by Gloria Swanson, D. W. Griffith, and others lost considerably more.

Before the release of *Steamboat*, Schenck, who had personally lost money in nearly everything that he had produced in the years 1925–27, had decided that he was going to abandon his own film production interests and devote all his time to running United Artists. Schenck was also strongly influenced by the publicly stated fiscal policies of the powerful Wall Street brokerage house Hayden, Stone and Company, who were acting as bankers for such large Hollywood firms as Associated–First National. Hayden, Stone deplored the high cost of feature films; their recommendations to the industry were to keep all budgets below $150,000 and to abandon the costliest kind of filmmaking: independent production, which had made possible the brilliance of Chaplin and Keaton.

This advice could scarcely be ignored by an industry that knew perfectly well that it would need to borrow many millions of dollars in the next two or three years for the rewiring of every motion picture theater in the United States. The Wall Street opposition virtually abolished the independent producers from the industry; only Lloyd and Chaplin, who could afford it, continued to make pictures their own way. For Keaton, it meant the end of his independent productions. In later years Buster told many of his interviewers that he "had made the greatest mistake of his life" when he decided to abandon his independent unit and sign a contract at MGM. He had no choice in the matter, for Joe Schenck had been virtually unique in Hollywood for his willingness to finance independent production. When Joe left the field, there was no one to take his place.

Buster also insisted that he had gone to New York in the fall of 1927 to see if Adolph Zukor would create an independent unit for him at Paramount. Zukor already had such a unit at Paramount, but this was the Harold Lloyd unit, financed totally by Harold Lloyd himself. It would have been easy for Buster to get himself a contract at any one of several studios, Fox, Pathé, Universal, or Warner Brothers, but it would have been an acting contract. He had no chance of getting the kind of arrangement he'd had with Joe over the years. In addition, the fact that Buster's recent films had lost money reduced his chances of anyone's financing an independent unit for him.

It was really a foregone conclusion that Buster would end up at MGM. Just a month or so before he signed the contract, photos appeared in the trade papers showing Buster with Nicholas Schenck, who ran MGM from the Loew offices in New York. People in the industry knew well what Buster's visit to Culver City portended. Buster may well have regarded his staggeringly huge increase in pay as real evidence of how favorably MGM regarded the return of its prodigal son. With Nick Schenck as his new boss, Buster may also have felt that it was still all in the family. But it really wasn't, as he found out within the first six months at Culver City.

Lou Anger, Nicholas Schenck, Louis B. Mayer, George C. Cryer, Joe Schenck, Lt. Gov. C. C. Young, Fred Niblo, Irving Thalberg, Jesse L. Laskey at MGM, 1928. *National Film Archive / Stills Library*

8
THE LION ROARS

[1]

He could have gone on his own, nobody asked
him to sign the contract at Metro. . . . Don't you
see, he was a child, with the mentality of a child. He
had no other world as far as I know. . . .
——Lawrence Weingarten, 1972

Buster was very sexy, very relaxed and easy with
women—the first sign of a man secure in his performance. I think he was capable of love but he was
possessed rather than choosing to possess. . . .
——Louise Brooks, 1977

Preliminary drafts of the first of Buster's MGM employment
contracts were drawn up by their legal department in early December 1927, but it was not until the twenty-sixth of January
1928 that Buster signed the ten-page agreement. It was a two-
year contract, and Buster was to receive $150,000 per year, or
$3,000 per week, with no payment in the tenth and twentieth
weeks.

Three thousand dollars was a lot of money at MGM in 1928,
the same amount that Irving Thalberg, head of all production at
the studio, was receiving when Buster joined the firm. There
were few actors drawing this kind of salary. John Gilbert was the
highest paid of all the MGM stars, receiving $10,000 per week,
an awesome amount. Garbo, the most popular of all the female
stars, was getting only one-half as much as Gilbert, $5,000 per
week all through the period 1927–32. But these two were the extraordinary exceptions; the majority of MGM's stars received far
less than Buster. Clark Gable, for example, started off at $650 a
week in 1930, rose to $1,150 in 1931, and was receiving $2,000
at the end of 1932.

Buster was to be starred in all his films, and he was obliged to make at least two a year; if more than two were made, he was to be paid an additional $50,000 per film. A connecting link was to be maintained with Joe Schenck, for in order to secure Buster's services, MGM agreed to pay Joe and the other shareholders in Buster Keaton Productions 25 percent of the net profits in Buster's MGM films. In turn, Buster was to continue receiving 25 percent of the profits of his old production company, an arrangement that continued for nearly all the time that Buster spent at MGM. This situation was similar to Arbuckle's in 1919, when Paramount paid his salary and financed the production of his films.

One proviso in the contract stipulated that Buster was not to be paid if he was "out" for any reason whatever for more than six consecutive working days, or for more than twenty-one days in any year. (This proviso was later invoked on several occasions.) Another important and fateful stipulation was that Buster was to "be consulted as to story and direction but the decision of the producer shall be final."

Working at MGM was a totally new experience for Buster, for he no longer had the fatherly figure of Joe Schenck to turn to when he had problems, and Nicholas Schenck spent most of his time in New York. His new employers, Irving Thalberg and Louis B. Mayer, were frequently too busy to give him much of their time. A great deal has been written about both of them, most of it extremely favorable to Thalberg and almost none of it kind to the man the English producer Michael Balcon liked to call "the unspeakable Mayer." Tradition has it that Mayer was a crude, tough, sentimental, totally obnoxious businessman. Thalberg, on the other hand, has emerged as the sensitive boy-wonder genius whom F. Scott Fitzgerald portrayed as Monroe Stahr in *The Last Tycoon*. In *Mayer and Thalberg: The Make Believe Saints,* Samuel Marx, for many years the head of MGM's story department, shows that despite their many differences they shared one common goal: profit for MGM. Marx quotes Eddie Mannix, the studio manager, as saying, "Thalberg was a sweet guy but he could piss ice water."

Buster had little to do with Mayer in the early years; their mutual lack of interest was clear from the start. As Buster saw things, Thalberg was his main friend at the studio. Thalberg was fond of Buster and put up with behavior from him that he would have found intolerable in anyone else. But this friendship never got much beyond some occasional bridge games and the day-to-day production problems that brought them together now and then. For Thalberg it was purely a matter of his time: nearly everyone at MGM wanted some of it, and he simply hadn't any to spare. As Buster Collier put it, "Buster had no one to look after him at MGM, a thing he really needed in a place like that. He was really all on his own, right from the start. And it never changed. Never."

When Keaton joined the firm at the beginning of 1928, it had existed as a corporate entity for only four years but had quickly risen to the top in every area of film production. MGM often spent a good deal more money on its productions than its competitors, and it usually showed. Their publicity department was second to none in the business. Its chief, Howard Dietz, was the author of the famous phrase "More Stars Than There Are in Heaven," which remained useful to MGM for forty years. There weren't as many stars in 1928 as later on, but they included, besides Garbo and Gilbert, Marian Davies, Ramon Navarro, William Haines, Lon Chaney, and Norma Shearer, with Buster their most recent acquisition. In the next few years the list would include Joan Crawford, Marie Dressler, Wallace Beery, Clark Gable, Robert Montgomery, and, quite briefly, Helen Hayes and the three Barrymores. The hits that had made MGM the success it was included *The Big Parade* (1925) with Gilbert and *Flesh and the Devil* with Garbo and Gilbert (1927). Their 1928 hits included Lon Chaney in *West of Zanzibar,* Monte Blue in *White Shadows in the South Seas,* Crawford in *Our Dancing Daughters,* and Marion Davies and William Haines in *Show People.*

With the exception of Davies and Dressler, none of the MGM stars did very much in the way of comedy. Buster Keaton was the studio's first real "comic," and it took some time for them to find out what to do with him. Thalberg finally decided to assign his brother-in-law, Lawrence Weingarten, to be Buster's producer. Weingarten actually had some experience in comedy, having directed several of MGM's Jackie Coogan films in the mid-twenties. He is perhaps best known today for his productions starring Katharine Hepburn and Spencer Tracy in the forties and fifties: *Adam's Rib* and *Pat and Mike*. He also produced *The Broadway Melody*, MGM's first real talkie, the archetypal musical comedy that won the Academy Award for the best picture of 1929 and made a staggering profit of over $1.5 million.

Buster's arrival at MGM did not go unnoticed by the media. The New York office of Loew's, Inc., the parent corporation of MGM, published an elaborate weekly house organ, *The Distributor*, which was also sent out to theater owners all over the country. While Buster was still completing the shooting of his first MGM film, *The Cameraman*, *The Distributor* published a feature story about their new star that, included some curious items:

> A new Buster Keaton has come back to the MGM fold. A Keaton . . . who convulsed the world with *The Navigator* is himself again. . . . eventually the load which Buster was carrying was too great. No one man could carry all the responsibilities of picture making as Buster had to. So grief finally slipped in. . . . Now, under MGM supervision, with production on the MGM lot, with MGM gag men and title writers to help and MGM technicians to guide him, Buster will again assume his rightful place at the top of the industry.

The Cameraman, 1928. *National Film Archive / Stills Library*

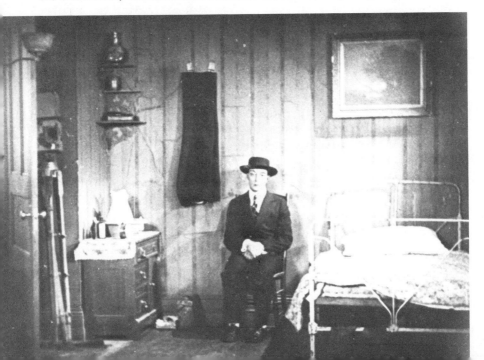

Buster may have been amused, or possibly annoyed, by reading this story, in which one of the few cinematic geniuses in film history is told in plain English by his employers that he can no longer bear the burden of making his own pictures and also told that the assembled might of MGM will now come to his rescue and show him the right road to true success.

In what might be called the initial "era of good feelings" between Buster and his new employers, he was allowed a reasonable amount of freedom. Clyde Bruckman supplied the basic story of *The Cameraman* in collaboration with Lew Lipton; the shooting script was assembled by Richard Schayer, an MGM scriptwriter who worked on five of Buster's films. Elgin Lessley and Reggie Lanning were the cameramen; Fred Gabourie was the technical director. In this first MGM feature Buster had been able to reassemble a good share of his old production crew.

As a director, Buster was given Edward Sedgwick, Jr., a fat, jolly Texan he had known from the time when he was a child in vaudeville. Sedgwick's boyhood had been similar to Buster's, for he had been one of the "Five Sedgwicks" (another family act) at an early age. Like Weingarten, Sedgwick was an old hand at films. One of his main claims to fame was his reputed discovery of both Tom Mix and Hoot Gibson at Fox in 1915. At Universal he had worked with Robert Julian on the Lon Chaney film *The Phantom of the Opera*. At MGM his specialty was comedy; with one exception he directed all eight of Buster's MGM films. Three years older than Buster, "Junior" Sedgwick was easy to get along with. He tended to let Buster do as he pleased, but that created some real problems, as Harold Goodwin recalls:

> We had no sooner started "The Cameraman" than trouble started. Sedgwick, whom I had made many pictures with, called me aside one day and confided, unbeknownst to B. K., that the front office had called him in. They wanted to know why we weren't following the script. Ed explained that often a situation arises that has comedy potential and B. K. liked to milk it for all it is worth. The brass wanted to know how they could budget a show if we didn't follow the script. Some thinking! . . .

This kind of thinking led to the construction of a fixed story line, which became increasingly complex. The basic simplicity of the stories in Buster's earlier films was replaced by more elaborate plots, full of twists and turns. Buster later recalled:

> Thalberg was in charge of production and he wanted—oh—I wasn't in trouble enough trying to manipulate a camera as a cameraman, trying to photograph current events as a news weekly cameraman. In *The Cameraman*, Thalberg wanted me involved with gangsters, and get in trouble with this one and that one, and that was my fight—to eliminate those extra things.

At MGM, Buster had to weave his improvised bits into the texture of the working script. He had some degree of success, for Goodwin claims that "two of the funniest scenes in the picture were the ones where he tried to open his piggie bank and the one where he shares a bathhouse cubicle as he tries to put on a bathing suit. These were not in the script."

In the improvised scene in the bathhouse, Buster is closeted with a short, stubby man, Edward Brophy, in his first screen role. As each man attempts to undress and don his swimsuit, their clothing becomes hopelessly and inextricably confused. The action was filmed in long takes of two or three minutes, each from the point of view of a stationary camera. It is one of those perfect sequences in Keaton's work, very similar in effect to that of the couple searching for each other on the abandoned ship in *The Navigator*, where absolutely precise, split-second timing is the essence of the comedy.

Despite Thalberg's wishes, the plot of *The Cameraman* is fairly simple: Buster is smitten by a pretty young secretary who works for the Hearst International Newsreel organization, at that time distributed by MGM. Quickly giving up his old occupation of humble tintype photographer, Buster buys a movie camera and starts bringing his work in to the office on speculation, with surprising footage as the result. It includes double-exposure shots of battleships making their way up Broadway, and badly focused glimpses of cars and pedestrians moving backward.

The Cameraman also contains some incredibly poignant scenes, showing conclusively that Keaton could easily give Chaplin strong competition in this area, just as he had in *Go West*. Buster's rival for the girl, Goodwin, takes her for a speedboat ride just off Balboa Beach. While showing off, he manages to overturn the boat, and swims ashore in a panic, leaving the helpless girl in the water. Having observed all this, Buster dives in and drags the girl, now unconscious, ashore. He runs up the beach to get something to revive her; in his absence Goodwin returns to greet the now slowly awakening girl, who accepts without question that it was Goodwin who had rescued her. When Buster returns, he is just in time to see his beloved walking off slowly in the arms of his rival. Buster, shot sideways in full figure, slowly sinks to his knees in complete, abject helplessness. It is heart-rending in its absolute simplicity.

The Cameraman, 1928. *National Film Archive / Stills Library*

Portions of *The Cameraman* were shot in New York, mainly because Buster wanted to see the original company performing in *Show Boat*. The Studio had been prompted perhaps by Harold Lloyd's having shot stretches of his *Speedy* in New York earlier that year, using locations in Coney Island, Penn Station, and Yankee Stadium. Comparatively little of New York can be seen in *The Cameraman;* the notable exception is the eerie baseball game in which Buster plays *all* the positions in a solitary game in a totally empty Yankee Stadium. Buster always claimed that the shooting in New York had to be sharply curtailed because too many people recognized him, a situation that did not arise with Harold Lloyd.

The Cameraman was completed rather quickly, for shooting

The Cameraman, 1928. *National Film Archive / Stills Library*

began on the first of May and was completed on the twenty-fifth of June at a cost of $362,565, roughly $50,000 less than *Steamboat Bill, Jr.* It was a triumph for Buster and did much to weaken the impression that he was in any way finished. The public and most of the critics loved the film and—at least momentarily —Buster was back in favor again, just as much as he had been at the time of *The Navigator.*

On the face of it, Buster seemed to have gotten off to a fine start at MGM. Despite the conference difficulties with Weingarten and Thalberg, *The Cameraman* was pretty much his own kind of picture; the real question in his mind was, would it be the last? By the summer of 1928 Buster realized that his old production staff was dwindling away: Clyde Bruckman, who had written a wonderful tong-war sequence for *The Cameraman* in Buster's bungalow, had left to begin directing for Harold Lloyd; Fred Gabourie would not be available for Buster's next film, *Spite Marriage,* nor would his favorite cameraman, Elgin Lessley. But the most crucial problem was that the studio insisted upon knowing how things were going to be *in advance of the shooting:* they wanted to see complete shooting scripts before a camera turned. Shooting scenes "off the cuff" was an unheard-of luxury at MGM. Buster's increasing inability to make his pictures in the old way was beginning to bother him badly, but as usual, he found he couldn't say much about it to anyone.

During the summer of 1928 Louise Brooks began seeing Keaton with some regularity, largely because of her current friendship with Buster Collier. The first two years of Louise's film career had been spent working for Paramount at their Eastern studio in Astoria, where she had made films like *It's The Old Army Game* with W. C. Fields. She had met Collier in New York when they had appeared in a film together, and they had resumed their friendship when she came to Hollywood to continue working as a contract player for Paramount. One summer evening in 1928 Louise and Collier attended a small, informal dinner party at the Italian Villa. Keaton seemed moody, restless, and even "a bit grim." After dinner he played bridge briefly before approaching Collier and telling him that he would like to be driven to the studio. Although it was long past midnight, Louise and Collier were

Louise Brooks in 1928. *Museum of Modern Art / Film Stills Archive*

At the Kennel with Jimmy and Bobby in 1932. *Museum of Modern Art / Film Stills Arch*

happy to oblige Buster's whim and agreed to drive him to MGM in Collier's roadster.

Buster remained silent all the way to the MGM lot at Culver City, where he led his guests to his newly acquired bungalow, just outside the studio gates. This was the structure he had dubbed "Keaton's Kennel" the moment he had first seen it. The bungalow served as Buster's dressing room, as well as his eating and sleeping quarters. It had become a second home for him, or perhaps his real home, for he would often spend the night there, either alone or with a girl. The bungalows were only given to MGM's major stars; at this time Buster's close friend Lew Cody had one, as did Garbo, William Haines, and John Gilbert.

At the bungalow Buster, Louise, and Collier all sat down in what passed for a living room, and Buster offered his friends a drink. The room was lined on all four sides with expensive, glass-covered bookcases, mostly empty; each door was divided into a dozen or so panes of glass. Buster rose suddenly from his chair and disappeared into the bedroom. He returned carrying a baseball bat. Without saying a word he began methodically to smash the panes of glass in the bookcases. There were hundreds of them, and it took some time to complete the job. Louise and Collier sat there speechless as the destruction proceeded. When the very last pane had been smashed in, Buster resumed his place in his chair and took up the conversation as if nothing had happened. When asked why the security police had not appeared on the scene, Buster's only matter-of-fact comment was, "If it had been a fire, they would have come to put it out. Otherwise, they don't care much about what happens in here."

Louise and Collier recall that Buster had been drinking steadily all night but that he had not seemed particularly drunk. Louise regards the scene as a symbolic act of destruction directed at Buster's employers at MGM: "Perhaps that was what he was doing the night he took a baseball bat to the glass doors in his bungalow . . . trying to break out of his cage, escape to creation. But he never made it. He had lost his magic power over booze." Collier recalls that evening also, saying, "Buster had a private fun factory when he was on his own with Joe Schenck, but at MGM he was just another employee, expensive yes, but still an employee."

In the fall of 1928 Buster was reminded again and again that he was indeed an employee, for he now began to receive still more of the "help" that the MGM publicity department had promised him in the pages of *The Distributor*. Nearly everyone at MGM liked Buster Keaton, and many of them had ideas for his next picture, all sorts of ideas. The man who was on the receiving end of these offers of help was Keaton's producer, Lawrence Weingarten. In later years Buster told his first biographer, Rudi Blesh, that he believed Thalberg had appointed Weingarten as his producer on simple grounds of nepotism—Weingarten had recently married Thalberg's young sister, Sylvia. This is a claim that can easily be disputed, for Weingarten had been directing Tim McCoy westerns for Harry Rapf since 1925. It was Weingarten's responsibility to find appropriate vehicles for Buster, but the real problem was that until 1928 the two men had worked under radically different conditions.

Until he joined MGM, Buster had worked in a climate of relative freedom from outside pressures. At MGM the studio required elaborate screenplays on which complete production costs could be based. MGM was extremely anxious to know in advance how and where its money was going to be spent; there was no allocation for the unexpected. William Goetz, who later founded Twentieth Century Pictures with Joseph Schenck, was the production manager on *The Cameraman*. Goodwin recalls some of these accountability problems:

> I had a run-in with Bill Goetz the first day and it never ended. He was our business manager and later married Mayer's daughter. He was young and inclined to be officious. When I went out of the boat and swam ashore fully clothed I ruined a pair of my shoes. I did that twice. Goetz refused to pay me for the shoes I ruined. An argument ensued and he told me that I wouldn't work on the lot again. I didn't for eight years. A funny thing, in 1938 we were both at Fox and became good friends. . . .

This restrictive system filled Buster with a steady sense of rage, which he expressed only when drinking.

At the end of his life in 1975, Lawrence Weingarten offered his own interpretation of the problems they had with Keaton. He

even claimed that the studio had regarded Buster as something
of a has-been at the time he joined MGM:

> When he came to us he had been working for Joseph M.
> Schenck in the early days of *The General* and *The Navigator,* and
> then his popularity started to wane, and Mr. Schenck was trying
> to find some way to get rid . . . of some of the contract. . . . So
> we took the contract. Now by this time poor Buster was pretty well
> broke. He'd made a lot of money, he'd married . . . Natalie Tal-
> madge, and was drinking pretty heavily. . . . In any event, he was
> evidently very unhappy, depressed, we had quite a problem with
> him.

The reference to Buster's being broke in 1928 seems wrong, but
most of Weingarten's account is accurate enough. He went on to
say:

> We had problems with all actors, didn't matter whether it was his
> drinking, or other types of temperament; I didn't mind that. I
> was terribly fond of him. He was a darling man. But we had
> troubles. We would find him someplace. . . .

Weingarten also indicated that Buster was often ill at ease with
the people he was now working with, many of whom were so
much better informed than he was. He felt that his lack of
schooling put him at a disadvantage.

Spite Marriage, Buster's second picture for MGM, finally went
into production on the nineteenth of November 1928 and was
finished on the twenty-fourth of December, a shooting time
of only five weeks. *Spite Marriage* cost only $282,215 to make, or
about $80,000 less than *The Cameraman.* The cost of the script
was significant, for whereas Bruckman had been paid $34,866
for *The Cameraman,* the use of MGM's regular, salaried
scriptwriters Richard Schayer, Lew Lipton, Ernest Pagano, and
Robert Hopkins cut the cost nearly in half to $18,265. But there
seems little doubt that the real savings were made by following
the script as written. In *Spite Marriage* there is only one particularly eccentric scene—aloft among the sails—like the solitary
baseball game in *The Cameraman.*

Buster was given the name Elmer in *Spite Marriage,* the name that was to be his in most of his MGM productions. Here he is a wistful pants presser in love with the beautiful and glamorous young actress Trilby Drew, played by Dorothy Sebastian. Trilby has nothing but scorn for Buster, but marries him out of spite in a moment of jealous rage with the man she really loves. The marriage starts off badly, for Trilby gets drunk on her wedding night and has to be put to bed by Keaton. For four or five inspired minutes Buster attempts to place his unconscious bride in her bed without awakening her. Her totally inert condition poses exquisite technical problems as he gamely goes about his business. At one point he folds her in a chair and tries to carry her across the room in it, but her dead weight keeps making her body slip down from the chair. In despair, he picks her up bodily and starts off toward the bed. When at long last he gets her placed there, he is dismayed to find that it is her feet that have wound up on the pillows; he has been so careful not to disturb her that he has completely reversed her body. The entire sequence is a piece of brilliantly executed choreography involving, as do all of Buster's best routines, miraculously split-second timing. This involved Dorothy as well, for she had to do exactly what Buster wanted her to do at precisely the right moment. (Buster performed this routine in the mid-fifties in Europe with his third wife, Eleanor, as his drunken partner.)

On the morning after the drunken night, Buster awakens to find his bride gone, but he is quickly reunited with her aboard a yacht manned by rumrunners. The gimmick by which Buster gets himself accidentally involved with gangsters en route to the yacht would seem to have been inspired by Thalberg's previous ideas for *The Cameraman.*

In order to get closer to his girl while she is onstage in the leading role in a Civil War melodrama, Buster agrees to take over the part of one of the minor actors in the play. There is a hilarious scene in which Buster attempts to create a false beard for his appearance onstage, but it is only a prelude to what happens once he gets there. First we see the entire scene as normally played *without* Buster's presence. Then he appears and wreaks havoc on the performance by missing all his cues and failing to do what is required of him. The full impact is greatly increased, of course, by one's knowledge of the way things should be going on a normal night. Presenting the scene twice is a tour de force requiring some patience, but the result is incomparable.

There is one bizarre episode in this film that concerns Keaton and his girl, Trilby, when they have been left alone together on the yacht. The weather suddenly turns bad, and both climb frantically to the top of the mainmast to strike the sails in order to ride out the coming storm. While they are aloft, Dorothy Sebastian keeps falling into the complex folds of the sails, and Keaton manages to rescue her in a strangely dreamlike series of events high up on the yardarm of the deserted vessel. The surrealist poetry of this scene reminds one of similar scenes in his earlier work; it has none of the "functional" quality of Buster's later MGM films.

The film concludes with the chief rumrunner's return to the boat and a violent fight between him and Buster, recalling the dressing-room incident in *Battling Butler*. In fact, the decision to have a sequence in which the boy and the girl find themselves on an otherwise empty boat is a reprise of *The Navigator*, while much of the backstage business at the beginning of the film is reminiscent of *The Playhouse*. Although Thalberg's insistence on a rigid plot can be seen here more plainly than in *The Cameraman*, *Spite Marriage* has many wonderful things about it, including a full display of Buster's acrobatic powers in the fight scenes on board the yacht.

One special aspect of *Spite Marriage* is that for the first time its heroine emerges as a fully developed character. Trilby Drew is far more believable than the earlier Keaton heroines. This may have been partly due to the fact that Dorothy Sebastian and Buster were in the midst of an affair that lasted for several years. Variously known as "Slam-bang Sebastian," "Little Alabam," or just "Slam," Dorothy was an extremely pretty girl from Birmingham, who had come to New York in 1924 as a showgirl in George White's *Scandals of 1924*, a show in which Louise Brooks and Dolores Costello also appeared. Louise found Dorothy adorable, as did a great many other people who still remember her. She was also a much better actress than any of Buster's previous leading ladies.

Dorothy Sebastian and Buster in *Spite Marriage*, 1929. *Museum of Modern Art / Film Stills Archive*

Dorothy Sebastian at MGM in 1929. *National Film Archive / Stills Library*

Buster fell in love with Dorothy. At last he had found a "fun girl," who loved practical jokes just as much as he did, a girl who would stay up half the night on the telephone in order to finish a game of "Battleship." Dorothy was as enthusiastic a drinker as Buster was, but had nowhere near his tolerance for alcohol. She had a disconcerting habit of falling down without warning after a few drinks, hence her nickname of "Slam."

Largely through her friendship with a well-known, diminutive British newspaper publisher, Dorothy obtained a Hollywood contract within a year after her arrival in New York. Many of her early films were made by the nearly forgotten firm of Tiffany-Stahl; by the beginning of 1928 Dorothy was considered to be one of their regular stars, a doubtful honor at a studio that was noted for not having any stars. She was sufficiently impressive in these films to be welcomed at MGM with a two-year contract as a stock player. She then appeared in a large number of MGM's important films of the time, including *A Woman of Affairs, Our Dancing Daughters, Our Blushing Brides,* and Buster's first sound film, *Free and Easy.*

Buster and Dorothy Sebastian's love for each other was not exclusive; as Louise Brooks remarked, they were not particularly possessive people. If either one found someone else of temporary interest, that was all right. Each got what he wanted from the other. Buster got a great deal of open, warm-hearted sex from a woman who made no other demands on him. Dorothy's warmth extended into every phase of her life; people still remember her loading an entire taxicab with her Christmas gifts and driving all over Beverly Hills on Christmas Day to deliver them.

Dorothy went to great lengths to exhibit a kind of mock jealousy. Buster had been spending some of his mornings in the bed of a woman whom Louise Keaton remembers as "Mrs. Neighbor Lady," and when Dorothy discovered that Buster and the lady were planning to spend a weekend at Palm Springs, she rented the attached house next to theirs and patiently waited for the couple's arrival. When Dorothy had reason to believe that things had become interestingly quiet next door, she began to bang the pots and pans in her kitchen as loudly as she could, keeping up the din until Buster and his lady drove away in disgust. Buster loved her all the more for pranks of this kind. She possessed all the qualities that Natalie lacked: wit, charm, gaiety, and, most of all, the joy in sex that Natalie had refused him.

Spite Marriage was completed the day before Christmas of 1928. With the exception of a brief (and silent) appearance in MGM's *Hollywood Revue of 1929,* Buster did not begin his next picture until November 11, 1929, a long wait between films, especially by 1929 standards. A great deal of this time was devoted to endless story conferences centering on the question: what should Buster do next? Part of the problem was that the sound revolution was just beginning to gather real momentum, although MGM was almost the last of the major studios to acknowledge its existence.

As 1928 ended, Buster had the comfort of knowing that he had made two first-rate films in his first year at MGM. Despite the dreary conferences, the requisitions in quadruplicate, the whole solid bureaucracy of the studio system, he had been able to turn out his kind of picture—not as good as *The General* or *The Navigator,* but better than *College.* Moreover, both *The Cameraman* and *Spite Marriage* made a lot more at the box office than any of his three United Artists films. *The Cameraman* grossed $797,000 (about twice that of *Steamboat Bill, Jr.*); and *Spite Marriage* did nearly as well, grossing $701,000. The only previous Keaton film to do this well was *Battling Butler* in 1926, an MGM release, perhaps demonstrating that MGM had more clout with the exhibitors than United Artists, as well as better publicity. The two most recent films showed a combined profit of $264,000, of which Buster Keaton Productions received $66,000 and Buster himself $16,500 in addition to his regular salary. On the surface, Buster's career seemed to have recovered from the slump it had entered in 1927. His home life was unsatisfactory, but at least he now had a regular woman who loved him. The only really new threat on the horizon was sound films, which MGM had finally begun to make, with some hesitation, in the very last days of 1928.

[2]

Everybody went sound-happy. They thought that because you were making a sound picture you had to talk all the time, you had to go to the verbal. . . .
—Harold Lloyd, 1969

Don't let them talk if they haven't anything to say.
—John Ford, 1929

Buster felt that anytime he wanted to pull himself together, he could do it . . . even if it took thirty days. The hangovers, that's what really did him in. Buster never really thought he'd get any older. . . .
—William Collier, 1977

In his later years Keaton often blamed his fall from stardom on the treatment he received at MGM, claiming over and over again that it was a question of "too many cooks" spoiling his pictures. Lawrence Weingarten, on the other hand, stressed that Buster was accustomed to working with a group, just as at MGM.

> He had as many people around him. . . . There weren't as many people to see, but there were . . . as many people involved in Joe Schenck's. . . . He had a director and writers. He had just as much leeway with us. Only in a big studio they were paying him his salary and they had to make a number of pictures over a number of years, that was the problem, that was always the problem with the star system. They paid large salaries and they had to make X number of pictures. We had to find the material, try to find the material.

Much of this is true, but what is left out here is the vital fact that Buster's original writers in the Schenck days were writers that he himself had hired. Now the ideas and gags were supplied by everyone, as Weingarten admits:

> The writers, the director, myself, and Buster, that's how we worked. Sometimes we'd have a couple of gag men. We had Al Boasberg on a couple of those pictures . . . there was Ralph Spence and Bob Hopkins and Lew Lipton. . . .

Weingarten also overlooks the fact that Buster was able to turn out two feature films per year on his own; at MGM, even with all the help he was getting, Keaton's output was the same.

Weingarten went on to say that, apart from Keaton's alcoholism, there was a real problem with Keaton's voice after the advent of sound:

> And for talkies, he couldn't talk. We had a very difficult time, because there were no inflections. . . . Then there was Charlie Chaplin who couldn't make the . . . times had changed, they were all from the same school. If anything we kept him [Keaton] alive longer than they were alive. Harold Lloyd went out of the picture immediately.

Weingarten is wrong here about Lloyd, who went on producing his own films until 1938, but is quite right when he claimed that Buster's sound films had actually made more money than had his silent features.

> Some of these pictures did much more than his original silent pictures, but he was the victim of change. He accused the studio of his gradual demise, but Harold Lloyd had his own studio and he left the picture, went down the drain . . .

Weingarten summed up his views on Buster's career by saying,

> . . . but I'm sure he was a victim of his times. He didn't have as much as Chaplin, or even Lloyd, in speaking. There were no intonations. As you remember, when he spoke, he spoke in a flat monotone . . . that was a part of his physical action, that monotone, the blank face. . . .

Weingarten's arguments led him into a labyrinth of contradictions. Even while insisting that it was Buster's voice that destroyed his career in sound films, he concedes that the MGM sound films he made in the thirties brought in more money than his silent features of the twenties.

What actually happened to Keaton in sound pictures had nothing to do with the quality of his voice. The myth of unacceptable or unsuitable voices has died hard over the years; there are many who still believe that both Lloyd and Keaton met extinction because of their voices. This view is so prevalent that even a man as knowledgeable about films as Weingarten believed it, but it simply isn't true.

Fear gripped many film actors in the second half of 1928 and into the first part of 1929, the last few months before the end of the silent era. The actors were agonizingly self-conscious about just *how* they were going to talk in these new sound films. The fears arose in part because of a calculated attempt on the part of the studios to sell the idea of talking pictures to the audiences by arousing their curiosity about what their favorite stars might sound like. The fan magazines were filled with endless stories about the dreaded "mike fright" that might wipe out famous careers in a week. At many of the studios the contract players were given highly publicized "voice tests" that proved next to nothing. These also seem to have been the products of the studio publicity departments.

The truth is that most of the silent stars survived the sound revolution; most of the ones that didn't left the screen for other reasons. Actresses like Pola Negri or Vilma Banky, and the German actor Emil Jannings (who refused to study English) were forced to leave because of their heavy European accents. And the fine silent comedian Raymond Griffith, whose weak vocal chords permitted him to speak only in a whisper, also left the screen at this time.

John Gilbert is the most highly publicized of all the leading stars whose decline was blamed on the coming of sound. Tradition has it that his voice struck many as too thin and reedy for that of a great lover, and it has been claimed that at the opening night of his first sound film, *His Glorious Night,* the audience responded to the sound of his passionate lovemaking with titters. Anita Loos explains that she always thought audiences began to laugh at these overly passionate lines simply because they came from someone's lips; as intertitles in a silent picture they were perfectly acceptable. Another legend is that Gilbert's voice was deliberately distorted on the sound track by the express order of his employer, Louis B. Mayer, who would stop at nothing to crush the career of a man he'd been feuding with for several years. However, not the slightest bit of evidence has ever been brought forward concerning the sabotaging of Gilbert's career by those who had considerably more to lose than he did in such an attempt. Thalberg kept on making Gilbert films and even tried to change his image to that of a lusty he-man type (in *Way for a Sailor*), but all to no avail, for by 1932 Gilbert's difficulties with his public were widely published in fan magazines and trade journals. And by that time the public infinitely preferred the talents of Clark Gable.

There were those who thought that the art of talking could be taught. Norma Talmadge fell into this trap and spent a lot of money on elocution lessons given by Laura Hope Crews, a well-known British actress of the day. The result was a kind of leaden, painfully spoken English that managed to please no one; it took just two of these sound films to convince her that her career was finished. Her sister Constance never bothered making the effort. Tradition again has it that Norma decided to take the lessons because she had a strong Brooklyn accent, but a number of people who knew all three of the Talmadge sisters in the twenties and after denied that she had such an accent.

It may well be that audiences felt intuitively that some of their old favorites belonged somehow to the past and that these sound pictures required a whole new pantheon of talent. Some of the great silent stars had begun to find it difficult to play the roles with which their audiences associated them: Mary Pickford and Norma Talmadge were thirty-six in 1929, while Douglas Fairbanks was forty-seven. Buster was thirty-four but still looked quite young. There were few signs of his heavy drinking on his face or in his incredibly swift and graceful movements. As for his voice, it turned out to be a deep bass, and in spite of Weingarten's remarks, there seem to have been no complaints at the time.

When the new talent did arrive, they spoke in a variety of ways, but quite unlike the cadenced, stagey quality of the elocution teachers. Actors like Barbara Stanwyck, James Cagney, and

Joan Blondell were all from Brooklyn, with accents to prove it, and the public loved them and their fast, wise-cracking speech rhythms. And some stars with foreign accents did manage to get accepted: Marlene Dietrich only began her American film career in 1930, and in that same year Garbo was bigger than ever after her sound debut in *Anna Christie*.

It took nearly nine months for the MGM story department to come up with an idea for Buster's first sound film. While in production it was called *On the Set,* but it was released as *Free and Easy* in early 1930. After months of conferences, Weingarten and Thalberg had decided that a musical comedy was the answer, for this was the peak of the "All Talking, All Singing, All Dancing" era, in which the studios were determined to prove

Free and Easy, 1930. National Film Archive / Stills Library

that their stars could do all three of these things on demand. Many silent stars made their sound debuts in musical pictures: Bebe Daniels in *Rio Rita* and Janet Gaynor in *Sunny Side Up.* MGM's house organ, *The Distributor,* ran a little story about Buster that drew attention to his vaudeville background: "The new Keaton in pictures will permit full play to the dialogue, singing and dancing talents which make him a stage winner." At the time this was written, Buster had not appeared on a stage in twelve years. A later story in *The Distributor* presented Buster "in a new kind of role—similar to the sort of pantomimic style of Fred Stone—acrobatic and other dancing which is literally breathtaking."

In *Free and Easy,* Buster again played an "Elmer" part, this time as a bumbling garage owner from Indiana who escorts his girl friend and her mother to Hollywood after the girl has won the "Miss Gopher Prairie" award. Elmer then takes his girl to MGM to get her a movie contract, and much of the film is devoted to Buster's running through the sound stages on the MGM lot. The basic idea was to show the glamorous side of MGM by having Buster burst into a set being used by a production company, wreck the shooting, and then run on to yet another set. The picture offered brief glimpses of William Haines, Fred Niblo, Cecil B. De Mille, and Lionel Barrymore directing a scene. Dorothy Sebastian made an appearance in a scene with Karl Dane. For the finale, Buster sings the title song, and loses his girl to Robert Montgomery. The final shot is of a suffering Buster in a huge close-up, wearing his clown makeup, in an unmistakable *Pagliacci*-like appeal to the audience.

Free and Easy runs for nearly two hours, cost nearly half a million dollars to produce, and is extraordinarily dull. Perhaps the saddest thing about it is how resolutely it ignores the essence of Buster's talents: there is really nothing for him to do in it but to act dumb and run. He sings and dances more than tolerably well, but there is no sign of the magic and poetry or the delicate precision of his best work. The picture remains as a morbid example of how badly Keaton's talents were understood by his employers.

MGM was not the only studio to make bad musicals at this

time—in fact, what we take for "badness" here is simply occasioned by changes in taste. James Cruze directed Eric von Stroheim in a 1929 musical drama, *The Great Gabbo;* the dance numbers in this film produce a great deal of giggling in modern audiences. The same is true of MGM's own Academy Award–winning *Broadway Melody of 1929,* which is intolerable by modern standards, especially the dancing, performed by hopelessly inept dancers who are incredibly plump.

The real problem was that Thalberg and Weingarten simply thought of Keaton as their comic actor who needed vehicles to show how funny he was. In this they were badly mistaken, for Keaton's talents, like Chaplin's, embraced a great deal more than acting. In effect, MGM's story department confined a great inventive talent in a straitjacket. Only part of the problem here was the medium's having become verbal; cutting through everything was MGM's conviction that they were dealing with just an actor, *a comic* and not the great and original filmmaker that he had been until this time.

Cecil B. De Mille was another filmmaker who suffered at the hands of MGM in the early days of the talkies. His sole aim was always to make commercially successful films, and he came to MGM in 1929 with just that in mind. He remained there for two unhappy years, making three expensive films, all of them disasters with both the public and the critics. De Mille blamed a lot of his troubles on the uncertainty and panic prevailing at the top levels of MGM. De Mille had come to MGM for essentially the same reasons as Buster:

> The trouble in 1928 was that I did not have enough "picture money" to be completely independent and make only the kind of picture I wanted to make. I never had, as a producer, that complete financial independence.

De Mille, too, encountered a basic misconception of his abilities, as this letter of January 1931 indicates:

> I cannot find any inspiration at all in the type of pictures that producers want me to make. They are in a state of panic and chaos. . . . I cannot find a producer who is willing to do anything but follow the mad rush for destruction.

Thalberg gave De Mille three films to direct: *Dynamite, Madame Satan,* and a remake of his famous 1913 film *The Squaw Man. Madame Satan* was a musical as awesomely bad as *Free and Easy.* At the end of his contract De Mille left MGM to return to Paramount, where he proceeded to make a lot of money for himself and his employers by using his real talents in making historical films.

Harold Lloyd was also having troubles adapting to sound films in 1929 and 1930. Lloyd's own total financial independence meant nothing, for both his problems and Buster's were the same, the death of the silent film and what to do about sound. When he spoke at the American Film Institute in 1969, Lloyd vividly recalled this troubled time and the difficulties he had encountered with his first sound film, *Welcome Danger,* at the beginning of 1929. It had originally been shot as a silent, but at the preview there was also a one-reel sound comedy on the bill,

> And they howled at this comedy. They had the punkest gags in it, but they were laughing at the pouring of water, the frying of eggs—it didn't matter—the clinking of ice in a glass. We said, "My God, we worked our hearts out to get laughs with thought-out gags, and look here: just because they've got some sound to it, they're roaring at these things. . . ."

Lloyd bowed to the inevitable and went back with his crew to convert the film into a talkie. With Buster's friend Clyde Bruckman as director, additional footage was shot in sound, but a good deal of the silent version was salvaged by dubbing the sound in where it seemed to need it:

> So, I had a silent technique to it, and oh, the dubbing was horrible. We didn't know what we were doing. We had a screen up there and we'd run the picture with "x" marks on it and just try to hit those things. Cutters didn't know much about cutting them in. . . .

Lloyd had tried to maintain his basic gag techniques from his silent days and simply "surround" these gags with the necessary dialogue to keep the story line moving. Lloyd's third sound film, *Movie Crazy,* came as close to succeeding in this attempt as any of his later films. However, neither Lloyd nor his public thought his sound films were up to the standards of his silent ones. He produced these films with his own money until 1938, but at a greatly reduced rate: only one every two years.

Keaton did not resist the coming of sound per se, but he was unhappy about the primitive technique of the early sound films which forced characters to talk incessantly. All the great silent comedy stars found themselves *having to say things—but what were they to say?* For a long time Chaplin simply refused to cope with the problem. His great wealth insured him against the necessity of making any sound films until 1936, when he sang a gibberish song in *Modern Times;* his first talking film was not until *The Great Dictator* of 1940.

Mayer and Thalberg were confident that Buster had succeeded in mastering the sound film, and MGM gave him a new two-year contract in July 1930, and a third contract as late as October 1932, at the end of the fourth year of sound films. By that time the star careers of the Talmadge sisters, John Gilbert, Harry Langdon, Mary Pickford, and Douglas Fairbanks had either come to a complete stop or were very close to doing so. Outwardly at least, things still looked good for Buster.

Buster's 1930 contract was very nearly the same as his 1928 one; his weekly pay remained at $3,000. He was to be paid an additional $12,500 for foreign-language versions of his pictures. In the early days of sound films, before the development of either dubbing or subtitling, many of the studios would make entirely new versions of their more important films for the foreign market, especially ones with stars like Garbo and Keaton, whose foreign grosses often equaled and sometimes surpassed their domestic ones. The foreign-language versions would be shot using the same sets as the original; entirely new directors would be hired to direct mostly French or German actors. The main stars would reenact their roles in the new language as best they could: Garbo spoke German with some fluency, while Keaton was able to speak his lines phonetically. In the next few years, Buster made Spanish versions of *Free and Easy* and *Doughboys,* French versions of *Parlor, Bedroom and Bath* and *The Passionate Plumber,* and a German version of *Doughboys.*

Buster was still extraordinarily active at the beginning of the thirties. He had bought himself one of the first of the famous

"Baby Austin" cars and delighted in going for long, fast drives through Beverly Hills in the small hours. Much more time-consuming than the car was his "land yacht," a monstrous vehicle that had originally been ordered from the Fifth Avenue Coach Company in New York by the then-president of the Pullman Company, who had placed it up for sale shortly after obtaining it. The land yacht was thirty feet long, could sleep six people in two bedrooms, possessed a kitchen and a dining room, and was probably unique, the kind of gadget that Buster loved. His manservant, Willy Caruthers, was the nominal chauffeur for the land yacht, in addition to his duties as bartender and cook. Keaton dubbed himself admiral of the strange craft, with his actor friend Lew Cody as vice admiral, and they borrowed suitable nautical costumes from the MGM wardrobe department. Once under way, extended trips in the land yacht were spoken of as real sea voyages, and all the correct nautical terms were used scrupulously.

Except for Louise, Buster saw much less now of his family than he had in the past. His brother, Harry, was twenty-six in 1930; Louise was twenty-four. Neither had ever prepared for careers of any sort, nor had they ever worked, for Buster considered himself the traditional "head of the clan," whose main task was to provide for all the members of his family. He finally managed to get Harry various jobs at MGM, including an apprenticeship in sound engineering under the hands of Thalberg's brother-in-law, Douglas Shearer, but Harry was not happy in this kind of work, or any other, for that matter.

Louise and her mother would occasionally visit the Italian Villa for lunch, as a prelude to long shopping expeditions in Beverly Hills. Joe Keaton was still living with his "Christian Science Lady" in downtown Los Angeles and came for dinner now and then. He could still perform his famous high kick, and he still looked like a banker in his Sunday best. Buster got his father on the MGM payroll, where he performed a variety of odd jobs for many years. Father and son maintained a healthy respect for each other's privacy. If Joe, who never returned to drinking, noticed his son's steadily increasing diet of alcohol, he said nothing about it.

[3]

Buster, in those days, was an alcoholic and he was in a place called The Keeley Cure, down on Wilshire Boulevard, that dried drunks out, when we invented that scene. That was the only problem I ever had with Buster Keaton. I didn't know it was a problem. . . .
—Lawrence Weingarten, 1974

Sound comedy is a different thing entirely. Sound comedy is about what people say, mostly, not what they do. We tried to combine both. . . .
—Lawrence Weingarten, 1972

It took four months to devise Buster's second sound film, *Doughboys,* which finally went into production on May 13, 1930. Buster always thought of it as a personal film because of its autobiographical elements. The story, as written by Al Boasberg and Sidney Lazarus, draws on some of Buster's experiences as an entertainer with the American forces in France in 1918. Cast as a wealthy, inept idler, Buster is inducted into the army by mistake. There is some moderately amusing material involving Elmer's basic training, but on the whole it is a predictable, plodding affair. As is so often the case with Buster's less successful films, there is one outstanding scene: an Apache dance in drag, performed in a show for the troops at the front. Here, for the duration of only three or four minutes, is the old Keaton, incredibly lithe and graceful. It is an electrifying sequence that permits him full use of his body, unencumbered by the banal dialogue that he had been given by scriptwriters Boasberg and Richard Schayer.

Doughboys cost a lot less than *Free and Easy,* only $276,000, and it made considerably more money, earning a profit of $141,000 compared with the minute $10,000 profit of the expensive musical. The budget for *Doughboys* became the norm for all Buster's MGM features. "A Keaton" had become a standardized product.

In 1958 Keaton offered his own version of the way he had dealt with the new sound medium at the beginning of the thirties:

> Sound didn't bother us at all. There was only one thing I wanted at all times, and insisted on: that you go ahead and talk in the most natural way in your situations. Don't give me puns. Don't give me jokes. No wisecracks . . . as soon as our plot is set and everything is going smooth, I'm always going to find places in the story where dialogue is not called for. . . . So you get those stretches in your picture of six, seven, eight, nine minutes where there isn't a word of dialogue. In those, we did our old routines. Then, when it was natural to talk, you talked. You didn't avoid it.

None of this sounds surprising today, but at MGM in 1930 more than a moment's silence was unthinkable. Opposition to Buster's ideas about making his films stiffened, and his views on the use of sound fell on increasingly deaf ears.

> But in every picture it got tougher. . . . There were too many cooks. Everybody at Metro was in my gag department, including Irving Thalberg. They'd laugh their heads off at dialogue written by all your new writers. They were joke happy. They didn't look for action, they were looking for funny things to say. You just kept fighting that, see. . . .

At no time in his later career did Buster have anything unkind to say about Thalberg, reserving most of his criticism for Weingarten, with some occasional remarks about "that SOB Louis B. Mayer!" There were times when Buster would go over Weingarten's head to Thalberg, but it didn't seem to do much good, for as he later said, "When I found out that they could write stories and material better than I could anyway, what was the use of my fighting with them?"

He did fight with them in the early years and managed to win at least some of the battles, as the excellence of *The Cameraman* and *Spite Marriage* indicates. But starting with *Free and Easy,* these struggles became ever harder to win, especially since by then he was either hungover or trying to dry out at Arrowhead Springs.

In the early summer of 1930 Buster received this telegram from the studio:

> YOU ARE INSTRUCTED TO REPORT TO US AT OUR CULVER CITY STUDIO AT TEN O'CLOCK A.M. WEDNESDAY JUNE FOURTH TO RESUME YOUR SERVICES IN OUR PHOTOPLAY TENTATIVELY TITLED MAN O WAR (STOP) YOU ARE FURTHER ADVISED THAT YOUR REFUSAL TO COMPLY THIS AFTERNOON HAS CAUSED US CONSIDERABLE LOSS AND FURTHER LOSS WILL BE CAUSED IN EVENT YOU FAIL TO COMPLY AND RESUME YOUR SERVICES.
> METRO-GOLDWYN-MAYER CORPORATION
> IRVING G. THALBERG, VICE PRESIDENT

Whether Buster's absence was responsible for the studio's abandoning *Man O' War* is uncertain, but the project was dropped.

Buster's ability to argue with his employers became progressively eroded for a number of reasons. For one, Thalberg and Weingarten, as well as the staff writers, were convinced they were giving Buster the best available material for his films. Secondly, Keaton was visibly affected by the amount of alcohol he was consuming. He was missing time from work, actually losing expensive days of production, behavior that he had always regarded as extremely unprofessional.

By the time of Buster's third sound film, *Parlor, Bedroom and Bath,* things were much worse.

> But I know for a finish, they were picking stories and material without consulting me, and I couldn't argue them out of it. They'd say, "This is funny," and I say, "It stinks"—it didn't make any difference, we did it anyhow. . . .

Weingarten, who was responsible for obtaining material for Keaton, frankly admitted that there were times when he simply didn't know what to do. In 1972 he recalled:

> We were desperate, we didn't know what to do. Sedgwick, the director, and I were riding down Hollywood Boulevard by the old El Capitan Theater which is now the Paramount. We saw a play, a matinee, an old Avery Hopwood play with Charlotte Greenwood. It said "Parlor, Bedroom and Bath." I said, "Eddie, let's go in and see this." We saw it and it appeared to be the genesis of an idea. So we bought the play for $6,000 including Charlotte Greenwood's salary. . . .

A third reason for Keaton's loss of bargaining power was the startling fact that his films of 1930 and 1931 actually made a lot more money than anything he had ever done before. The total grosses for *Doughboys* and *Sidewalks of New York,* which Buster made in 1931, were $814,000 and $855,000, earning net profits of $141,000 and $196,000. Since these two films had cost only $276,000 apiece, the profit margin here was so great that it would have been nearly impossible to shake MGM's faith in the kind of film they were now making for Buster. None of Buster's films from the silent days had ever done this well, with the single exception of *Battling Butler,* which had grossed $749,000. To MGM, a net profit of nearly $200,000 on an investment of only $276,000 was extremely impressive, especially in the darkest days of the depression, when admission prices fell to the level of a dime. With figures like these in Thalberg's hands, it seemed foolish of Buster to argue with him about quality. All right, Thalberg would have answered, the pictures are terrible, but the American public loves them.

Many of Buster's fellow stars at MGM were not doing nearly as well. The Jean Harlow vehicle *Red-Headed Woman,* on which F. Scott Fitzgerald had worked for a month, made a net profit of only $69,000, while Eugene O'Neill's *Strange Interlude,* with Gable and Norma Shearer, showed $90,000. *A Free Soul,* with Gable, Shearer, Leslie Howard, and Lionel Barrymore, produced a profit of $244,000, while Noel Coward's *Private Lives* with Shearer and Robert Montgomery made $256,000. But these last two films had cost more than half as much to produce. A number of MGM's films were actually showing heavy losses at the box office, with the John Gilbert film *Way For a Sailor* losing $606,000 and Tod Browning's *Freaks* $164,000. *Rasputin and the Empress,* starring all three of the Barrymores, lost $185,000, partially due to the loss of a libel suit brought by the heirs of the Russian royal family.

Buster was truly caught in a trap from which there seemed to be no escape. Why didn't he attempt a shift to another studio where things might have been different, where he might have had more voice in what he appeared in? There is no indication that he made any active efforts to do so; perhaps his close friend Joseph Schenck advised him to continue on at MGM. Where else was he going to earn $3,000 a week, plus a share of the profits? After 1931 the Depression began to affect the film industry powerfully, so that by the end of 1932 Paramount, RKO, and Fox were all in some form of bankruptcy or receivership proceedings. MGM was in the soundest financial shape of all the Hollywood studios. There was really nowhere for him to go. It may well be too that Buster realized that the problems he was facing at MGM were exactly the same problems he would meet all over again at Universal or Warner Brothers: what does a silent comedian do in the sound era?

Buster Collier still thinks that many of Keaton's difficulties at MGM arose from his being so very much on his own there. He had no theatrical agent to argue for him, no strong family to support him. He had plenty of friends, but there was virtually no one in whom to confide. He and Natalie had little to say to each other, and rather than going home to the Italian Villa, he often preferred to sleep at his bungalow on the lot, or in his land yacht, seldom alone. Buster's drinking as well as his many infidelities were put up with by Natalie, who was still curiously passive about these matters.

Sometime in the fall of 1931 Collier went on a duck-hunting trip with Buster to Bakersfield, California. Ducks were not really so much on Collier's mind as a desire to be left alone for a few days with his old friend so that he could talk to Keaton about his drinking. Buster's heavy consumption of alcohol was by now fairly well known in Hollywood. As he remembers it today, Collier thinks he was approached by Constance Talmadge, acting on behalf of the Talmadge family, to see if "he couldn't do something about Buster's drinking." In any event, Collier had decided that a few days out in the open air were what his friend needed; only when they had gotten away from the distractions of Hollywood could he freely broach the real reason for the duck hunt.

Collier agreed to meet Keaton at MGM early on a Friday evening, and the two friends would then drive on down to Bakersfield. The evening arrived, but Collier was disappointed to find that Buster had brought along some female company for the trip, a pretty young starlet from Paramount. Keaton hastily explained that she wouldn't be a bother, she wouldn't get in the way, that she'd be invisible. Fully convinced that she would be very much in the way, Collier could only accept Buster's fait accompli with as much grace as he could muster.

The trip to Bakersfield was taken in Buster's land yacht, with Willy Caruthers driving. Collier noticed that while the girl was scarcely invisible, she certainly had absolutely nothing to say, not a word. When they arrived at their destination for the night, Caruthers served them dinner. Collier and Keaton stayed up talking in the kitchen until about midnight; the girl had gone back into Buster's bedroom an hour or so earlier. Collier kept trying to get Buster to go to bed, but he kept on saying, "Time for just one more drink, and then we'll go to bed. Okay?" Under the circumstances, it had to be okay, so Collier stayed up until about two, and then he finally went to bed, leaving Buster sitting up with a drink in his hand.

The plan was to arise at about four fifteen to try their luck at the duck blind; miraculously both men woke up in time to get started. It had begun raining during the night, and they slogged along in silence through the mud until they reached the duck blind. They sat there in silence, in the dark, waiting for the dawn. Suddenly Keaton groaned aloud, whispering to Collier: "I've got to stand up! Listen, my legs, I've got no circulation." Then quite loudly he cried out, "It's killing me, help me up!" Collier helped Buster to his feet to see what was causing the pain.

In the dim glow of his flashlight, Collier noticed that Buster's hunting boots seemed extraordinarily tight. Buster cautiously began to explore the length of his leg; suddenly he began to laugh. In the frenzy of getting up and out of the land yacht in time, he had put on the girl's boots instead of his own; he had had so much to drink the night before that he had been oblivious to the pain it must have caused. In the end they had to cut them off his legs with a knife.

By now the chances of getting any ducks that morning seemed remote. Collier took this opportunity to talk about Buster's drinking. He didn't get very far, for Buster's response was immediate: "Listen! If you were sent up here to me to have this big thing out with me, and tell me how I'm doin' wrong, you're just wastin' your time. I know the only person in the world can cure me of that is me! So listen, I know what I'm doin'."

Keaton said all this with such deadly vehemence that Collier gave up the idea of saying any more; he realized that he could do nothing, nor, probably, could anyone else. The two men finally rose to their feet, with Buster now ready for a morning pick-me-up and some breakfast. Buster drank a lot that afternoon, and they all went to bed early. The next morning there were no ducks to be had. They drove back to Hollywood on Sunday afternoon; it was the first and last time that Collier broached the matter of alcohol to Keaton.

9

THE LION HAS TEETH

After that, everything happened. I got to the stage
where I didn't care whether school kept or
not. . . .
　　　　　　　　　　　　　　　　—Keaton, 1958

Buster was really too nice a guy, just too nice. . . .
　　　　　　　　　　　　　　　—Gilbert Roland, 1977

In early February of 1931 Keaton's name appeared on the front
page of the *Los Angeles Times,* as well as in a great many other
papers throughout the country. The *New York Times* headlined
the story:

EX-FILM BEAUTY CLAWS
KEATON, MOVIE CLOWN

Kathleen Key Wrecked His
Dressing Room When Refused
$20,000, He Charges

The woman was a young actress of large proportions whose
screen career had faltered because of her inability to control her
weight. Buster told the Los Angeles reporters that he had en-
couraged Miss Key to lose weight and that she bet him $500 she
could lose twenty pounds in ten days. She lost her bet, dropping
only six pounds, but Buster agreed to pay her anyway. By the
time Buster had instructed his lawyer to prepare a check for her,
she later claimed the agreed sum had been $5,000. When she
came to Buster's bungalow at MGM for the money, Buster offered her a check for this amount, but she refused it and told

him she wanted an additional $20,000. Buster lost his temper and told her he would not pay her a penny, tearing up his check as he spoke. Suddenly the girl went berserk, scratching and clawing at Buster until his face was covered with bloody scratch marks. She then turned her attention to his dressing room, which she proceeded to wreck thoroughly. Buster said later: "But when the lady picked up a pair of long shears and lunged at me with them, I belted her in the jaw in self-defense." Willy Caruthers and the comedian Gus Edwards called for help: "At this point a couple of Culver City policemen arrived. They turned out to be unlucky cops. When they tried to drag her away, she kicked one in the genitals and took a backhand swipe at the other, giving him a black eye." The girl was taken to the Culver City Police Station but was not held because Buster refused to press charges. The following day she claimed that her jaw had been broken and threatened to sue both Buster and MGM.

Thalberg and Mayer were convinced that there had been more than just a friendly bet between Buster and Miss Key. For reasons that remain obscure, but perhaps because they suspected a liaison, they felt that anything else she might have to say to the press would be damaging to the studio. Their solution was simple: pay her $10,000 to leave town and keep her mouth shut. Buster later said that he had been forced to pay Miss Key through the law offices of Lord, Wacker, and Lord, MGM's attorneys in Los Angeles; however, there is no record of his salary having been docked by this amount.

A few weeks later MGM's publicity department decided to make use of the episode to convey the idea that Buster was a Casanova, a living danger to female virtue, and printed a mock waiver form to be signed by women reckless enough to enter "Keaton's Kennel." The waiver was promptly reprinted in one of the fan magazines:

Culver City, _____ 19__

> The undersigned hereby deposes and states that she is in the spot designated as "Keaton's Kennel" at her own risk and in consideration agrees that she will under no circumstances sue for any damages, either actual or punitive, arising out of any injury, bro-

ken limbs, loss of virtue, etc. or any other mishap sustained upon said premises. And she further undertakes that she hereby waives all right, legal or otherwise, to bring legal action in any court for any cause whatsoever arising from her presence in the "Kennel."

This has the familiar ring of Joe Keaton back in his German-American Doctors days in 1910, and it is likely that Buster had a hand in its composition, although the words are clearly the product of MGM's publicity department.

The stories about Buster and Miss Key did nothing to help the marriage of the Keatons. His absences from the Italian Villa had become longer and more frequent, and he invariably refused to tell Natalie where he had been or where he intended going. She was perfectly aware that these absences were caused by the steady stream of women in his life. Peg and her other daughters had become less tolerant than in the early days of the marriage and were beginning to consider Buster's infidelities an affront to the Talmadge family name. They urged Natalie to do something about the situation, but she remained reluctant because of their two boys, who adored Buster.

There were money problems as well. Natalie complained a good deal, but Buster refused to discuss it. Despite his $3,000 a week salary, a great many of their bills, including taxes, never got paid. The money Buster made at MGM was spent as fast as he made it. In early 1932 he bought a one-hundred-foot yacht for Natalie for $25,000, a bargain price, but the upkeep for the vessel was enormous. Natalie must have wished for a return to the days when Buster's paychecks were payable to her, but this situation did not prevail at MGM. Another reason for the financial squeeze was that Buster was such a soft touch, always ready to say yes if anyone asked him for money.

There had been some attempt at a reconciliation in the fall of 1930 when he and Natalie spent nearly three months touring Europe, part of the time in the company of Norma and her lover, Gilbert Roland, who acted as a guide for the party. The expenses for the European trip were partly underwritten by the $10,000-bonus that Mayer and Thalberg had given Buster for his work in *Doughboys*. But apparently the trip did nothing to

Buster and Natalie in Berlin, 1930. *Wide World*

improve the quality of the marriage, and they never rediscovered the feelings they once had for each other.

Immediately after his return from Europe, Buster was shown
the working script for his next film, *Parlor, Bedroom and Bath,* to
which he took an instant dislike. The script was based on the
1917 Broadway farce by Charles W. Bell and Mack Swan. This is
the same play that Weingarten saw in a 1930 revival on Hollywood Boulevard. Weingarten claimed that he had bought it for
Buster on the spot, but this is unlikely, for the play had been
filmed previously by MGM in 1920. Buster's basic objection to
the play was the fact that it was a farce comedy, a form of entertainment for which he had little regard.

Buster once gave a reasonable definition of farce comedy.
They were all, he said, based on a "simple misunderstanding or
mistaken identity":

> There are always a couple of characters in the show, who if they
> would come out and say, "Wait a minute, this is the case," all the
> problems would be solved. Then there's farce tempo. In all farce
> stories, everybody works faster than they do when they're telling a
> legitimate story. They take things bigger. People get hysterical
> easily. . . .

Buster felt that he "shouldn't have been put into anything that
was a farce. Because I don't work that way. Life is too serious to
do farce comedy."

Buster's theatrical agent for fifteen years, Ben Pearson, states
that Buster had an almost infallible instinct for what would work
and what would not in virtually every form of entertainment. He
could take one look at a play, a film, or a TV drama, and tell you
with extraordinary precision exactly what was good or bad about
it. Buster was absolutely right about the script of *Parlor, Bedroom
and Bath* being wrong for him. But when he tried to argue with
Weingarten and Thalberg about this project and others like it,
his complete lack of formal education did him a great disservice,
for he simply didn't have the command of language to change
their minds: he simply *knew* it was wrong. Forty years later,
Weingarten went out of his way to mention Buster's educational
weakness: "He was a sweet fellow. But here's a boy had never
gone to school, I don't think he was ever in a school. . . ."

Parlor, Bedroom and Bath turned out to be just as fast and hysterical as Buster had predicted. The picture involved three other
comedians besides Buster: Reginald Denny, Cliff Edwards, and
Ed Brophy. In addition to Charlotte Greenwood, now best
known for her performance as Aunt Eller in *Oklahoma!,* there
were four girls in the film. The whole point of the story was to
have Buster pretend to be an incredibly gifted lover of all the
women in the picture. There is a great deal of frantic running
around, lots of fast talk, and very little real comedy. The picture
was retitled for England *Romeo in Pajamas,* a title that at least
conveyed what the film was about. The scene in which Buster is
given a professional "lesson in love" by the lanky, agile Miss
Greenwood is quite good, but there is little else to praise. Buster
had talked Thalberg into allowing the opening sequence of the
film to be shot at the Italian Villa, and there is an excellent view

of the villa as it was in the winter of 1930 in a spectacular chase in which Buster runs down the steps of his house to the swimming pool at the bottom. The chase sequence in *Parlor, Bedroom and Bath* was filmed silently: few talkies were made out-of-doors at this time because of the cumbersome recording system then in use. There is one highly topical gag in the film: Buster is asked to "say something!" He shyly replies: "I'm not much good at talkin'!"

By the spring of 1931, Keaton's bungalow was a subject of some irritation to Louis B. Mayer, who felt that it was a hotbed of studio unrest, a place where the hard drinkers, all possible troublemakers, hung out. Buster loved to entertain in the grand manner, and lunch at his bungalow was a memorable experience. The liquor flowed freely there, at a time when the consumption of alcohol was still technically a crime. Mayer also disapproved of the sexual goings-on: the most attractive girls on the lot always seemed to be there. Many parties would go on all through the night. Mayer disliked the situation intensely and used Eddie Mannix to keep him posted about what went on at Buster's Kennel.

Edgar Mannix, always "Eddie" to everyone who knew him, was a one-man police force. A tall, imposingly tough Irishman with a face that reminded many of a happy bulldog, Mannix had started out in the Loew-Schenck hierarchy by working as a bouncer at the Schencks' Palisades Amusement Park in New Jersey. One of his many jobs at MGM was to take care of potentially dangerous situations created by such troublesome stars as John Gilbert, Jean Harlow, and John Barrymore. But Mannix, like everyone at MGM except Mayer, found it very hard to get angry with Buster, whatever the provocation, not even when he ruined an expensive take on a swimming pool set by suddenly jumping into the pool himself. This was a common response. Gilbert Roland, who appeared with Buster in *The Passionate Plumber* (1932), recalls Buster's incredible sweetness; it was almost impossible for anyone to dislike him.

Buster's future at MGM depended wholly upon Weingarten, Thalberg, and Mayer. He regularly asked Thalberg for a production unit all his own with which he could deliver his two contract films each year, but, just as regularly, Thalberg turned him down. The only independent unit on the lot was the Marian Davies Cosmopolitan Productions unit, which was partly subsidized by William Randolph Hearst. As Buster had no grasp of finances, it is not likely that either Thalberg or Mayer believed that he could produce his own films successfully.

Buster also complained about his writers' refusal to give him scenes involving the dangerous physical stunts of his silent films. He was told that if there were to be any such scenes, a suitable double would be found to do them: MGM's insurance policies on its stars did not permit them to take any dangerous risks. This news was terribly discouraging for a man as intensely physical as Keaton; he argued this point with Thalberg again and again, but to no avail. He was completely caught up in the MGM factory system.

Sidewalks of New York is surely the worst of all Keaton's sound features, the only other candidate being *What, No Beer?* (1933). Sedgwick was not available for *Sidewalks,* and it was directed by Jules White and Zion Meyers, a team who had been making a profitable series of shorts for MGM featuring talking dogs (the films were referred to in the trade papers as "All Barkle Comedies"). Buster hated *Sidewalks* as much as he had *Parlor, Bedroom and Bath.* "I knew before the camera was put up for the first scene that it was practically impossible to get a good motion picture. . . . Everything happened, and it was no good. Absolutely impossible."

Sidewalks features an insipid revival of Buster's old Rollo Treadway character from *The Navigator* in a story about a dim-witted millionaire who courts a tough girl of the slums, played by Anita Page. The girl has a young brother who has become involved with criminals. To win the girl, Buster offers to set up an athletic club for the boy and his friends in order to woo them away from the criminal life. Boxing is the main sport at the new club, and the story reuses some of the boxing material from *Battling Butler.* There is only one scene in the entire film with any real life, a brief one at the end in which again, as in *Doughboys,* Buster dances. In spite of its dullness and predictability, it nevertheless grossed $855,000, with a net profit of $196,000.

The financial success of *Sidewalks* can best be explained as a triumph of the Loew's distribution system. It seems clear they had no illusions about the film, for instead of opening up in New York at the Capital Theater, as was the custom for new Keaton films, *Sidewalks* was quietly premiered at Loew's 175th Street in Washington Heights. Loew's was selling these new Keaton films to his old audience, which kept hoping in vain for better things. The European grosses, too, were as big as ever, actually exceeding the domestic ones: there was a great deal of curiosity in Europe about Buster's sound films, which he satisfied by his appearances in the foreign-language versions. He liked making these films.

> Oh, I was speaking Spanish. I spoke French, too. I even did one for Metro in German, *Parlor, Bedroom and Bath* in German! I memorized a sentence at a time, see. I did that also in French and Spanish. It was awfully hard work, because by the time I'd satisfied the Spanish dialogue supervisor, I'd then get the French cast, and by the time I'd get to the German I'd hear the German supervisor say, "Oh, I understand him very well, only he's speaking with a French-Spanish accent. . . ."

The manager of MGM's Paris exchange, George Kahn, was quite aware of how poor *Sidewalks of New York* was, remarking on it in a cable to Louis B. Mayer at the time Buster's next film, *The Passionate Plumber,* was going into production:

> MAKE PARTICULAR EFFORT HAVE PASSIONATE PLUMBER DIALOGUE MOST HUMOROUS POSSIBLE. KEATON'S LAST VERY WEAK. . . .

The cable may have had some effect, for considerably more effort went into this film, which was based on Jacques Deval's comedy *Her Cardboard Lover.* A great deal of time and money was spent in providing new material for Buster, for in addition to the basic scenario cost of $33,000, MGM spent $15,000 or so in buying what the company records indicate as "three scenes for Keaton."

In *The Passionate Plumber,* Buster was tacitly given Jimmy Durante as his co-star. This was the first of their three joint appearances. The decision to combine the talents of "Schnozzola" Durante, the fiercely energetic, long-nosed nightclub comedian, with those of Buster Keaton now seems a strange one. Some people felt that Durante was brought in to fill out Buster's pictures, to give them an extra dimension, but this was firmly denied by Weingarten.

> No. Keaton was doing a certain amount of business. And we thought that Durante . . . in this particular role, would be fine, that's all. We weren't thinking of bolstering him. There were a number of pictures made, we tried our best. If it wasn't good enough, that's another thing. But we didn't set out to destroy Buster. . . .

There is no reason to doubt Weingarten's sincerity here; no one at MGM was interested in destroying Buster. The destruction of Buster's career was caused by his worsening alcoholism and his inability to regain control over the *kind* of pictures in which he appeared.

In *The Passionate Plumber* Buster is again used as a bogus or decoy lover for a wealthy girl who wants to make her real lover, Gilbert Roland, sufficiently jealous that he will assert his love for her. There is more vitality in *The Passionate Plumber* than in any of the other Keaton sound films. Part of its charm lies in the supporting cast, and there are a number of extremely funny scenes between Roland and his Hispanic girl, played by Mona Maris. On two separate occasions Miss Maris assaults Roland with a violent, unending stream of Spanish invective; she then stops and exclaims, "Oh, if you could only understand Spanish!" Since Roland was the Spanish lover incarnate for forty years, the joke still works. Roland has told me that the joke was improvised by Miss Maris and himself while the picture was in production.

During the film, Roland challenges Buster to a duel. With Durante as his completely incompetent second, Buster converts the affair into a parody of all the dueling scenes ever shot, for he proceeds to do everything totally wrong, starting with his attempt to shoot Roland in the back as he begins walking away for the count of ten.

There are some superb glimpses of Buster's ability to move

Buster and Irene Purcell in *The Passionate Plumber*, 1932. *Maryann Chach*

quickly and gracefully. At the very beginning of the film, Buster,
cast as an American plumber working in Paris, is brought to the
girl's house by her chauffeur, played by Durante. The door is
opened by the maid (Polly Moran), who eyes Buster with some
suspicion. Staring at each other intently, the two proceed in the
direction of a vast, curving staircase. They hesitate at the bottom
of the stairwell; Moran takes a step or two, then turns back to see
if Buster is still behind her. At that instant, with almost blinding
speed, Buster manages to pass Moran and is at the top as if by a
miracle. The sequence is shot with full figures, without fakery,

Buster, Jimmy Durante, and Gilbert Roland in *The Passionate Plumber,* 1932.
Maryann Chach

just the way Buster had made his own films for Schenck. Later
on in the film, in a sequence set in Monte Carlo, Buster gracefully flees a stream of pursuers by making his way under and
over all the roulette tables in the huge room. He finally runs up
a huge flight of stairs, at the top of which is the camera, recording his astounding burst of speed. This sequence still produces
applause at the relatively few screenings the film receives.

Buster was unhappy working with Durante for two reasons.
He was aware that Mayer had high hopes for "Schnozzola," and
that he was being given parts in Buster's films as a showcase for
his talent. Buster was quite sure that he and Durante didn't
belong in the same picture:

Then, of course, when you give me a Jimmy Durante—they brought him in there to play a part in a picture with me. Well, Durante just can't keep quiet. He's going to talk no matter what happens. You can't direct him any other way. Louis B. Mayer liked him very much; it could have been that he was brought out to replace me, I don't know. . . .

What actually happened in *The Passionate Plumber* is what happened in nearly every film Durante appeared in: he played himself and seemed to have little to do with anyone else in the cast.

Buster disliked working with Durante for personal as well as professional reasons. Durante invariably punctuated all his conversations with Buster by punching him on the upper arms and chest. Since Durante was, in Buster's words, "strong as a bull," this constant rain of punches really hurt, but Buster was simply too polite to tell him to stop. The punching continued unabated for the next year.

The shooting of *The Passionate Plumber* proceeded with great speed and took only nineteen days to complete. This was the last of Buster's films at MGM to be completed on time, for 1932 was to be a year of personal disasters for Buster, disasters that inevitably resulted in delays in the production of his films. The few moments when he had been allowed to show what he could do in films like *The Passionate Plumber* were not enough for him. But he found it almost impossible to communicate to anyone that he longed for the days when he and his team were responsible for the kinds of pictures they had made in the twenties. Instead, he became increasingly angry and resentful, and some of this anger spilled over into his life at home.

In early April of 1932 the Los Angeles newspapers were filled with a number of stories about Buster's alleged "kidnapping" of his two sons, Jimmy and Bobby, then nine and eight years of age. The incident had come about in part from Natalie's angry departure from the Italian Villa on Friday evening, the twenty-fifth of March. She and Buster had quarreled bitterly over his intention to take the two boys with him on a trip to Mexico. She was probably opposed to the trip because Buster was drinking heavily at the time. When she had not returned home by Monday morning, Buster took his two boys over to the MGM commissary for lunch and then to Clover Field in Santa Monica. At the field he engaged the services of a pilot who agreed to take Buster's party to Aguascalientes in Mexico. Willy Caruthers and the boy's governess, Consuelo Costello, also went along. The plane hired for the trip was one the boys had seen being flown by a friend of Buster's, the actor Hoot Gibson. Buster's basic explanation for the trip, or so he told the newspaper reporters, was "to show who wears the trousers around our house. I just wanted to see who's boss. I didn't know I'd stir up a miniature war in doing it, though. Why, I wouldn't have been surprised if they'd called out the Army, Navy, and Marine Corps to greet me in San Diego."

Natalie had been informed about the trip and did everything she could to prevent it, engaging the help of Constance, who contacted the district attorney's office in San Diego, a necessary stopover point to clear Mexican customs. She also contacted Eddie Mannix at the studio, who had reasons of his own to suspect that something was odd about Buster's flight to Mexico. When the plane landed at the San Diego airport, the police were there to prevent any more flying that day. The following day Buster and his entourage returned to Beverly Hills in a hired car, per Natalie's specific instructions. She had claimed that she had been in deadly fear for the safety of her children and had managed to convince the authorities, with the aid of Mannix and Constance, that her fears were well founded. When Buster got back to his house on Tuesday evening, Natalie was still missing, presumably staying at Constance's house.

Then Buster, with the strenuous help of the MGM publicity department, attempted to make a joke out of the entire rift between Natalie and himself. He summoned all the Los Angeles reporters to the house and had himself photographed on the front lawn with the two boys in the pose of a grieving father "waiting for the return of mom." Buster was quoted as saying: "She knows I adore her. I don't think this is anything but stubbornness on her part. I've been a bad boy I guess, but gee, I wish she'd come home. I've called Constance's home but got no answer and I can't get an answer at my mother's place. This is my punishment, I guess."

By Thursday afternoon, the papers reported, everything was

again peaceful at the Keaton home; Natalie had returned and all was forgiven. What is understandably left out of all these newspaper stories is the fact that Buster had not been reporting for work at the studio since the previous Monday, the twenty-eighth of March. The preliminary work on Buster's next film, *Speak Easily,* was in progress, but Buster had again simply refused to appear at the studio, just as he had done back in the summer of 1930. Mayer was angry and sent Buster a telegram on Tuesday afternoon:

YOU ARE HEREBY INSTRUCTED TO REPORT TO THE OF-FICE OF MR. MANNIX AT THE STUDIO AT HALF PAST TWO IN THE AFTERNOON ON WEDNESDAY MARCH THIRTIETH NINETEEN THIRTY TWO
METRO GOLDWYN MAYER CORPORATION
LOUIS B. MAYER
VICE PRESIDENT

Buster ignored the wire, just as he ignored all official communications. At the end of that week, the week of Buster's proposed trip to Mexico, Mayer sent him a registered letter, which began by advising Buster to read his contract, particularly paragraph 10:

MARCH 29, 1932 WE INSTRUCTED YOU TO REPORT TO MR. MANNIX'S OFFICE AT OUR STUDIO ON MARCH 30, 1932 AT 2:30 P.M. YOU DID NOT COMPLY WITH SUCH IN-STRUCTION AND HAVE AT ALL TIMES SINCE THEN FAILED TO RENDER YOUR REQUIRED SERVICE FOR US.

THIS IS TO INFORM YOU THAT, PURSUANT TO THE PROVISIONS OF PARAGRAPH 10 OF SAID CONTRACT, WE SHALL REFUSE TO PAY YOU ANY COMPENSATION COM-MENCING AS OF MARCH 30, 1932, AND CONTINUING THEREAFTER UNTIL YOU ARE READY, WILLING AND ABLE TO RENDER YOUR REQUIRED SERVICES FOR US IN ACCORDANCE WITH THE TERMS OF YOUR SAID CON-TRACT. . . .

Mayer's letter had no more effect than his telegram, for Buster did not report back to work until Thursday, the fourteenth of April. He was given a formal suspension of thirteen working

days for his failure to report. During the days he was absent some hard thinking about Buster's future at the studio must have taken place, for the legal department of MGM prepared a series of memos for Mannix, Thalberg, and Mayer outlining the contractual situation with Buster as it then existed. At that time, Keaton's contract of July 1930 was due to expire shortly; Thalberg and Mayer were concerned whether *Speak Easily* could be made in time under the terms of that contract. What gave them cause for worry was the fact that Buster had started returning his weekly paychecks to the studio. The studio manager, M. E. Greenwood, wrote a memo to his superiors:

> He has returned his paychecks for the five days to March 29th and for the two weeks ending April 20th and April 27th. He has given no specific reason, but I think what he has in his mind is that he will complete his next scheduled picture and then demand compensation for the suspended period. About two weeks ago he contended to me that if he made two English language pictures during the year, he was entitled to the $150,000 irrespective of any suspensions without compensation. Under his first contract of January 26, 1928 this was true of suspensions account of incapacity, but not true as to suspensions account of refusal, but under the contract of July 9, 1930 it is not true as to any and all suspensions. He contends the understanding was that his contract of July 9, 1930 was to have been the same in this respect as the contract of January 26, 1928. Even so *refusal or failure* to comply would be subject to suspension without pay. . . .

It is likely that Buster's decision to refuse his paychecks was based on the advice he received from a man whom he had hired as his business manager, Jack Codd. On May fourth the three checks were sent by registered mail to Codd's office in Beverly Hills, but Buster refused to cash them. There was not the slightest doubt that MGM was fully in the right in refusing to pay Buster for the time he either refused to appear or simply couldn't because of physical incapacity. His decision to take the line he did was ill-advised: Mayer was particularly incensed by Buster's stubbornness.

Buster was regularly finishing off more than a bottle of liquor a day. It seems obvious that his kidnapping venture was al-

Buster in his kennel, 1932. *Rudi Blesh*

coholically inspired, as was the openly defiant attitude he took at MGM by refusing to appear for work. After Buster's return to work on the fourteenth of April, preparations for *Speak Easily* went ahead and the picture started shooting on the ninth of May. The whole problem of Buster's withheld pay of $6,500 was left up in the air.

Louise recalls driving out to see her brother the week following the aborted plane trip. It was a bright Sunday afternoon at the Italian Villa, but the place seemed absolutely deserted. On Sunday afternoons in the past there had always been a throng of guests sampling Buster's barbecue specialties; now there was not a sound to be heard. She finally found Buster sitting by his swimming pool in the company of an attractive blonde whom he promptly introduced to Louise as his "hired call girl for the day." Buster was drinking from a bottle of bourbon he had carried down to the pool with him; he wasn't really drunk, as Louise remembers, but he was high enough to speak far more frankly than usual. He kept railing on about Natalie's prevention of the trip to Mexico. He stopped suddenly, turned to the girl sitting beside them, and told her in his gravest tone: "Your services are no longer required—you are now discharged." The puzzled girl nodded her head and began walking up the steps to the house. Buster then told his sister that Natalie had again left, taking the two boys with her, and had no intention of returning. He also told Louise that he had packed up some of Natalie's clothing and given it to the call girl the previous night. He went on about Natalie's implacable bitterness, often blaming himself for it, but insisted that he was as fond of her as he had ever been. He finally lapsed into silence as they sat there together by the empty pool. Louise said good-bye and left; it was her last visit to the Italian Villa. Her final image was of Buster sitting in the approaching dusk, staring into the pool, with the half-finished bottle of bourbon in his hand.

Buster's extreme reluctance to appear in *Speak Easily* had arisen for several reasons. The most important in his view was that this would be the fourth film in a row that cast him as a bumbling, witless character. It also would be his second appearance with Durante as the virtual co-star of the picture. Actually,

Buster was quite contradictory about *Speak Easily*, telling Charles Samuels that Durante had been "very good in the one picture we made together that had quality . . . *Speak Easily*, which was based on a Clarence Buddington Kelland story and a sound comedy plot." As for his being cast as a bumbling, witless character, nearly all of his silent pictures had him playing roles of this kind; there was really nothing new about this except for the fact that he was now playing bumblers who talked. Under Keaton's direction the story of *Speak Easily* could undoubtedly have become a typical Keaton silent film, but as a talkie at MGM it left him little to do but mouth the lines written for him. The physical Keaton, the Keaton of spectacular inventions, was absent.

Speak Easily deals with a shy professor of classics who believes that he has inherited three-quarters of a million dollars. The professor (Keaton) leaves his college and falls in with a traveling show directed by Durante. The show is in dire financial straits; Buster promises to give them money, and they all set off for New York to put on the show. Thelma Todd attempts to seduce him with the aid of her own charms plus booze. Buster's main task in the final part of the film is to reduce the opening night to a shambles because of his assorted *gaucheries;* the audience is convulsed, and the show is a smash.

The story of *Speak Easily* met Keaton's own high standards, so it is puzzling that the film is not a lot better than it is. Why doesn't the seduction scene between Thelma Todd and Buster work as well as the scenes between Todd and Groucho Marx in *Horse Feathers* and *Monkey Business?* The simplest answer is that the Todd-Marx sequences are of the essence of sound comedy, whereas the scene in *Speak Easily* with Todd and Buster is flat and dull; this is just not Buster's element. The scriptwriters, Ralph Spence and Laurence E. Johnson, are just not as witty as S. J. Perelman and his collaborators; *Speak Easily* also suffers from the fact that Buster was not in good physical shape during the shooting of the picture. Now, for the first time, he wears a slightly flustered, hazy look. As he later said, his timing had begun to leave him.

Efforts were made to accommodate Buster during the shooting of *Speak Easily*. The first half of the picture was shot without incident and on May 27 Thalberg authorized the payment in full of the money that had been kept back because of Buster's failures to report for work in April. But by the twenty-eighth, Buster was "unable to shoot" for two days in a row; he may have done some celebrating over finally getting the money. All together, eleven production days of *Speak Easily* were lost. The production cost of the film finally rose to $420,000, making it the second most expensive of all the Keaton films, partly because of the expense of carrying the members of the cast who sat around waiting for Buster to resume shooting. *Speak Easily* eventually cost $30,000 more than the Jean Harlow–Clark Gable film *Red Dust,* which was in production at the same time.

When Thalberg became aware of the lengthened shooting schedule for *Speak Easily,* thirty-four days rather than twenty-three, he demanded that Greenwood furnish him with a bill of

Buster, Thelma Todd, and Jimmy Durante in *Speak Easily. National Film Archive / Stills Library*

particulars about the actual amount of money the studio had lost because of Buster's inability to shoot. The memo that Greenwood furnished Thalberg indicated that Buster's conduct had cost MGM about $33,000. Nothing further was done at the time, but neither Thalberg nor Mayer forgot it. With the completion of *Speak Easily* on June 17, 1932, Buster's 1930 contract was on the verge of expiration; there were indications that his new contract was not going to be quite the same as the earlier ones. It was at this point in Keaton's life that Natalie decided to divorce him.

[2]

The persecution tactics indulged in by the plaintiff have been motivated by her sister, Norma Talmadge, who for years has evidenced a violent dislike for me. The plaintiff has always been dominated by the advice and guidance of her sister.

—Keaton, 1936

Given the unpaid debts, the heavy drinking, and the succession of other women, the only surprising thing about Natalie's decision is that it did not come earlier.

When she did sue him for divorce on July 25, 1932, she employed the services of the trial lawyer Jerry Giesler, whose later fame arose from his defense of Errol Flynn in his statutory rape case in the 1940s. In order to obtain a clear-cut verdict of adultery against a spouse in those days it was often necessary for the wronged party to bring detectives and photographers along to record the transgression. By the time *Speak Easily* was finished in mid-June, Buster was dividing his nights between the land yacht and his bungalow at the studio. He also spent time on the real yacht, the expensive hundred-foot craft that he had bought for Natalie the previous year. One night in early July, after another

of Natalie's stormy departures, Buster picked up a girl and
brought her back with him to the Italian Villa. He gave the girl
her choice of anything she wanted from Natalie's vast collection
of clothing. The girl made a hasty selection, packed several bags,
and the couple left for the yacht to spend the night. Sometime
after midnight, Natalie and Constance, accompanied by two detectives and Natalie's attorney, boarded the craft. The landing
party found what they expected to find: Buster in bed with a
naked girl, supplying them with ample legal proof of infidelity.
Buster could never recall this episode with any clarity, for he had
been drinking steadily for several days—the main reason for
Natalie's departure from the Italian Villa. He did recall that he
had not made love to the girl; he also vaguely remembered that
the two detectives quietly sorted out the various items of Natalie's clothing that he had given her. The visitors left the boat with
all the evidence they needed, as well as the clothing.

To win a divorce suit on grounds of adultery, it was necessary
for Buster to respond to the charges; since he didn't, Natalie and
her lawyer changed the plea to "mental cruelty." When she filed
her petition for divorce, Natalie mentioned the abortive spring
plane trip, as well as "the humiliation" she had received at the
hands of a drunken Buster during a trip she had taken with him
in March. She also cited his frequent absences from the house.
Following his usual procedure with legal matters, Buster totally
ignored all aspects of the divorce proceedings. Under the circumstances of his default, Natalie was awarded an interlocutory
degree of divorce on August 9, 1932. She demanded no alimony
whatever but did obtain a settlement of $300 per month for
child support of the two boys, to start on the first of November
of that year.

Buster told Rudi Blesh and Charles Samuels that Natalie took
nearly everything he had at the time of the divorce, the implica-
tion being that Natalie was a rapacious monster. She wasn't, for
Buster kept the entire amount of available cash, which seems to
have been $12,000, or about a month's pay. Natalie was clearly
entitled to as much alimony as the court allowed; she asked for
none. This was an act of great kindness on her part. Despite her
bitterness, she was not willing to saddle him with these payments

for the rest of his life. The divorce settlement contained not a single word about the disposition of the Italian Villa; normally there would have been a stipulation as to who would get the house. Since the matter was never brought up in the proceedings, it would appear that the house had actually been Natalie's property from the very beginning, dating back to the days when she received all the money Buster earned.

In fact, the Italian Villa was almost more of a liability than an asset; without Buster's money to run the place it would have been impossible for Natalie to go on living there, even if she had wanted to. She attempted to sell it immediately, but this was the bitter depression summer of 1932. There were few offers for a mansion of this size, and they were all at a fraction of the price originally paid in 1925; the assessed value of the land had fallen from $36,000 to $25,000.

It was not until the spring of 1933 that Natalie was able to sell the Italian Villa, to the dance team of Fanchon and Marco, with a good deal of the proceeds going to pay the accumulated back taxes plus a hoard of other debts. Buster had paid no income taxes for 1932; in order to pacify the government, Natalie agreed to have her new house attached as security for the unpaid tax bill. The new house was a small one that Constance had bought for her at Tuna Beach, as well as setting up for her a trust fund of $200 per month for the rest of her life. The Tuna Beach house was a summer house; Natalie then got herself a two-bedroom apartment in Santa Monica in which she lived until her death in 1969.

The combination of Buster's total inability to deal with money, plus the drinking and all that it involved, had produced a financially chaotic situation. The Talmadge family was convinced that Buster would not be in a position to support his children in the future. They set up another trust fund for the education of the two boys, who were sent to the Black Fox Military Academy in the fall. Buster was granted visitation privileges but did not take advantage of them. What he wanted to do was to take the boys on camping trips, but Natalie had expressly forbidden them.

The market for yachts was scarcely brisk that summer either. Natalie impulsively rented the boat to some rumrunners who operated off Catalina Island. The yacht was intercepted by the Coast Guard on its very first run but luckily managed to escape in the fog. This frightened Natalie, and she immediately sold the boat for far less than the $25,000 Buster had originally paid for it.

Buster bought himself a small house in Cheviot Hills, adjacent to the golf course of the California Country Club. Despite his troubles, he was still very much a major star at MGM, with a $3,000-a-week contract in full effect and with talk of a new one in the works. Materially he was much better off than Natalie, who now had no prospects at all; hence the trust fund activities on her behalf. Physically and emotionally, Buster was in very bad shape. Some hoped that he would pull himself together, but many had given up all hope.

He took the divorce very badly. The loss of Natalie, the two boys, the house, everything all at once, was almost more than he could bear. He found it impossible to sleep and drank just to put himself out. His friends suddenly noticed how terrible he began to look. Some of them, like Buster Collier, sensed that he was very close to disaster.

[3]

Who's going to look after Buster?
—Louise Keaton, 1932

Buster was working for the most financially stable firm in the film industry, for MGM withstood the effects of the Great Depression with greater resilience than any of the other Hollywood studios. Nineteen thirty-two was the year of Hoovervilles and breadlines all over the United States, twelve million people were unemployed, and the Bonus Army marched on Washington that summer. The downward trend of the economy seemed absolutely irreversible; it was indeed, as Edmund Wilson called it, the time of *The American Earthquake.* In films, Paramount had entered a state of receivership, as had Fox Films, which had been taken over by Wall Street investment firms after its founder, William Fox, was deposed. By the end of 1932 RKO Radio Pictures was in perilous shape, tottering on the brink of bankruptcy. The trade papers were filled with stories that things were not going well at Warner Brothers and Universal.

Many of the Hollywood studios, particularly Fox and Paramount, had invested millions of dollars in wiring their theaters for sound films. The money was spent in the last good flush days before the full effects of the depression began to invade every phase of life. By the summer of 1932 the American public was ready enough for sound films, but large segments of that audience did not have enough money to pay for the tickets. Paid admissions dropped from 90 million in 1930 to 60 million in 1932. Admission prices dropped sharply during the year, and dime admissions were not uncommon; the entire film industry was in a state of acute panic. Unlike most of the competition, MGM continued to show high profits on their operations, for they had produced a number of films in 1931 and 1932 that achieved enormous success: *As You Desire Me,* with Garbo and von Stroheim; *The Champ,* with Wallace Beery and Jackie Cooper; *Tarzan the Ape Man* and *Tugboat Annie,* with Marie Dressler and Beery; and *Grand Hotel,* with an all-star cast. Each of these films made a net profit of over half a million dollars, and three of them neared the million mark. Not one was personally produced by Thalberg, but as nominal head of all production at MGM he was given most of the credit for the studio's output. His own personal productions at this time included *Private Lives, Strange Interlude,* and *Freaks;* the first two films achieved modest success, but the last was a complete failure.

From the outside, things were going very well at MGM that summer, but a bitter dispute had opened up between Louis B. Mayer and his "boy wonder," Thalberg, the man whom he had hired away from Universal at the age of twenty-four to become head of all production at MGM. The trouble between them, which was to have a strong effect on Buster, had begun in 1929 when Nicholas Schenck attempted to sell control of Loew's, Inc., the parent company of MGM, to William Fox. The three men running MGM at the time—Mayer, Thalberg, and their chief counsel, J. Robert Rubin—were appalled by Schenck's decision, feeling that their work in building up MGM had merely served to make Schenck wealthier than he had any right to be. When the deal finally fell through, Schenck tried to pacify Thalberg, believing him to be the most important of the three. This involved a reshuffling of the size of Mayer's and Thalberg's slices of the profits: Mayer found that he had to reduce his share of the profits from 53 percent to 43 percent in order to raise Thalberg's slice from 20 to 30 percent, with Rubin remaining at 27 percent. Mayer realized two things at this time: that he couldn't trust Schenck, and that his "boy wonder" thought his contribution to the company was at least as great as his own. At the same time, Schenck went out of his way to irritate Mayer, whom he had never liked.

By the summer of 1932 the profit pie had to be recut, largely because of the great success of *Grand Hotel*. This time Mayer was forced to split the difference with Thalberg, both men now to receive 37½ percent of the net profits of the firm. Later in the fall Thalberg threatened to resign for reasons that were probably more to do with his frail health than anything else. Schenck lured him into staying on by giving him a chance to buy large blocks of Loew's stock far below the current market price; Mayer was given the same deal, but on a lesser amount of stock. According to Thalberg's biographer, Bob Thomas, from this time on Mayer and Thalberg began to regard each other as enemies. F. Scott Fitzgerald uses their quarrel in *The Last Tycoon,* in which Mayer and Thalberg become Bradogue and Monroe Stahr.

Buster always believed that Thalberg had a special affection for him. This "affection" has been greatly exaggerated by many who have written about Keaton. Actually, Thalberg usually sided with Weingarten against Keaton and rejected Buster's repeated requests to have his own production unit at the studio. He was no sentimentalist; he simply regarded Buster as first-class star material that could be shaped to a mold suitable to MGM. And he saw no reason why he should not churn out two films a year.

When he did support him it was often for sound, practical reasons—and just as often Buster let him down. Buster's talent was for the bizarre, the unexpected, the excitement of doing something *new*. Like Chaplin, Keaton was an artist who delivered custom-made products to his audience; unlike Chaplin, Keaton's audience was never sufficiently large to guarantee him his artistic freedom.

Thalberg liked Buster well enough to listen to him whenever he came to his office, a privilege denied to many of MGM's chief attractions, stars as well as writers. In later years Buster often recalled an elaborate story idea for a film that he concocted for Thalberg's approval at about this time. It was to be a full-length parody of MGM's greatest hit of the year, *Grand Hotel*. Buster's film was to be set in a skid-row hotel called the Grand Mills Hotel, after the name of a well-known New York flophouse. Besides Keaton himself in the Lionel Barrymore role, the film would star Marie Dressler in the ballerina role originally played by Garbo, with Jimmy Durante cast in the John Barrymore part as the count. Buster dwelled on the comic possibilities of Jimmy Durante holding Marie Dressler, sixty-three at the time, in his arms. Not surprisingly, Thalberg thought the project would be a disaster and turned it down.

Speculation about unproduced films is risky, but on the face of it, the idea seems scarcely worthy of the Keaton who had made *Our Hospitality*, *The Navigator*, and *The General*. If he actually did present an idea like this to Thalberg, it may indicate something of the change in Keaton's outlook—he was "giving them what you think they want." After all, he had seen his *Sidewalks of New York* gross nearly a million; if that's what they like, how about *Grand Mills Hotel?*

Buster's drinking was assuming ever more dangerous proportions. Both Harold Goodwin and Buster Collier recall that he would disappear for four or five days or even a week on extended drinking bouts. Afterwards, he would be white-faced and unbearably tense. He began to have blackouts, periods of time when he simply couldn't recall what he had said or done. He was arrested on one occasion in Arizona when he arrived in a quiet little town and proceeded to "shoot up the place" at 2:00 A.M. He continued to spend his money as fast as he got each of his weekly $2,985 paychecks.* The drying-out establishments at Arrowhead Springs were a constant drain on his finances and he continued to give a lot of his money away to friends.

Mayer and Thalberg may have had some doubts about giving Buster another contract that summer of 1932. By then a number of their major stars had lost their public and dropped by the wayside, among them John Gilbert and William Haines. Gilbert had his own problem with alcohol, and his pictures lost huge sums of money, caused in part by the size of his salary. Keaton was different: he had not lost his public, and though the $100,000 to $200,000 profits on his films were not in the *Grand Hotel* league, they were more than just respectable: they were the backbone of MGM's annual output, not only in the United States but all over the world. The Keaton films were a staple for a firm that had its losers: *The Guardsman,* starring the Lunts, lost just under $100,000; *The Wet Parade,* with Walter Huston, lost $112,000. It was obvious that the "new Keaton," which is the way the studio referred to the newly created "Keaton-Durante" team in *The Passionate Plumber* and *Speak Easily,* could not be ignored. The exhibitors liked these pictures and were asking for more. *Speak Easily* had grossed nearly three-quarters of a million dollars. (It only showed a $33,000 profit, mainly because of Buster's delays in shooting.) Thalberg, at least, thought Buster was still a good investment, provided he could be kept relatively sober.

Buster's 1930 contract was due to expire on October 15, 1932, and in the middle of August, Thalberg decided to proceed with a new one. Under normal circumstances, a new Keaton film would have gone into production that summer, but it would have cost MGM $50,000 more than under the new contract that Thalberg had in mind. He decided to wait.

This contract contained a pay-back system set up to recompense the studio for its losses during the shooting of *Speak Easily.* Keaton's weekly salary was still $3,000, but he was to receive only $2,400, a cut of 20 percent, until the $33,000 had been paid back in full. Buster had no objection to this, finding it only fair.

*Fifteen dollars was deducted each week for the Motion Picture Relief Fund.

Greenwood, the studio manager, noted that Keaton "has been very amiable and is leaving it to us to be considerate as well as equitable." What did bother him was that MGM was no longer under obligation to star him in his films; the new contract made a point of the fact that he could be starred or co-starred as the studio saw fit. This contract made it possible for MGM to have Jimmy Durante as the official co-star of their films together. It is impossible to say with any certainty whether Mayer had a hand in drawing up this contract, but it is likely that he did. This part of the deal infuriated Buster. Nicholas Schenck, too, was probably consulted on the terms of the contract, for the profit-sharing arrangements between MGM and Buster Keaton Productions were now in abeyance for Buster's new films. He had lost his special status at the studio; he was truly just another employee.

The new contract also specified that there would be no limit to the number of pictures made under its terms, and there was to be no extra money for appearing in foreign-language versions. All in all, it was a serious comedown for Buster; it was really both a reprimand and a warning. The studio was simply not going to put up with any more of Buster's absences—if he was going to be away, he would pay for it. MGM considered Durante fully Keaton's equal and wanted to be able to indicate it on the film credits. It was only a one-year contract, demonstrating Mayer and Thalberg's uneasiness about giving him one at this time; all the others had been for two years.

The new Keaton-Durante film was *What, No Beer?*, which went into production on the seventeenth of December 1932. Like *Sidewalks of New York*, the new script was an original concoction on the part of the MGM scriptwriters Carey Wilson and Robert Hopkins, and Buster hated it quite as much as the other Durante scripts. Buster is another "stupid Elmer," this time a taxidermist who has saved some money by hiding it in the carcasses of the animals he has stuffed. His friend Jimmy Potts (Durante) conceives the idea of illicitly making real beer, using Buster's money for capital. The plot of *What, No Beer?* is tedious, and the picture is filled with endless talk.

As always, there is one magical moment. This time it occurs just after Buster has stupidly allowed a whole truckload of beer

What, No Beer? 1933. *Maryann Chach*

barrels to roll off the truck he has been driving. His bootlegger enemies are at the bottom of the hill, waiting to close in on him. The barrels, scores of them, are seen ominously and quietly poised at the top of the hill, just before they are to begin the long roll down; the camera lingers on the scene longer than it might, almost caressingly. When the barrels start rolling down the hill, many watchers are reminded strongly of the great days of silent comedy, for this entire scene is performed without a word of dialogue. It recalls the superb scene in *Seven Chances* in which Buster flees down the mountain followed by women and boulders. It is nice to think that the barrel scene in *What, No Beer?* was created by Buster; it lasts only a minute or so, but it is the only memorable thing in the entire picture.

What, No Beer? reveals all too clearly what had happened to Keaton in the six months since he made *Speak Easily* in the spring. In many of the scenes Buster gives the impression of being under the effect of sedatives. He seems shrunken, hollow-eyed, and considerably older. He told Samuels and Blesh that he finished off a bottle of booze daily during the shooting of the film, which dragged on for more than six weeks.

A little over a week after *What, No Beer?* went into production, Thalberg suffered a major heart attack, an illness that had a lot to do with Buster's fate at MGM. There had been a tremendous Christmas party that year at the studio that started on Christmas Eve and was still going the next day. The workers at MGM, at every level, really had something to celebrate, for their studio was doing better than any other in Hollywood. Thalberg became overly tired by all the congratulations and expressions of good-will as he made his way around the studio. When he finally got home to Santa Monica late on Christmas Eve, he had a heart attack and collapsed. His wife, Norma Shearer, on the urgent advice of their doctor forbade any visits or phone calls, but the moment Nicholas Schenck heard the news he caught the first train from New York.

Buster also collapsed that night, partly from the effects of booze and partly from a tough acrobatic trick that he was attempting to perform. He cracked his head badly on the floor and lost consciousness for many hours. The people with him thought he had fallen asleep and just left him lying on the floor; in the drunken uproar of the party nobody was paying much attention to sleeping bodies. He did not awaken until late the next afternoon with an unbearable headache that lasted for days.

Mayer and Schenck decided to bring in David O. Selznick as an independent producer, a replacement for Thalberg. Selznick had made quite a name for himself at RKO, with films like *A Bill of Divorcement* and *King Kong,* which was shortly to be released. He was willing to come to MGM even if it meant working for his father-in-law, Louis B. Mayer, for RKO seemed to be in a state of imminent collapse. Thalberg was furious and remained at home in Santa Monica. He felt betrayed by Mayer, who had hired his son-in-law to supplant him as head of production. Nepotism had come full circle at MGM.

On January 13, 1933, there was a story in *Variety* about the condition of Thalberg's health. It stated he was sick at home and that "he may return in four weeks." No visitors were allowed. A day or so later Thalberg indicated to both Schenck and Mayer that he had no intention of returning to work until he had recovered some measure of his health; he told them that he was going to take his fully authorized six-month vacation in Bad Nauheim in Germany. This news threw Schenck and Mayer into a panic, for Selznick was certainly not on a par with Thalberg. Mayer hastily assembled an executive board to run the studio in Thalberg's absence. It included Mayer himself, Walter Wanger, Harry Rapf, Eddie Mannix, and Hunt Stromberg. At the end of the month the list was augmented by Bernard Hyman and Selznick. For a week or so Mayer had attempted to include Howard Hawks on his board, but he refused the offer, preferring to finish the shooting of his *Today We Live,* the film based on William Faulkner's "Turnabout."

It was at this point that Buster disappeared from the studio. Shortly before the beginning of the New Year he took a plane trip to Mexico, accompanied by a beautiful woman named Mae Scribbens. One morning in Mexico City, after a heavy night of drinking, he woke up to find her in bed with him. She and Buster were married in Ensenada, California, on the eighth of January at a time when Buster was in an alcoholic blackout of several days' duration. He could never remember anything about the marriage as long as he lived. Meanwhile, time was being lost on *What, No Beer?;* Weingarten later claimed that they simply "shot around Buster."

In the last days of January there was a great deal of panic in Hollywood. Mayer was extraordinarily tense about the situation—and he didn't know what to do about Buster Keaton. Buster had never been Mayer's favorite, the drinking was causing real problems, and the Mexico trip was the last straw. In the absence of Thalberg, Mayer began to consider firing him. It took him more than two weeks to make up his mind. He had no doubt that if he went ahead it would cost MGM money, for the Keaton-Durante team had begun to catch on heavily with the public. *Variety*'s annual poll of star popularity showed them in ninth place at MGM. On the strength of the box-office returns of *Speak Easily,* MGM had run full-page ads in all the trade papers for the next film starring the team. It was to be called *Buddies* and would include twelve-year-old Jackie Cooper.

Buster told a story in later years indicating that he had been fired at Mayer's whim. Mayer requested that he appear for some simulated shooting at the studio on a certain Saturday in January. This shooting was to be done for the benefit of some important visiting dignitaries who would think they were seeing the real thing. Buster claimed he refused Mayer's request because he was scheduled to be the mascot at a football game that day between UCLA and St. Mary's. As Buster told it, Mayer then fired him by writing him a letter which is supposed to have read: "Your services at MGM are no longer required." The facts are somewhat different.

The football game was probably the least of Mayer's worries. It is obvious that Mayer did not wish to fire Keaton if it could possibly be avoided: this had been basically the same position taken by Thalberg, and there was really no disagreement about it. But by the nineteenth of January, with still another nine days to go on *What, No Beer?*, George Cohen of MGM's legal department had sent Greenwood a rough draft of Buster's termination notice. He accompanied it with a note that stated:

> The second sentence of the first paragraph may be omitted if you so desire, although by reason of the fact that it particularly specifies intoxication I think it makes the notice more specific in that respect.

The letter specifying why Buster's contract was being abrogated was never sent. The final day of shooting on *What, No Beer?* was the twenty-eighth of January. *Buddies* was scheduled to begin shooting only a few days later. Buster was in no shape to start the new film, and Mayer immediately wrote the termination letter himself. It was a short one and was delivered to Buster's bungalow by two men on his staff.

> You are hereby notified that for good and sufficient cause we hereby terminate the contract with you dated October 5, 1932.
> Yours very truly,
> METRO-GOLDWYN-MAYER CORPORATION
> By Louis B. Mayer
> Vice President.

Scrawled across the bottom of the carbon of the letter are these words: "Served on Keaton by Lou Edelmen & Frank Davis about noon Feb. 2, 1933."

If Thalberg had been around, Mayer might possibly have changed his mind about firing Buster at that time, but it was bound to happen sooner or later. When Thalberg and his wife sailed from New York on the *Europa* on the twenty-first of February, they were accompanied by Joseph Schenck. Buster's old friend and Thalberg had much to talk about. It was the end of Buster's career as a star at MGM and the beginning of a long descent.

Buster and
Mae Scribbens,
January, 1933.
Wide World

10

DOWN AND UP AGAIN

It only takes about two bad pictures in a row to put
the skids under you.

—Keaton, 1958

Mae Scribbens, Buster's second wife, was a practical nurse who
specialized in the care of alcoholic patients. She was twenty-eight,
just Buster's height, an extremely good-looking brunette, and
very much interested in marriage. Her previous patient had
been the wide-mouthed comedian Joe E. Brown, who had
required her services more than once. She had made strong efforts to land Brown, but he managed to slip through the net she
had cast for him. Buster was not so lucky. As he told it later, he
could never recall much about meeting Mae in those last days at
MGM.

Doctor Harry Martin, the husband of columnist Louella Parsons, specialized in the treatment of alcoholic withdrawal. In the
fall of 1932 Dr. Martin had sent Buster to sulfur caves around
Arrowhead Springs for a series of drying-out sessions, which
never accomplished much, for Buster had no intention of changing his drinking habits. By then only a few drinks could send
him into a blackout period that might last for several days. Mae
was sent along to watch over Buster on one of these visits and
remained on with him after their return to his new house on
Queensbury Drive. Within a week or so she was acting as his
valet, girl friend, nurse, and chief dispenser of the alcohol that
she kept under lock and key. By arrangement with Dr. Martin,
Mae administered two ounces every four hours; if this regimen
were kept up for a few days, there was some chance of Buster's
avoiding his around-the-clock drinking pattern. *What, No Beer?*

had been filmed under these conditions. This method of withdrawal failed, for Buster invariably escaped from the house when he couldn't stand the wait for his dosage.

At one point he managed to flee the house when Mae was sleeping and walked over to the nearby country club. After three or four drinks at the bar he nearly passed out but managed to get back to the house safely. Frightened by this, Mae decided to place Buster in an expensive drying-out establishment that specialized in aversion therapy. The notion behind this method was to give the patient a drink every hour or so, but always a different one, so that in time the patient would come to dread the bottles being offered him. The cure was a failure, for the patients merely longed for the time when they could again select drinks of their own choice. Buster hated the place and managed to escape while incarcerated in a straitjacket. He claimed that he did so by employing Houdini's secret methods of escape from confinement. He escaped from the establishment by sliding down a rain pipe in the dark, a full four stories to the ground, and then making his way through empty, wet streets back to his house in the rain.

It will be recalled that in late December 1932, while still working at MGM, Buster had asked Mae to go to Mexico with him; she had been quite agreeable and the two set off. In later years Buster had no memory of asking her anything; he told Harold Goodwin that his first real memory of Mae was of waking up in bed with her. Buster decided that he had to marry Mae, although it is much more likely that she asked him. On their way back from Mexico they were married at Ensenada, California, on January 8, 1933, despite the fact that Buster's interlocutory divorce decree was not yet final. He married Mae for the second time ten months later at Ventura on October 17.

The immediate blow of being fired by Mayer must have been hard to bear, for MGM had been Buster's real home for many years. But if he felt despair, he didn't talk about it, nor did he seem particularly bitter about his fall from stardom. He tended to be stoical about it, feeling that a good part of his troubles had been self-inflicted. He later referred to Mayer as "that louse

Looey B. Mayer," or "that SOB Mayer." He also felt that there had been too much of Thalberg's nepotism at MGM, especially with Weingarten. He was curiously contradictory about his MGM films, only singling out *Sidewalks of New York* and *What, No Beer?* as being really dreadful and asserting that the others weren't all that bad.

The Keaton family was unhappily reunited in the spring of 1933 when Myra and her other two children, Harry and Louise, moved into the house with Mae and Buster. Myra found it hard to accept her son's reduced status in the world. The family was convinced that Mae was simply not capable of taking care of Buster, which was probably true, for Mae never realized how dependent he really was.

Buster told both Samuels and Blesh a story about Edward Sedgwick's being dispatched to his new home in Cheviot Hills sometime that spring to convey the news that Thalberg had relented and had decided to go ahead with the *Grand Mills Hotel* project. This is doubtful, for Thalberg was in Europe from February through the late summer of 1933; it is equally doubtful that he would have changed his mind about the project. If MGM was making overtures, they may well have come from Mayer, for *What, No Beer?* had done sensational business on its opening at the Capital Theater in New York. Its run was extended for a second week, a rare occurrence during the Depression. The film grossed $633,000 and made a profit of $118,000. Keaton was still a box-office draw, and Mayer was no fool in money matters; if Keaton could work, Mayer would not stand in his way. But Buster became violently angry at the feelers from the studio and told Sedgwick to tell Thalberg *and* Mayer to go to hell.

The success of *What, No Beer?* resulted in an offer to appear as the star of a feature film to be made by a new, independent firm, Kennedy Productions of St. Petersburg, Florida. The director was to be Marshal Neilan, famous a decade earlier for his work with Mary Pickford. The script was by Lew Lipton, who had written the story for *Spite Marriage*. Best of all, the pay was the same $3,000 a week that Buster had received at MGM. With Harry Keaton as their chauffeur, Mae and Buster drove to Florida to encounter a series of disasters. Neilan was in worse

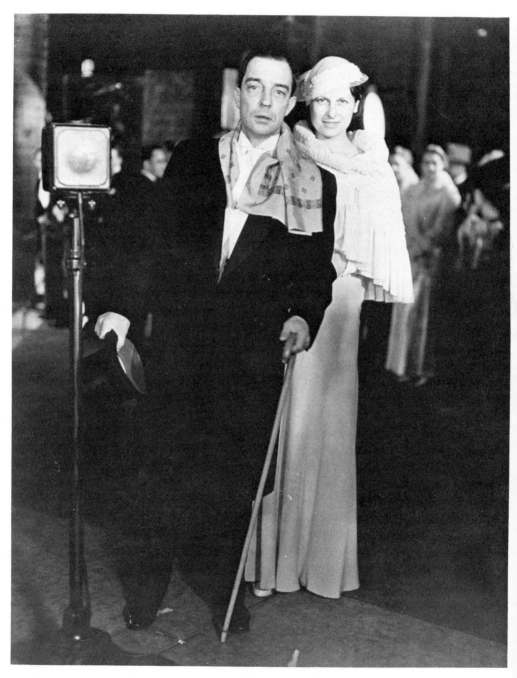

Buster and Mae, 1933. *Museum of Modern Art / Film Stills Archive*

shape than Buster from alcohol, but this was only the beginning. The semitropical heat of St. Petersburg in April was enough to melt the emulsion off the film, and there were millions of mosquitoes, day and night. Everything went wrong that could go wrong, and the production was abandoned after the ninth week. Buster received every cent of his $27,000, despite his having told the producers that the film was doomed from the start. Before leaving Florida, Neilan set up a deal for Buster to star in a film based on Otto Soglow's newspaper cartoon *The Little King*. This picture was to be shot, for reasons now unknown, in Havana, Cuba; nothing ever came of this venture.

None of the major producing firms in Hollywood were willing to offer Buster a contract in 1933; his reputation as a hopeless drinker was firmly established. But for Keaton, a life without work was no life at all; he indicated that he would take anything available. That autumn he earned $8,000 by appearing in a vaudeville show at the Hippodrome Theater in Baltimore. He had not appeared in vaudeville since the beginning of 1917, and he was quite nervous about it. The show was reasonably successful, but vaudeville was clearly in its final decline, and there were no more offers after Baltimore, so Buster returned to Hollywood.

The big money stopped after the Florida fiasco, and for several months almost nothing came in except the small monthly checks from Buster Keaton Productions in New York, his share of the profits on the silent films of the twenties. His old films were still being shown in countries like Japan that did not begin making sound films until well into the 1930s. But Mae kept Buster's family afloat with her powers of sexual attraction—in an afternoon at the Biltmore Hotel she could pick up a hundred dollars or so. Louise Keaton recalls one long afternoon when she waited for Mae to pay seven or eight visits to the rooms of "some of my good men friends."

Mae had some other qualities that displeased Buster. When money got really tight, and there were no gentlemen friends at the hotel, she would order expensive furniture from one of the department stores (a grand piano on one occasion), charge it to Buster, and then sell it quickly at a greatly reduced rate for spot

Buster and Mae, 1934. *Museum of Modern Art / Film Stills Archive*

cash. The department stores couldn't easily repossess their merchandise, and there was some talk of prosecution, but nothing came of it.

Nineteen thirty-three was a bad year for Buster. On June 25 Roscoe Arbuckle died of a heart attack in New York. He had been sufficiently rehabilitated for Warner Brothers to use his name as the star in a series of two-reel comedies he had made for them in Brooklyn. Arbuckle had also gone back into vaudeville; prior to the shorts for Warner Brothers he had directed a number of two-reelers in Hollywood for RKO and Educational Pictures. Educational was the organization that undertook the production of Arbuckle's Reel Comedies back in 1922 when Joe Schenck had them financed by contributions from the industry. Now, in 1933 with his old friend dead in New York, Buster received a proposal from Earle Hammons, the president of Educational, to make a series of two-reelers for them, "just like old times."

The logo of Educational Pictures was an Aladdin's lamp with a wisp of smoke issuing forth; their trademark was "the Spice of the Program." In 1933 Educational was close to the bottom in Hollywood filmmaking. The only thing that was "just like old times" about Buster's Educational films was that they were two-reel films. The total budget per film was $20,000, with Buster receiving $5,000 of this amount. The films were known in the trade as cheapies, cheaters, and various other disparaging names. They were made in two or three days, with the shooting sometimes continuing until two in the morning in order not to exceed the tiny budget. Charles Lamont was the director of twelve of these films that Buster started making at the end of 1933. He remembers Buster as extremely withdrawn in those days, not exactly unsociable, but hard to know. He had very definite ideas about how certain things should be done, and if he didn't get his way, he would often sulk and go out for a walk in the apple orchard that was near the Educational Studios. The Educational films are, on the whole, mechanical, cliché-ridden, and totally predictable pictures. Occasionally, as in *The Gold Ghost* or *Grand Slam Opera*, there are flashes of the old, inventive Keaton, but they are rare.

The Educational shorts were shot in groups of two at a time, leaving Buster with plenty of time on his hands. He filled it with endless games of solitaire. Mostly he stayed at home, where he had his mother to cook for him and Louise and Harry to talk to during the long days. He was still seeing Dorothy Sebastian, who had married the actor William Boyd in 1932. Her own screen career had floundered, and Buster got her a job as his leading lady in the second of his Educational pictures, *Allez-Oop*.

Love Nest on Wheels, 1937: Al St. John, Myra Keaton, Diana Lewis, unknown, Buster, Harry Keaton, Bud Jamison, unknown. *Rudi Blesh*

Buster's income for 1933 was $47,400, quite a falling off from the $147,300 of 1932, but still an impressive sum in the Depression years. He was facing a lot of suits for unpaid bills, including his unpaid federal income taxes, which amounted to $28,000. There were a great many other suits and claims against Buster, some dating back to 1932. In self-defense, he declared personal bankruptcy, listing liabilities of $308,832 and assets of $13,000; this move succeeded in reducing the pressure being exerted by his creditors. He gradually repaid nearly everything he owed, with his brother, Harry, handling all his financial affairs for him.

Willy Caruthers, Buster's servant since the end of the twenties, stayed on with "little Bussy," as he called him, until it became impossible for Buster to pay his weekly salary. In the mid-thirties Willy was converted to the religious movement led by Father Divine in Harlem. He changed his name to Ely Prosper; his wife changed hers to Lotus Flower. Willy made a new life and vowed to change his evil, thieving ways, for over the years he had been stealing from Buster. He attempted to make restitution for everything; figuring that he had stolen 287 chickens over the years, he returned exactly this number. After leaving Buster, Willy took a job with the Southern Pacific Railroad. When times got harder for Buster, Willy and his wife came once a week to clean his house from top to bottom. Like Buster, Willy always drove a Cadillac, even in the worst of times; one maddening year Buster could not afford a new one, but Willy managed to get himself one.

After making his first two Educational shorts, Buster received an offer to make a feature film in Paris for a fixed price of $15,000. The offer came from Seymour Nebenzal, the owner of Nero Films, who was world famous for producing G. W. Pabst's *Pandora's Box* and *Kameradschaft*, Fritz Lang's *M* and *The Last Will of Dr. Mabuse*. American-born Nebenzal had operated in Berlin until Hitler's rise to power in 1933 and had then moved to Paris. Like many other prominent filmmakers in Europe, Nebenzal had some awareness of Buster's troubles at MGM, but he was willing to take a chance in producing the kind of film he thought appropriate for Buster's talents. The result was *Le Roi des Champs Elysées*, or *The Champ of the Champs Elysées*, and it gave Buster the kind of script he'd been wanting for the last four years.

Le Roi's script was quite deliberately written in such a way that it allowed Keaton to "keep quiet with lots of sound all around me." There are entire scenes in this film in which Buster says absolutely nothing—he has a chance to do the things he wanted to do. Whenever he did speak, his voice was dubbed in French. Nebenzal was famous for the artistic freedom he allowed the people working for him, and he was willing to cooperate with Buster as well as he could; Arnold Lipp's script is the best evidence of this.

Buster plays two roles in the film. We first see him as a nice young man whose job it is to dress up as a millionaire and ride around Paris throwing away bogus thousand-franc notes. He also plays the part of a not-so-nice American gangster, his exact double, who has just escaped from jail. One day the money giver accidentally gets his hands on real money and throws it away; he gives the heroine of the film a few thousand francs to pay her rent. The fiasco with the francs has cost him his job, and his mother gets him a small part in a play at the theater where she works. During the intermission the nice Buster is seized by the mobsters, who think he is their chief. They take him to their hideaway, where, predictably enough, the real gangster is present. The rest of the film is a dizzying series of close calls as the two Busters narrowly miss each other; the gangster's girl is bewildered by her lover's abrupt changes of mood from lust to apathy.

There are some wonderful moments in the film, particularly a scene in which Buster attempts in vain to get onstage to deliver his lines and is foiled by getting himself trapped on a ladder. There are many little touches to the film that seem unmistakably Keaton's; in one scene outside a church a young bridegroom stares at the money that Buster has placed in his hand, turns his gaze to the plain bride soon to be his, and starts running down the street, shouting "Saved, Saved!"

The Buster Keaton of *Le Roi* is only thirty-nine, yet he looks older. More importantly, the infinite grace of his earlier films has disappeared. Despite all the good things about the picture, it leaves one with the conviction that a certain measure of Keaton's special greatness lay in the fact of his youth. This Buster is funny enough, but there is very little of the sheer magic and excitement found in all of his films through the end of the silent era.

Le Roi can be seen as a test case of whether or not Buster could make a first-rate sound film in 1934. To help him in Paris he had a sympathetic producer who allowed him to have the silence he wanted to work in; he was given a story far better then some he'd inherited in the twenties. Against him he had his drinking to contend with, his aging, and what appears to be a definite loss of his inventive powers. But how much of this loss of inventive power was due to the inherent limitations of sound film? The other two great comic geniuses of the silent era, Chaplin and Lloyd, showed some degree of impoverishment in all their sound films. Chaplin's greatest moment after his last completely silent film, *City Lights,* was the scene in *The Great Dictator* (1940) where he plays and dances with a huge balloon in complete silence before it explodes in his face. A talking Chaplin never had the power to move an audience as much as the silent, unbelievably graceful Chaplin. The same was true of Lloyd, for in none of his sound films was he able to act with the beautiful purity he had in silent films. Chaplin and Lloyd were both their own producers, while Buster never possessed this degree of freedom. If Lloyd and Chaplin could never rise to their former heights, there is no reason to suppose Keaton could do any better; in fact, it is amazing that he achieved what he did.

With Max Nosseck directing, *Le Roi* is at least as good as the very best of Buster's MGM sound films. It was given worldwide distribution by Paramount, but no American distributor cared to risk investing in it; relatively few foreign films were shown in the United States in the thirties unless they had received sensational reviews or had scored a huge box-office triumph in Europe. The film has been unearthed only recently by William Everson, who rightly claims that it shows that all of Buster's sound films are not as bad as they are reputed to be.

Before he had quite completed the French film, Buster received an offer from Sam Spiegel and his British and Continental Film Corporation to star in another feature film, this time in England. Buster would be paid only $12,000, but he accepted, for he needed every penny he could get to live and to pay his debts. The surviving shooting script, the director's copy, indicates that *The Invader* was based on a story devised by Keaton himself, although he ultimately received no screen credit. The shooting script was written by Walter Greenwood, the author of the immensely popular British novel of the thirties *Love on the Dole*. The plot of *The Invader* is almost unbearably thin: Buster plays Leander Proudfoot, a wealthy yachtsman who has anchored his craft in a small, sleepy port in Spain. A pretty Spanish girl with two men in her life decides to use the smitten Buster as a foil in her scheme to play her lovers off against each other.

The director was Adrian Brunel, best known for his films *The Constant Nymph* and *The Vortex*. His son Christopher recalls his father's account of the troubles he had in making *The Invader*. Brunel had greatly admired Keaton and eagerly looked forward to working with him. On the morning of his first encounter with Buster, Brunel was quietly slipped a note by Sam Spiegel's assistant, Ward Wing, which read, DON'T LET HIM DRINK!

Adrian Brunel directing Buster in *The Invader*, London, 1935. *Christopher Brunel*

Brunel got the message, but it didn't make much difference, for Buster drank heavily all through the shooting. In his autobiography, *Nice Work,* Brunel was quite circumspect about his difficulties in directing Buster in *The Invader,* consistently calling it *The Intruder:* "And, of course, we had Buster Keaton. Buster was ill most of the time, but he was a grand trouper; it was bad luck that he should have got into this galère." Brunel described his various problems in a very guarded manner, for many of the people concerned with the film were still alive at the time he wrote his book: "My difficulties involved people struggling or not, with their own peculiarities, such as financial recklessness, writing phoney cheques, lack of sexual control, and disturbing addictions. . . ."

The film was underfinanced from the start. Many of those concerned with making it never got paid; Brunel received one-third of the amount he had contracted for. The backers had decided that the film needed at least one musical production number, so they invited a dozen pretty girls down from the West End of London for two weeks of rehearsing before shooting the number. The girls were nice, but they couldn't dance, and their appearance in the film used up 20 percent of the budget. The set on which the girls did their number was so tiny that they dwarfed it completely; this is the only funny thing in the film.

Buster wanted some of the scenes to be shot outdoors. Brunel was glad to oblige, but there are almost no exterior shots because of the constant drilling and blasting required for the construction of a new highway nearby. Sound recording was still largely confined to the studio. The cameraman was Eugene Schufftan, one of the best in Europe. He was famous for his lighting effects; Brunel admired them until he realized how dark and atmospheric they were, totally inappropriate for a broad comedy. But it was too late, and the picture went on as scheduled.

When the picture was finished, it was discovered that it ran for only sixty minutes. Brunel had been telling the backers that it would be too short, but they didn't believe him. When the distributors refused to take the film because of its length, a woman was engaged to put back every cut-out piece of film she could find to beef up the footage until it was six thousand feet long.

This meant, for instance, that when in our version a character dashed from a room, banging the door after him, and he was then seen in the hall haring away from the banged door, you would see in this childish new version the first part of the man going from the room and added to the shot would be five or six seconds of *shut door,* followed by the character just completing the action of shutting the door the other side and dashing off! This sort of thing went on throughout the film. . . .

The Invader was scarcely seen in England, for its intended distributor turned it down. No American distributor would touch it until the following year, when M. H. Hoffberg bought it and changed the title to *An Old Spanish Custom.* This didn't help much, for the film was rarely seen in the United States. It was the last of Buster's feature films to be made. He cannot have been unaware that these two comeback efforts in Europe had failed to accomplish their purpose, and when he and Mae returned to the United States in 1935, there was more bad news.

Mae opened up a beauty shop, calling it predictably MRS. BUSTER KEATON'S BEAUTY SHOPPE; this enterprise lasted only a few months before Mae was back in business down at the Biltmore. Buster's future in films looked uncertain, and Mae began to think she'd had enough of him. That summer she sued him for divorce, naming an old friend of theirs, Mrs. Leah Sewell, as corespondent. Mae charged that Buster and her good friend Leah had "committed adultery at Santa Barbara on the 4th of July 1935 through the 7th, as well as at her home on the 14th of July." Her lawyer asked "that the plaintiff be awarded a reasonable sum commensurate with the ability of the defendant to pay. . . ."

Buster did exactly the same thing as when Natalie sued him for divorce—nothing. Under the circumstances Mae's attorney then had to take a new action against Buster, this time based on his "indifference." When it was all over, Mae was awarded the sum of $2,000, payable in four installments, to be doled out from Buster's next few checks from Educational. She demonstrated her eccentricity to the end. The divorce decree specified that the community property was to be divided equally; Mae divided it just that way, including the silverware and the dishes, taking with her exactly half of each set. But she also took Buster's dog, Elmer—out of sheer spite, Buster thought. The final decree of divorce was October 14, 1936. Buster was again a free man.

---

[2]

The one thing you don't need right now is another drink.

—Myra Keaton, 1935

You are all right as long as you can drink and wake up without a hangover. You are still all right if you can fight off the tearing desire for an eye-opener . . . that eye-opener that brings such relief but doesn't last long enough, and leads you into taking another and another until you find yourself waking up with a hangover all over again. . . . Keep it up a while and whenever a couple of little things go wrong, you find yourself saying the hell with it and getting drunk to help you forget. And that's the final step that brings you to the police station or the psychopathic ward. . . .

—Keaton, 1959

Buster acquired an agent in 1935, the first time he'd had one since the days of Max Hart back in 1917. This was Leo Morrison, who was to represent him for the next fifteen years. Besides acting as his agent, Morrison also acted as Buster's financial manager, a service that he desperately needed. Shortly after his return from England with Mae, Natalie brought action against him for being delinquent in his monthly payments of $300 for the support of the two boys. Buster's income for 1934 had been $44,500, dropping slightly in 1935 to $42,500. Natalie charged that Buster had been guilty of "extravagant living and purchases in France and England." She was furious when she discovered that Buster's money was going into Mae's beauty shop, telling Louise that if he could afford that kind of waste he could easily pay $300 a month to support his two children. Morrison then worked out a deal with the court, whereby Buster's $5,000 checks from Educational Films would be placed in his hands so that all the outstanding debts could be paid, including Natalie's back payments and his own commissions.

Buster was forty on the fourth of October that year. His behavior in the face of bad news was always as stoical as the characters he portrayed in his films, yet at no time in his life did he have more reason to feel depressed. His career as a film star was over; the comeback pictures had flopped, and there was seemingly no chance of his ever producing "his kind" of pictures again. His only future lay in turning out the cheap Educational shorts, and he was convinced that almost no one would ever see them.

Buster's social life was scant. Buster Collier saw very little of his old friend at this time, for the experience was depressing. Many of Keaton's best friends were dying off: after Arbuckle's death in 1933, Lew Cody died suddenly the following year, John Gilbert just as suddenly in 1936.

Buster was drinking so much it often took days for him to be in any condition to shoot the films at Educational. His periods of around-the-clock drinking were usually of three or four days' duration. He would leave his house and appear at bars around town until some good-natured cop drove him home in the small hours of the morning. He was seldom violent and seems never to have been arrested on these excursions. Sometime in the middle of October he began drinking heavily and did not stop until he was taken to the Veterans Hospital at Sawtelle, a few miles from Los Angeles. Dr. John Shuman, an old family friend, had realized that something had to be done to avert a terrible period of alcohol withdrawal, and he decided to get his friend into a hospital. Buster was taken there unconscious. The next morning he had to be physically restrained by several of the attendants. He was still extraordinarily strong, and it required great efforts to keep him down until a sedative was injected.

Newspapers all over the country carried headlines reading,

KEATON IN STRAITJACKET IN MENTAL HOSPITAL. The headlines brought Mae back into his life, for she appeared at the hospital to grant an interview with the press. She was quoted as saying, "We'll make up and I'll nurse him back to health. I know I can help him. I nursed him through a similar collapse three years ago and I can do it again." Nothing came of Mae's offer of help; sick or well, Buster was totally disenchanted with her and told her so.

He remained in the hospital for two weeks. Alcoholism was not recognized as a disease in 1935 and was commonly regarded as merely the symptom of some emotional disturbance. Since the psychiatrists at the hospital could find no trace of any such disturbance, he was discharged. The two-week stay at the hospital accomplished a minor miracle in Buster's life, however, for he stopped drinking after his release. The doctors at Sawtelle, especially Dr. Shuman, had finally got it into his head that he simply *couldn't* drink anymore, that he'd reached a stage where he'd soon kill himself. Buster listened calmly and did not drink for the next five years.

One sign of his better health can be seen in his next Educational film, *Grand Slam Opera*, for which he received the co-writing credit, the only one of these films for which he did anything but act. It is a satire of the popular radio show the Major Bowes Amateur Hour; in it Buster performs a series of ethnic dances with great agility. But there was very little he could do to liven up these shoddy productions in any significant way; their main function in his life was to pay his bills, which kept piling up.

By the fall of 1936 Buster was again in arrears on Natalie's monthly payments, this time in the amount of $4,500. On Norma's advice, Natalie decided to take Buster to court in New York City, where he was shooting four of the Educationals. She attempted to attach his wages, but her motion was blocked on appeal when Buster's attorney tried to demonstrate that Natalie was making more than he was. The reverse was true, for Buster had earned $42,500 in 1935, while Natalie had made $23,000, all of it coming from trust funds and rent from her house on Tuna Beach. When it looked as if the New York judge was going to hold back virtually everything he had earned in New York, Buster told the reporters: "You tell the judge that if Natalie will let me alone for awhile, I'll be on my feet again. . . . She knows I'm broke. She knows I'm trying to get back in the money again and when I do she knows I'll square everything with her." He also told the reporter, "I got this job with Educational Pictures because I went on the wagon. I haven't had a drink since last Christmas day. If Natalie will let me alone so I can work, I'll never take another drink." Buster's appeal worked, and the whole affair was shifted to the California courts, where it dragged on for a year. Early in 1937 his monthly payments to Natalie were reduced to $100. Buster was convinced that Natalie's taking him to court was motivated solely by the strong, continuing influence of Norma, whom he claimed had always hated him.

Harold Goodwin, the villain of *College* and *The Cameraman,* had not seen much of Buster since the end of the twenties. He ran into Buster and Louise on the local golf course and soon began to see a lot of the Keaton family, for Harold loved bridge as much as Buster did. At one time in 1936, the year that Buster's income fell to $15,000, he was unable to pay his taxes. Goodwin was acting in a film over at Fox, and he and Buster had lunch at the studio. After talking it over, Buster took Harold with him to see another old friend, Joe Schenck, now the president of the newly created Twentieth Century–Fox. Schenck saw them immediately, and Buster started to explain how badly off he was. Schenck interrupted him by producing his checkbook, pulled out a check, signed it, and gave it to Buster. "Fill in whatever you need, Buster," he said. Buster told him he needed a thousand, but Joe kept repeating, "Whatever you need, Buster, whatever you need," as he walked with them to the door. Buster filled in the amount for a thousand; it got him through the year, which had been the worst he had known financially.

Then Educational Pictures went out of business, so 1937 was even worse. Buster had hated the films, but they had been his sole source of income for nearly two years. He was unemployed for a longer time in 1937 than at any time since the spring of 1917. There were no jobs to be had in all of Hollywood, or so his agent, Leo Morrison, claimed. At this point Buster went back to work for MGM, as did F. Scott Fitzgerald, then living in Tryon, North Carolina. Fitzgerald was also going through the worst year in his history. Both men had suffered physical collapse, seemingly irreversible failure in their careers, and unremitting bad luck in almost everything they touched. It was mainly the influence of studio friends that got both men on the MGM payroll just one week apart in the summer of 1937.

Buster always credited Eddie Mannix with getting him his job as a gag writer at MGM, but it was really the collective work of many of his old friends who were still working at the studio, among them the directors Ed Sedgwick, Charles Reisner, Jack Conway, and Robert Z. Leonard. All of them were fully aware of how valuable Buster's suggestions could be in their films, and his contributions were worth every cent MGM paid him.

He began working at MGM on the twenty-fourth of June at a salary of $200 per week. His tiny office was located just inside the studio gates, not far from where his bungalow had been only four years earlier. One of his jobs in this first term of employment was to supply all the gags for a Clark Gable film, *Too Hot to Handle,* directed by Jack Conway. The opening sequence concerned the adventures of a newsreel cameraman in the troubled East; it was exactly the type of film that required the services of the maker of *The Cameraman.* Buster liked the work as well as he liked the regular paychecks. The only drawback to the job was the dull intervals between assignments; he would then sit in his office, playing solitaire, or chatting with his old friends from the better days. He wasn't bitter about earning $200 a week; he did everything he could to earn it. This involved strife with Groucho Marx, who found Buster's sense of humor totally unsuitable for his films. Buster had never cared for Groucho, claiming that any man who taught his grandchild to cheat at cards was as bad as they come. Groucho looked on Buster as an unfunny *shikour* from the past.

In September 1938, Joe Schenck's Twentieth Century–Fox engaged Buster to be the chief gagman for a series of B pictures featuring "the Jones family." In addition to providing the gags, Buster created the story line for the series of Jones family pictures that were produced with Jed Prouty and Spring Byington as

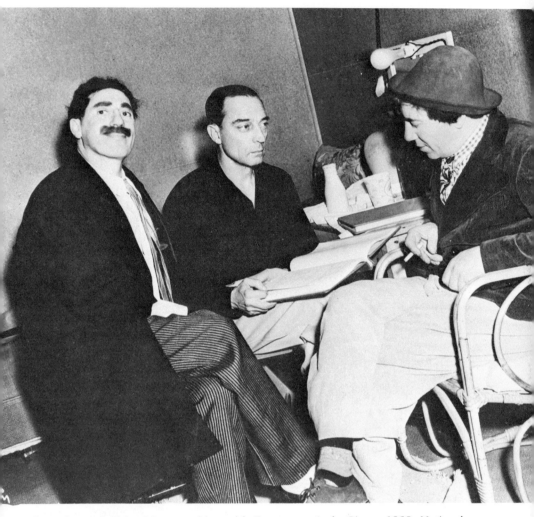

Groucho and Chico Marx working with Buster on *At the Circus,* 1939. *National Film Archive / Stills Library*

Mr. and Mrs. Jones. These were genre films about happenings in the life of a "typical" American family, quite similar in format to the sit-coms of American television in the late seventies. This was again bread-and-butter work, but it paid better than MGM—$300 a week. When the second Jones picture was finished, Buster returned to his MGM job at his newly established salary of $300.

In 1939 Buster appeared in a feature film that attracted some attention. This was Joe Schenck's Twentieth Century–Fox film *Hollywood Cavalcade,* an amusing picture about the early days of filmmaking. The scenes involving the evolution of silent comedy techniques were directed by Mal St. Clair, who had directed *The Goat* and *The Blacksmith* with Keaton back in the twenties. In the film Buster was at least given a significant role to play—himself. In one scene he was required to show the actress Alice Faye how to throw a custard pie. Buster did this scene brilliantly—no one else has ever thrown a pie this well—but the irony was that Buster had never thrown a single pie at anyone in his entire silent film career. Seeing that Buster looked alive and reasonably well, a number of directors began to use him in character parts. There were two such films made in 1940: *The Villain Still Pursued Her,* directed by Master Francis Cline from the old days, and *Li'l Abner,* both for RKO. Buster's face was gradually becoming familiar again.

At the end of 1939 Buster was hired by Columbia to act in a series of two-reelers for them. He wanted to perform rather than write gags for other comedians, so he accepted the Columbia offer of $2,500 per film, exactly one-half of what he had been getting from Educational. These films, all ten of them, were made for a totally undiscriminating audience. They were atrocious, and Buster hoped that few people would ever see them. With a single exception, all the Columbia shorts were directed by Jules White, the man who had been responsible for Buster's *Sidewalks of New York* at MGM in 1931. White's style had not grown any more subtle over the years, and the Columbia shorts represent the absolute bottom of Buster's career in films. Two were released in 1939, five in 1940, and the final three in 1941. A number of them were written by Clyde Bruckman, but this didn't help, for Bruckman's work had deteriorated sharply during the thirties. If anything, these Columbia two-reelers only tended to reinforce the growing notion that Buster's talents belonged to an earlier, cruder age of filmmaking; there were now many people who believed that Keaton had been a pie-throwing comedian with Mack Sennett.

Hollywood Cavalcade, 1939. Rudi Blesh

In a very real sense, Buster Keaton had become a living anachronism in the Hollywood of the late thirties. Except for a few sporadic screenings of *The Navigator* and *The General* at the Museum of Modern Art in New York, Buster's work was now the concern of a scattered handful of silent-film enthusiasts. The films were hard to come by in these years. Someone told Buster in 1937 that a failure in the cooling system of the vaults where the negatives of all his silent films had been stored had resulted in their total destruction. Except for the films that he had personally retained for his own collection, Buster believed for the next decade that most of his best work had perished. Luckily this was not true, for these negatives were actually just a block or two from where he worked—at MGM.

All his feature films from 1920 through 1926 were safe in MGM's vaults, as well as his first eight two-reelers. MGM did not own these films; the basic contracts between MGM and Joe Schenck had provided that the films were to be returned to him eventually, but by the late thirties all these agreements were so old that the films were just left sitting in the vault, where they remained until their resurrection in the sixties and seventies. MGM was scarcely aware of their existence, for they had agreed to distribute them and nothing else. As luck would have it, they preserved them and reentered them for copyright renewal, just as if they had been their own films.

Buster was unaware of any of this. One of the most painful things for him in these years was the increasing difficulty he encountered in proving just how good his best work had been. Very few people went out of their way to view silent films in these years. Many in the industry considered Buster to be just another has-been from the golden twenties. If people asked who Buster Keaton was, the answer might have been: "Yeah, Keaton, a silent comic. . . . Not like Chaplin or Lloyd at all . . . a little like Harry Langdon in some ways, but not really . . . hard to describe Keaton . . . Oh, he never smiled."

In May 1940 Buster married his third wife, Eleanor Norris. It was the best thing that had happened to him in a decade. They had first met at the end of 1938 when Buster's brother, Harry, brought her over to the house one night. Eleanor had dated an

Eleanor in 1940.
Eleanor Keaton

Eleanor and Buster applying for a marriage license, May 22, 1940. *Wide World*

acquaintance of Harry's who had told her that Buster Keaton knew more about bridge than just about anyone else in Hollywood; Eleanor wanted to play bridge well, and Buster had not lost his enthusiasm for the game. She began her lessons that first night. Eleanor had been aware of Buster for at least a year, for she had seen him in line at the MGM commissary nearly every day. She had been working as a contract dancer for the studio for nearly two years at that time. Her first thought when she saw the small figure in the line was, "There goes Buster Keaton!" She had never seen any of his films but had recognized his face from newspaper photographs from the time of her childhood.

Eleanor grew up in Hollywood. She was born in a house on Hollywood Boulevard about two blocks west of the Roosevelt Hotel. Her father, an electrician at Warner Brothers, was killed in a freak accident in 1929, leaving his wife to bring up Eleanor and her sister, Jane, on a tiny pension from the studio. Eleanor studied dancing from an early age, quitting school at not quite sixteen to embark with five other girls on an around-the-world trip as part of a nightclub act called "Six Blondes from Hollywood." At seventeen she was working at Harry Richman's nightclub in New York. At MGM she danced in films like *Rosalie* and *Born to Dance.*

She quickly realized that Buster needed a "gofer" just as much as he needed a girl friend or a wife. To Eleanor a gofer meant a combination valet, cook, housekeeper, bill payer, constant reminder, and anything else that seemed appropriate to the job. She took it all on, starting the twenty-ninth of May 1940, despite a great deal of advice from both her own friends and Buster's that it was idiotic to marry an aging, alcoholic ex–movie star twice her age whose future looked decidedly dim. At the time of the wedding, Eleanor was just twenty-one, whereas Buster was nearing forty-five. She listened to the advice carefully and married him. The marriage proposal was in the form of a duet, for one night she asked him, "Do you think there would be anything wrong if . . ." He interrupted her with ". . . we got married?" There was nothing wrong and they were.

The wedding itself had some of the elements of an early two-reeler. The ceremony was conducted in the judge's chambers in the Los Angeles courthouse. It was a fine day in May, and all the windows were left wide open. The judge turned out to be the younger brother of Harry Brand, the Schenck executive who had supervised Buster's *Steamboat Bill, Jr.* Eleanor was accompanied by her mother, and Judge Brand assumed that Buster wished to marry Mrs. Norris, who seemed much closer in age to him than Eleanor. Totally ignoring Eleanor, the judge attempted to marry her mother to Buster. When the identity situation was cleared up, the judge remained flustered and addressed Eleanor as Morris throughout the rest of the ceremony. Halfway through, ear-splitting sounds of what seemed to be all the fire-fighting equipment in Los Angeles assailed the ears of the wedding party and didn't let up until the couple were finally pronounced man and wife by a screaming judge.

Eleanor was extremely pretty, and Buster's ability to capture such an attractive young wife did a lot for his battered self-esteem. It isn't like Eleanor Keaton to speak openly about love and affection, but it seems clear that Buster found in Eleanor the deep affection that Buster Collier claimed he'd always been looking for, which had been lacking in his first two marriages. Sharply laconic in manner, Eleanor quickly adapted herself to the ways of a man famous for his long silences. Besides all her household duties at Cheviot Hills, she kept on with her dancing job at MGM. She got along extraordinarily well with Buster's family, with the exception of Harry Keaton, who had not yet found his life's work. Myra and Louise were convinced that this was the marriage that would last. As for old Joe Keaton, who still appeared at holiday times, she found him to be "a hard guy, nice in some ways, but a hard guy."

Buster later claimed that he had not had a drink in over four years when he married Eleanor in 1940. Feeling in better shape than he had for a long time, he persuaded himself that he might again undertake a little social drinking. The results were predictably catastrophic. Just one or two drinks were enough to get him on a period of extended drinking that would last for several days, followed by a painful withdrawal period of another few days before he was himself again. In the next twenty years there were a number of these disturbing episodes.

The house on Victoria Avenue. *Louise Keaton*

Back in the twenties Buster had bought his mother a large house on Victoria Avenue, where she lived with Louise and Harry until the beginning of the war. At that time he sold his Cheviot Hills home and moved in with his mother, not wishing to leave her alone, for Harry and Louise had gone to Las Vegas to get jobs in the war plants operating there. They remained in Nevada until the end of the war and then returned home to the Victoria house. Harry returned with a wife and two small children. He still had no occupation to speak of, and Buster was now the sole support of his mother, Louise, and his brother's family of four. Eleanor cooked and kept house for the entire tribe; she had got pretty much what she had bargained for. Buster's income in these years averaged about $15,000 a year, or about $75,000 in modern currency. Most of the money came from his gag-writing job at MGM, but Buster took any acting job he could get, for there were deadly dull periods in between jobs at the studio. He was not choosy about the acting jobs: work was work.

Producers were eager to see Buster on the screen again. In 1946 Alexander Salkind persuaded him to come down to Mexico City to star in his film version of the Bluebeard story. The result was *El Moderno Barba Azul,* a film that few people have ever seen, but which is reputedly extremely poor.

In 1945–46 MGM decided to perform what Eleanor calls "the blood purge," firing a great many of their supporting players and contract dancers, Eleanor among them. The studio feared that the all-time high admission rate for films during the war would soon sink and decided to trim its personnel accordingly. This left Buster with another mouth to feed, but the ending of the war in Europe suddenly opened an entirely new kind of life for him in the theater: the Cirque Medrano in Paris.

Jaimé Salvator, Buster, Eleanor, unknown, Alexander Saltsman in Mexico City, 1946. *Eleanor Keaton*

11

UP AND RUNNING
TO THE END

[1]

His act . . . a presser's boy, morose and detached,
attempting to deliver a dress suit while the circus is
going on—seemed the best thing I had seen him do.
—Edmund Wilson, 1957

The French had remembered Buster with more fondness than
his own countrymen. His appearances at the famous Cirque Medrano triggered a series of events that eventually resulted in his
second climb to international fame, the rebirth of a man thought
dead by many. Buster loved the Medrano, and he kept coming
back to it whenever he had the chance in the years between 1947
and 1954. At first he was a little unsure of himself, for with the
exception of his brief 1933 appearance in Baltimore, he had not
appeared on the vaudeville stage since the last days of "The
Three Keatons" in 1917. He worked out a number of routines
that he felt would go over in Paris, including "putting the girl to
bed," which he had done with Dorothy Sebastian in *Spite Marriage* and now performed with Eleanor. He also revived the
comic dueling sequence that he and Gilbert Roland had shot for
The Passionate Plumber.

Edmund Wilson wrote about Keaton in the late fifties for the
first time since his review of *Go West* in 1925: "In February 1954
I saw Buster Keaton perform at the Cirque Medrano in Paris,
and was confirmed in my opinion of twenty-eight years before
that Hollywood had not made the best of him. He is a pantomime clown of the first order. . . ." Wilson went on to indict
Hollywood in familiar language: "His loss of reputation in the
United States and his appearance in an engagement abroad is

256

Paris, 1947. *Eleanor Keaton*

only another example of the perversion and waste of talent for which Hollywood has been responsible."

The novelist Paul Gallico described Buster's delivery boy routine: "A sad-faced little fellow wearing a flat porkpie hat, string tie, too big clothes, and flap shoes. He was carrying a mouldy-looking dress suit on a hanger, obviously looking for a cleaner. Before he had done, the suit was a wreck on the arena floor and the audience was in hysterics." The French had always had a high regard for the clown they called Malec, and his live appearances resulted in his being favorably compared with the great clowns Grock and Orlando.

Le Cirque Medrano, 1947. *Eleanor Keaton*

After their success at the Medrano, Buster and Eleanor began to appear in variety shows in Italy, as well as in England and Scotland. In Milan one night they were performing the "putting the girl to bed" number on a slippery stage. Buster lost his grip on Eleanor's shoulders, and the next thing she recalled was waking in darkness and hearing voices. She was stunned for a few seconds, but Buster dragged her out from under the bed where she had slid and the show continued. They appeared together on variety bills in England with famous old stars such as Hetty King, George Robey, Wee Georgie Wood, Dolly Harmer, and Billy Danvers. They had all been headliners from Buster's early days on the stage, and he enjoyed working with them now, so many years later.

In September 1950 Buster performed the last of his gag-writing chores at MGM, for he no longer needed the money. The first sure signs of the reflowering of his reputation had already begun, signaled by the publication in *Life* of James Agee's famous 1949 essay "Comedy's Greatest Era." When Agee wrote his essay, Buster had slipped into at least partial oblivion. Although Agee found conversation with Buster not as engrossing as with Chaplin, he loved Buster's work. In the course of the article Agee mentioned the fact that Buster had "gallantly" refused to consider himself retired, a fact that did not go unnoticed in Hollywood. Agee's tribute to the silent era contained the strongest case ever made for the work of the four great silent comedians: Chaplin, Lloyd, Langdon, and Keaton. Langdon was dead; Chaplin and Lloyd needed no help from anyone. It was

Wee Georgie Wood, Buster, Hetty King, Sir George Robey, Dolly Harmer, and Billy Danvers, 1951. *David Robinson*

Buster who derived the most benefit from Agee, mainly in the form of being offered work in films again.

His cameo performance in Billy Wilder's *Sunset Boulevard* (1950) helped him greatly. Buster was cast as himself, along with Anna Q. Nilsson and H. B. Warner. He is seen playing bridge with these two stars of the twenties, along with Gloria Swanson, who plays the part of Norma Desmond, an archetypal silent star who is planning a mad, impossible comeback. Her loyal butler and devoted slave is portrayed magnificently by Erich von Stroheim in a film that was a huge success at the time of its first appearance. It is of interest today largely because of the presence of Swanson, von Stroheim, and Buster, who speaks only one strangely symbolic line during the bridge game, "Pass."

It was Harold Lloyd, Buster's great rival from the twenties, who was responsible for Keaton's getting into television in Los Angeles in 1949. Lloyd was then represented by Ben Pearson, who had obtained for him the job of master of ceremonies on the Old Gold radio show. In the course of a talk about the future of TV, Lloyd asked Pearson if he knew very much about the new medium. When Pearson said he didn't, Lloyd suddenly observed that "it's Buster Keaton that ought to be on television—all those sight gags!" Pearson agreed immediately and asked Lloyd how he might contact Buster. Lloyd advised him to begin with Clyde Bruckman, who had remained friendly with Buster over the years, and the following day Bruckman came around to Pearson's office in Santa Monica. Bruckman had sunk very low in

Hollywood at that time. In the mid-forties he had contracted to supply the actress Joan Davis with some gag material for a Universal film, and he gave her some of the identical routines he had worked out for Harold Lloyd in the early thirties. Lloyd promptly sued Universal and won, collecting several million dollars, and Bruckman became totally unemployable as a screenwriter. He drank heavily and usually had a pint bottle protruding from his jacket pocket. He told Pearson that he and Buster could easily put together a presentation for KTTV and promised to send Buster over the next day; Pearson had no idea about Buster's present condition and wanted to judge for himself. When Buster arrived, he had almost nothing to say, except that he "needed $250 for next week's expenses." Pearson saw no difficulties and agreed to meet him and Bruckman at his house the following night.

It was a strange evening for Pearson. When he arrived, a slightly eerie bridge game was going on in the large living room, not unlike the one in *Sunset Boulevard.* The players this night were Betty Compson, Norman Kerry, Florence Vidor, and Minta Durfee, all of whose starring careers had ended with the twenties. It was not uncommon for Buster to have these card games with his contemporaries at his house. Myra Keaton could be heard practicing her saxophone, and Eleanor, Louise, and Harry Keaton were all there too in the big rambling house. Myra was insatiably curious about everything and everybody who came to the house, and she often would be found listening behind doorways, her broom clutched in her hands.

When he'd become accustomed to the curious atmosphere of Buster's home, Pearson told him what KTTV had in mind: $1,000 a week for a half-hour weekly comedy series. Bruckman would write the scripts, and Harold Goodwin would be the straight man in the skits that required one. Buster agreed, and the Buster Keaton Comedy Show became quite popular on the West Coast. The show was filmed each week, but it was extremely expensive to produce and lasted only six months. From the very start Buster made it clear that he had no intention of providing new gags for the shows. He believed that he had developed a more than adequate repertoire of gags over the years and saw no need for creating new material. Bruckman's writing was mostly on the order of introductory spoken material to set the scene for the classic comedy routines. He proved to be unreliable at delivering his material on time, and Harold Goodwin was often given the job at the last moment. As the show increased in popularity, Master Eddie Cline, from the days of Buster's great shorts in the twenties, was also brought in to help.

Buster had taken an avid delight in watching TV from the start, remaining glued to his tiny set. In between jobs he would stare at the set he purchased in 1948 for as long as eight and nine hours at a stretch, smoking constantly, playing one of his endless games of solitaire, while keeping up a flow of conversation with whoever was in the room about how the performers were or were not "doing it right." The initial success of the Buster Keaton Comedy Show made it possible for Pearson to get Buster on all of the popular shows of the day, most of them originating in New York. He appeared ten times on the Ed Sullivan Show, a dozen or more times on Garry Moore's show, as well as "This Is Your Life" and "Candid Camera."

Garry Moore recalls the alarming seriousness with which Buster took his New York TV programs in the late fifties and early sixties. Moore was always afraid that Buster would hurt himself seriously while performing one of his celebrated acrobatic feats. He was taken aback when Buster had trouble jumping through a hoop, for he could not go through smoothly and kept hitting the edge with his shoes. Moore claimed that he couldn't stop Buster from doing it over and over until Buster's shins were literally bloody. Moore became so terrified that he stopped having Buster on the show.

In the early fifties Buster's activities were about equally divided between his TV appearances and the variety stage in Europe. Within a few years, his income had risen to between $50,000 and $60,000 a year from the fees for his appearances, plus the commercials. He no longer thought much about pictures and was surprised when Ben Pearson told him in 1952 that Chaplin wanted him for a few scenes in his production of *Lime-*

light. Pearson went to visit Chaplin in his old studio at La Brea and Sunset, where the first thing Chaplin told him was that the fee for Buster's services was nonnegotiable—$1,000 for either one or two days' work. He was to play the part of Chaplin's assistant in a nostalgic vaudeville number in which Buster was to feel free to improvise whatever seemed appropriate.

James and Mia Agee were present as Chaplin's guests for the shooting of the sequences of *Limelight* in which Buster appeared, and Agee's widow recalls the tremendous effect he had on Chaplin's production crew. Improvising everything he did that day, Buster was simply overpowering. In Mia Agee's opinion, Chaplin chose not to use all of the best of Buster's material in the final print of *Limelight.*

There is an incredibly poignant scene in the film in which the two greatest comic geniuses in film history chat quietly in their dressing room, with Buster lamenting the fact that "he never thought he'd come to this!" When the two begin their "concert," Chaplin sings and plays the violin while Buster accompanies him at the piano. Buster pretends to be extremely near-sighted and keeps managing to get his sheet music into a fantastic sort of circular motion that is counterbalanced by the constant spinning of the piano stool he is sitting on. It is a prodigious piece of invention on Buster's part, and confirms the fact that Buster could still be a master of timing and could still, in spite of his fifty-seven years, do uncanny things with his body. He had slept very little the night before arriving at Chaplin's studio, suffering preperformance nerves, which never left him.

When Pearson told Buster that he thought Chaplin's offer had been on the cheap side for a billed appearance in a feature film, Buster frankly admitted that he would have done it for nothing. It had been twenty years since he had seen Chaplin, and he thoroughly enjoyed working with the man he considered to be the very best in the business, the master. This was one occasion when he did not ask Pearson, as he usually did when discussing an offer, "Did they ask for me?" or "Did you suggest my name?" At fifty-seven he suddenly found that he had not been forgotten after all; it was hard to believe.

Limelight, 1952. *RBC Films*

Not long after his marriage to Eleanor in 1940, Buster reestablished contact with his two sons for the first time since the divorce in 1932. The initiative was not Buster's but his oldest son Bobby's, who decided to visit his father when he had reached his eighteenth birthday. He had not dared to do so before this because Buster's name was largely a term of abuse in his mother's home. Bobby Talmadge, for that was now his legal name, tracked Buster down by way of his car-buying habits. He went to the biggest Cadillac dealer in Los Angeles, who supplied him with Buster's address on Victoria. Louise Keaton recalls seeing a young man standing hesitantly at the screen door at the side of the house. She shouted Bobby's name and Buster came to the door, where he calmly shook hands with the son he had not seen in eight years.

After a year or two Buster was seeing his sons regularly. They were both married and eventually had eleven children between them. Natalie, who had become something of a recluse, went on living in her apartment in Santa Monica.

Buster and Eleanor spent several months each year in Europe right through the early fifties, traveling from town to town with a number of variety shows. Outside London one night in 1956 Eleanor got a cable telling Buster that Myra Keaton had died at the age of seventy-three. Eleanor was fearful that the news would throw Buster into a drinking binge, but nothing of the kind happened. He went out for a long walk by himself, four or five hours at least, before returning to the hotel, his eyes red-rimmed from weeping. He had always been closer to Myra than to his father, and Joe's death in 1945, after he had been knocked down by a speeding car, had not moved him very much. The two had made their peace many years before.

After the great success in 1955 of the film *I'll Cry Tomorrow,* which was based on Gerald Frank's ghostwritten autobiography of the singer Lillian Roth, who had suffered a long battle with alcohol, Sidney Sheldon decided that a film based on Buster's troubled life might have an equally large audience. Donald O'Connor, best known for his performance as a singer and dancer in *Singin' in the Rain,* was hired to play Buster, and Keaton was hired as technical director on the picture. As technical director his job was to teach O'Connor how to duplicate some of his best routines, such as the sinking of the *Damfino* in *The Boat.* O'Connor tried hard, but it was impossible for anyone to portray Keaton's movements. The picture was insufferable and had very little to do with Buster's actual life. Buster and Eleanor sat quietly in the darkness at the premiere of the picture, hoping that no one would ask them what they thought of *The Buster Keaton Story.* Eleanor recalls that "my stomach turned over, it was so awful!"

Paramount gave Buster a down payment of $60,000 for the film rights to his life story, and with this money Buster bought the house that he lived in until his death. He called it his "ranch." Located at Woodland Hills in the San Fernando Valley, it was bought from his old friend Harold Goodwin, who had now taken to the realty business. After showing Buster and Eleanor a number of houses, Goodwin took them to an address on Sylvan Way. Buster knew this was the house he wanted before he had even left the car, saying, "This is it. I don't have to go inside!" When he did enter, the old-fashioned stove in the den made it a certainty that he would buy the house. It was everything he had ever wanted, and there was plenty of room for a garden and a pool in the back; he could barbecue again.

It was usually Eleanor who made the friendships during Buster's last years, for he remained as shy or indifferent to most people as he had been in the past. But in the early sixties he became good friends with Lee Cox, a script girl at KTTV, and her husband, Bill Cox, the novelist and screenwriter. The Coxes became very close to the Keatons, as did the actor Dick Foran and his wife. At Woodland Hills, Buster and Eleanor did a lot more entertaining than they had at the house on Victoria Avenue.

In the late fifties Buster returned to the American stage to tour in plays such as *Merton of the Movies* and *Once Upon a Mattress*. It was while touring with *Merton* that he met Jane Dula, the actress from New York who became a close friend of both Keatons and, like the Coxes, remained so until the very last day of Buster's life. Jane and Buster had a student/teacher relationship, in which he taught her a lot about timing in comedy. She might never have had more than a casual knowledge of the Keatons if someone hadn't given her a bottle of Scotch on opening night. Anxious to share it, she asked where it could be consumed. Buster and Eleanor suggested their trailer, and an instant party resulted.

Jane recalls Buster's extraordinary kindness to her, even to the extent of sharing his father's hangover cure with her. When she needed the cure, Buster told her to mix together one raw egg, a glass of cold beer, and tomato ketchup. She remembers him telling her the recipe with "his eyes burning right into my soul!" The remedy worked miracles, and Jane was soon able to sit down and play a game of bridge with both Keatons. Like so many of Buster's friends, Jane stresses the fact that "his mind was always working!" His conversation was filled with practical stage lore, particular mechanical problems connected with the

Jane Dula and Buster in *Merton of the Movies,* 1958. *Jane Dula*

current production, and extended comments on the great comics.

In his talks with Jane Dula, the subject of Natalie Talmadge would come up from time to time. At no time did Buster say anything hostile or derogatory. He was aware that she had continued to live in her apartment at Santa Monica, alone most of the time and drinking heavily. By the 1940s she had become quite alcoholic, and her situation became so bad that Bobby Keaton took an apartment just above Natalie's to watch over her. Louise kept in touch with Natalie by phone, a practice that had started at the time of the death of Myra Keaton in 1956, which Natalie had taken very badly. Louise visited Natalie only once in these last years. Things started off well, but within half an hour Natalie had launched into one of her "Son of a bitch, Buster!" routines, and Louise responded by saying "Good-bye now, Nat!" and left.

Buster never grasped the fact that it was unsafe for him to drink at any time. After completing his cameo role in *Around the World in Eighty Days,* he suffered a series of near-fatal esophagus hemorrhages and was admitted to Wadsworth Veterans' Hospital at Sawtelle. He was placed on the critical list and told that if he continued to drink, he would surely be dead in a very short time. This warning kept him away from spirits for a good part of his last years, but not entirely. To the very end he would ask doctors, after a physical exam, if he could drink again. Some must have said yes, for he often did.

Buster appeared in a wide variety of cameo roles in many films in the late fifties and through the mid-sixties. They included expensive, all-star vehicles such as *It's a Mad, Mad, Mad, Mad World* and *A Funny Thing Happened on the Way to the Forum,* and quickie, low-budget American International films with titles such as *How to Stuff a Wild Bikini* and *Beach Blanket Bingo.* One of these was a film called *Ten Girls Ago,* which featured Bert Lahr and Eddie Foy, Jr. Shot in Canada, the film was never completed because the producers ran out of money. As far as Buster was concerned, all these films were work, and he accepted all the offers made him, regardless of who was in the film or where it was being made.

Penelope Gilliatt visited Buster and Eleanor at Woodland Hills in 1963. She found him eager to talk about filmmaking and was struck by his passion for work. When asked to attend the premiere of *It's a Mad, Mad, Mad, Mad World,* Buster was determined to go, despite Eleanor's wishes that he stay home because of his health:

> "We have aisle seats," he says.
> "You're not well," she says.
> "I can take my cough mixture," he says. "I can take a small container. I can get ready to move in a hurry."

Eleanor and Buster arriving in Rochester, New York, for his "George Award" in 1956.
Louise Brooks

The most notable of the films made in Keaton's last years was Samuel Beckett's *Film,* directed by Alan Schneider. Buster had been given *Waiting for Godot* to read some years before, but turned it down because he didn't understand it. *Film* had been written for the Irish actor Jack MacGowran, who had agreed to take the role, but at the last moment he turned it down to accept an important role in Tony Richardson's *Tom Jones. Film* was being produced by Barney Rosset's Evergreen Films, and there was a great deal of debate as to who should replace MacGowran. It was Beckett who thought of Keaton, and Alan Schneider was dispatched to visit him in Woodland Hills with a copy of the script. Buster read it and was just as doubtful about *Film* as he had been

Production staff for *Film*, New York City, June 1964: Samuel Beckett, Alan Schneider, unknown, Buster, Joel Glickman. *National Film Archive / Stills Library*

about *Waiting for Godot,* but he accepted the offer of $5,000 for what amounted to two weeks' shooting in New York.

Alan Schneider was concerned about Buster's health and the potentially harmful effect on him of the heat of the New York streets. But there were no problems and Buster carried out his tasks energetically. Beckett had come to the United States for the first time to see the shooting of his script. At the end of each day's work he was driven back to Barney Rosset's house in the Hamptons, totally unwilling to meet his many admirers in the city. He did come around to see Buster at his hotel just before the shooting began, in his usual corner suite at the St. Moritz, and it was here that the two first met. Beckett proved to be as shy as Buster, and they had very little to say to each other.

Film called for Boris Kaufman's camera to follow Buster through the streets from the rear so that we never see his face. Various people in the street gasp in horror as they catch a

Between takes on *Film*, 1964. *National Film Archive / Stills Library*

glimpse of the man coming toward them. Buster arrives at the building where he lives and enters his apartment. He immediately shoos his cat and dog from the room and covers up the goldfish bowl so that its occupant cannot see him: *no one* must see him. After tearing up his family pictures, Buster is finally trapped by the camera; his expression of sheer living horror is frighteningly well done. The picture has found few supporters, many finding it a freakish tour de force, but there is a terrible urgency about the film; the fact that you know that the figure up there on the screen with his face hidden is Buster Keaton helps establish the strangeness that Beckett wanted to achieve. Buster himself did not care for the film, but his explanation as to "what it all meant" was as good as anyone else's: "What I think it means is that a man can keep away from everybody, but he can't get away from himself."

Buster had lunch every day with Beckett, Schneider, and the whole crew during those two weeks in June 1964. A number of scenes were shot on the Upper West Side, in the 140s, near the Hudson River. At a nearby restaurant Buster would hold forth on the great days in the twenties when he had his own production unit and made films like *The Navigator* and *The General.* Yet there was no trace of defeat or sadness in his manner. Beckett would listen intently to Buster's stories, a small smile of pure delight on his face.

That same year the National Film Board of Canada, in conjunction with the Canadian National Railways, produced a two-and-a-half reel film starring Buster in which he takes a scenic trip all over Canada on a handcar. The filming of the picture was documented by a film shot at the same time: *Buster Rides Again,* in which he also discussed the making of his early films.

The Railroader, 1964.
Louise Keaton

His appearances in pictures such as *Limelight* and *Film* served to convince increasingly large numbers of people that Keaton was a living legend, but his films remained largely unavailable. Until the end of the fifties it was difficult to see many of his best films of the twenties; with the exception of *The Navigator* and *The General*, none of them had been shown publicly for thirty years. In a 1952 article Walter Kerr advised his readers to seek out Keaton's films, as they were in the process of vanishing forever because of the disintegration of the nitrate stock on which they had been printed. Films shot on nitrate stock rarely last more than forty years, and by 1960 Kerr's prediction had begun to come true. It might have been totally fulfilled had it not been for a series of fortuitous events.

One night in the mid-fifties Eleanor and Buster attended a showing of *The General* at the Coronet Theater in Los Angeles, a house that specialized in old films. The owner of the theater, Raymond Rohauer, recognized Keaton and at the end of the show asked him if he still possessed any of his old films. Buster gave him details of the ones he had kept all those years, and within a short time Rohauer got the films transferred to safety stock. He then began a long and complicated series of negotiations whereby whatever rights still existed in the films were eventually acquired from Leopold Friedman, who was acting as surviving trustee in liquidation of Buster Keaton Productions, Inc. MGM, the distributor of the first eight of Buster's two-reelers and all of his feature films, from *The Three Ages* in 1923 through *Battling Butler* (1926), had dutifully filed renewals for all the copyrights in these films just as if they had been their own films. The short films released through First National and the three United Artists features (*The General, College,* and *Steamboat Bill, Jr.*) did not have their copyrights renewed because there was no one in these firms who remembered them.

Other Keaton films were found in the Italian villa, which had passed through a number of hands after its purchase by Fanchon and Marco. It was acquired in the fifties by the actor James Mason and his wife Pamela. To his considerable surprise, Mason discovered that the small projection room that Buster had used to show films to his friends contained several dozen cans of film, positive prints of high quality. It was this find, together with the negatives and positives from MGM, which allowed for the eventual rerelease of many of Keaton's films. Eventually MGM transferred its own Keaton films to safety stock, but only just in time, for on December 5, 1957, their laboratory had issued these reports on the first two: *The Cameraman:* "Negative is unprintable, first reel is missing." *Spite Marriage:* "Negative is unprintable, torn perforations and is excessively shrunken."

Joe Schenck, the man who had financed all these films, had attempted on several occasions to help Buster when he needed it. In 1948 Buster attempted to sell the plot of *The Navigator* to Warner Brothers for a remake to star Danny Kaye. Schenck wrote to the New York office of Buster Keaton Productions: "I gave Buster an option on *Navigator* for $5,000 for 6 months. Know it's low, but want to give him an opportunity to make some money." Strangely enough, his wish was denied by his associates in New York, who pointed out to Joe that such a small amount was unfair to the stockholders, and the remake fell through. In 1957, after retiring as chairman of the board of Twentieth Century–Fox, Joe, at the age of eighty, suffered a stroke that kept him bedridden at the Beverly Hilton Hotel in Beverly Hills for the rest of his life. He also lost the power of speech, and only his smile served to convey to his visitors that he'd recognized them. Buster paid many visits to Joe's suite at the hotel, often not quite sure if his old friend knew him or not, but eventually he convinced himself that he did. Joe died in 1961 at eighty-four, leaving his estate to his brother, Nicholas.

The Talmadge sisters did not fare well in the 1930s, for the film careers of Norma and Constance came to an abrupt end with the advent of sound. After two unsuccessful sound films (*New York Nights, DuBarry: Woman of Passion*) Norma never again appeared before a camera. She did not give up her stardom without a fight, for she was the mistress of ceremonies on several radio shows in the late thirties and early forties. After divorcing Joe Schenck in 1934, Norma married the singing comedian George Jessel. Their marriage did not last long, and she finally married the doctor who had been supplying her with the narcotics she had become dependent on by the end of the forties. She died in 1957, leaving most of her estate to Buster's two boys.

Constance made no effort to appear in sound films. After the end of her fourth marriage, she commuted between her suite at the Beverly Hilton and a similar suite at the Drake Hotel in New York City. In time she became as much of an alcoholic as Natalie. When Constance died at the end of 1974, she left an estate of over a million dollars, most of it again going to Bobby and Jimmy. Natalie, a total recluse to the end, died in her apartment in 1969. All three Talmadge sisters are buried in the same crypt as their mother in Los Angeles.

The saddest end of all Buster's friends was Clyde Bruckman's. Completely discouraged by his inability to find work, he borrowed Buster's pistol and killed himself in a telephone booth on Santa Monica Boulevard in 1955. He had told his wife in a note that he was going out to a telephone booth because he did not wish to mess up their apartment.

All through the sixties Buster was invited to speak at various gatherings of film enthusiasts all over the world. The high moment of this critical homage was his appearance at the Venice Film Festival in September 1965. The occasion was the first European showing of *Film*, at which he received a long standing

ovation from the hundreds of people who had packed their way into the auditorium. He was visibly moved, and there were tears in his eyes. The next day he spoke to his interviewers as one who was still thinking about how to make films: "If I were going to show you this hotel lobby where we are now, for instance, I'd go back and then move in closer. But the main thing is that I want you to be familiar with the atmosphere, so you know what my location is and where I am. . . ."

Buster's feeling for *where* things should be in the picture was displayed in his final years by the dozens of commercials he made for American television, in which he nearly always had his way with the directors of these films or videotapes as to just where and how the camera should be placed. It was his right.

Bill Cox was writing television scripts for the popular Western series *Wagon Train*. Cox thought his friend the actor Ward Bond, who appeared in so many of John Ford's films, might like to appear with Keaton in one of the episodes. Bond was eager to do so, and Buster and Cox set out to contrive an episode on Sunday afternoon at Buster's home in Woodland Hills. Cox taped a great deal of the talk that day, and it is facinating to hear Buster gradually arrive at the main structural line of the proposed episode, in which he sees himself as a Pinkerton detective in disguise, on the trail of a murderer in the Old West. The high point of the story was to come at the moment when Buster tries to arrest Ward Bond as the criminal he has been seeking. Buster's voice bubbles over with laughter and excitement as he conceives the idea of his handcuffing the huge and burly Bond.

Bill Cox once tried to sum up Buster in a letter to a friend:

> He was simple and complex. He was clever and naive. His tastes were those of the turn of the century American lower class . . . but he played bridge for big stakes against Culbertson, Jacoby— and the Hillcrest crowd. He would rather have been a big league baseball player or a cameraman than a motion picture star—but his oral reminiscences were almost entirely of the old vaudeville days with Ma and Pa.

Cox made a number of recordings of Buster in his later years at Woodland Hills. Some of them give clear proof of the amaz-

At the Cinemateque, Paris, 1962. *Pierre Sauvage*

At the Bronx Zoo, New York
City, 1960. *Eleanor Keaton*

ing quality of Buster's memory in his late 60s. He could recall
every single line of the parody lyrics of songs that had been popular when he was a child of six and seven. He sang a number of
these songs in a wonderful cockney accent, which was the way he
had originally heard them. He is in superb form in his rendition
of a parody film version of "Oh by Jingo!" which became "Tia
Juana's the location for me!"

These long informal evenings at Buster's were regularly attended by Foran and his wife, the Coxes, Louise Keaton, Jane
Dula, and the Earle twins, attractive girls who had hopes of success in the theater. Buster would play his ukulele for hours and
sing these old songs of forty, fifty, and even sixty years ago, with
tremendous joy and verve. More and more in these last years his
thoughts turned back to his boyhood on the American vaudeville
stage. Buster may have been permanently damaged in many
ways by the treatment he received there, but that life was pre-
cious to him, and at the end he recalled it with great and continuing pleasure. Many of Buster's listeners were astounded by
how much he could remember from this early period of his life.

Buster is often regarded as a tragic figure, and there is much
in his best work that suggests some truth in this judgment. But it
was definitely not Buster's own way of regarding himself and his
life. In response to an interviewer's question about how he felt
about his smashed career and all the bad things that had gone
with it, Buster's answer was unhesitating: "I've had a very interesting career. I have no complaints!" I think he meant it.

[2]

Heat won't do any good. It's something that heat can't help.

—Keaton, 1966

Buster felt weak and tired after completion of *The Scribe,* an industrial safety film he made in Toronto at the beginning of October 1965. His "cigarette cough" had become much worse. After he had a checkup at the local hospital Eleanor was told that he had terminal cancer of the lung and that his life expectancy was about three months. The doctors at the hospital told her that acute headaches could be expected at the end. Eleanor decided not to tell Buster anything about the diagnosis. He blamed his heavy cough on smoking; he had been suffering from emphysema for several years, but that had not noticeably affected his habit of smoking three and up to four packs a day. Buster just felt that he was tired and decided to take it easy for a while. He took on no new working assignments in November and December. When the Coxes came to visit one night and Lee recommended the use of a heating pad, Buster told them that it wouldn't do him any good. Eleanor realized then that he knew the truth.

The end came almost as scheduled. Jane Dula came over for Sunday brunch on the thirtieth of January in 1966. During their usual bridge game both Eleanor and she noticed that Buster's scoring was highly erratic. He had trouble concentrating and didn't seem to care much about the game. They soon stopped playing, and Buster went into the adjoining room to resume one of his unfinished solitaire games. Half an hour later they heard a choking and gasping sound and rushed in to find him unconscious. He was taken to the hospital immediately and spent the night there. Buster refused to stay in bed during most of the night, repeatedly asking Chick, his male nurse, the question: "Why don't I just give up? Why don't I?" In the morning the doctors told Eleanor that there was nothing they could do for him and advised her to take him home.

Jane Dula had stayed overnight at the Keaton's, and she and Eleanor drove him home. Chick, Eleanor, and Jane attempted to talk him into getting into bed, but he refused to lie down. All that long afternoon Buster kept walking about his house, up-stairs and downstairs. He was fully conscious but frequently was unaware of where he was or who was with him. Jane had to leave for her home in the late afternoon, and for the first time in her life she was heartily embraced by her friend and teacher of eight years. When he said good-bye to her at the door, it was with more emotion than she had ever heard in his voice before. She left and wept as she drove back to Los Angeles. Buster finally got into his bed during the late evening after Chick went home.

At about six thirty in the morning the night nurse called Chick, who came over to the house immediately and confirmed that Buster was dead. He awakened Eleanor at once, and she said "He's gone." He was, but his films remain a permanent legacy.

Buster's seventieth birthday, Woodland Hills, October 5, 1965. *Eleanor Keaton*

APPENDICES

"BUSTER KEATON TAKES A WALK"

A FARCE BY
FEDERICO GARCIA LORCA

Translation and introduction by A. L. Lloyd

IN 1930 Garcia Lorca left proud, grave, unhurried Andalusia and found himself in New York. He was appalled. For him it was "a Senegal with machinery." He wrote a group of tormented surrealist poems in which he set down his terror of the concrete canyons of the city where men stagger "unslept like those who've just come from a bloody shipwreck." When his horror had eased a bit, it amused him to recall his favorite American fool, Buster Keaton, and to imagine him making an innocent's journey through the desperate landscape. It was probably shortly after finishing the agonized *Poeta en Nueva York* that he wrote the sweet little squib—dadaist, surrealist, "absurd," called *El Paseo de Buster Keaton*. It remained unnoticed among his papers (missing inclusion in the *Obras Completas* published by Losada in Buenos Aires) until it appeared in the small collection of *Tres Farsas* (Coleccion Teatro de Bolsillo, Mexico City, 1959).

Characters: Buster Keaton
               The cock
               The owl
               A Negro
               An American woman
               A young girl

COCK: Cock a doodle doo.
           Enter Buster Keaton with his four sons, hand in hand.

KEATON: My poor little boys. (*He draws a wooden sword and kills them*).

COCK: Cock a doodle doo.

KEATON (*counting the corpses on the ground*): One, two, three and four. *He takes a bicycle and rides away. Among old car tires and petrol cans a Negro is eating his straw hat.*

KEATON: What a marvelous afternoon.
A parrot flutters about in the neutral-colored sky.

KEATON: It's great, riding a bicycle.

OWL: Chirri chirri chirri chi.

KEATON: How sweetly the birds sing.

OWL: Chirrrrrrr.

KEATON: Stupendous.
A pause. Impassively, Buster Keaton rides through the rushes and across the rye patch. The countryside grows smaller under the wheels of his bicycle. The machine takes on a single dimension. It could enter a book, stretch out in a bake oven. Buster Keaton's bicycle hasn't a caramel saddle and pedals of sugar, of the sort that wicked men might wish for. It is a bicycle like any other, except that it is the only one that's permeated with innocence. Adam and Eve would run in terror if they saw a glass of water, but on the other hand they would stroke Keaton's bicycle.

KEATON: Ah love, love!
Buster Keaton falls off. The bicycle runs away from him. It chases after two huge gray butterflies. It goes like a madman, half a millimeter off the ground.

KEATON (*picking himself up*): I've nothing to say. What was I saying?

A VOICE: You're crazy.

KEATON: O.K.
He walks on. His sad infinite eyes, like those of a new-born beast of burden, are dreaming of lilies, angels and silk sashes. His eyes are like the bottom of a glass, like a mad child's. Very ugly. Very beautiful. An ostrich's eyes. Human eyes in the exact balance of melancholy. In the distance, Philadelphia can be seen. The inhabitants of this city know the old poem of the Singer sewing machine and how it circulates among the hothouse roses, yet they never understand the subtle poetic dif-

ference between a cup of hot tea and a cup of cold tea. Philadelphia shines in the distance.

KEATON: This is a garden.

An American woman with celluloid eyes comes through the grass.

WOMAN: Good evening.

Buster Keaton smiles, and looks at the woman's shoes in close-up. What shoes! We ought never to have introduced those shoes! It took the hides of three crocodiles to make them.

KEATON: I wish—

WOMAN: Do you have a sword decorated with myrtle leaves?

Buster Keaton lets his shoulders droop and raises his right foot.

WOMAN: Do you have a ring with a poisoned stone?

Buster Keaton slowly closes his eyes and raises his left foot.

WOMAN: What about it?

Four seraphim with wings of heavenly gauze dance among the flowers. The girls of the city are playing the piano as if they were riding bicycles. The waltzes, the moon, the motor-boats, shake our friend's delicate heart. To everyone's surprise, autumn has invaded the garden like water in the geometrical plot of a sugar-lump.

KEATON (*sighing*): I wish I were a swan. But I can't be even though I'd like to. Because what have I done with my hat? Where are my paper collar and my watered-silk tie? What a calamity!

A young girl, wasp-waisted, with beehive coiffure, enters on a bicycle. She has the head of a nightingale.

YOUNG GIRL: Whom have I the honor of greeting?

KEATON (*with a bow*): Buster Keaton.

The young girl falters and falls off her bicycle. Her striped stockings tremble in the grass like two dying zebras. Simultaneously, in a thousand cinemas, a gramophone is announcing: There are no nightingales in America.

KEATON (*kneeling*): Miss Elinor! Forgive me! It wasn't me, Miss Elinor! (*lower*) Miss! (*very quietly*) Miss! (*He kisses her.*)

Over the horizon of Philadelphia shines the glittering star of the police.

FILMOGRAPHY
COMPILED BY MARYANN CHACH

Arbuckle Comedy Shorts, 1917–20

All films: 2 reels. Produced by Comique Film Corp. Released by Paramount Pictures. Except where noted, all films were written and directed by Roscoe Arbuckle. Cast—Arbuckle, Keaton, and Al St. John (except for *The Garage*).

Summaries drawn from the trade journal *Moving Picture World*'s (*MPW*) reviews are included for missing films (*).

For a comprehensive listing of Arbuckle's films, see the filmography compiled by Samuel A. Gill for David A. Yallop's *The Day The Laughter Stopped: The True Story of Fatty Arbuckle* (St. Martin's Press, 1976).

1917
The Butcher Boy.
> Rel. April 23; © Apr. 12, 1917; LP 10592.
> Story: Joe Roach. Scenario editor: Herbert Warren. Photog.: Frank D. Williams.
> Cast: Josephine Stevens, Arthur Earle, Agnes Neilson, Joe Bordeau, Luke (dog).

*A Reckless Romeo.
> Rel. May 21; no copyright.
> Story: Joe Roach. Scenario editor: Herbert Warren. Photog.: Frank D. Williams.
> Cast: Alice Lake, Corinne Parquet, Agnes Neilson.
> Summary: Fatty takes his family to a moving-picture house, where to his horror an indiscretion (a dalliance with a girl) is revealed on the screen before his mother-in-law (*MPW*, May 19, 1917, p. 1,153).

*The Rough House.
> Rel. June 25; © June 20, 1917; LP 10972.
> Story: Joe Roach. Scenario editor: Herbert Warren. Photog.: Frank D. Williams.

Cast: Alice Lake.

Summary: Mr. & Mrs. Rough live happily in a house by the sea until Mrs. Rough's mother arrives and stays for a few weeks. Mother-in-law immediately begins to disturb the tranquility of the household. Also includes a cabaret scene and a conflagration in a bedroom (*MPW*, June 16, 1917, p. 1,809).

His Wedding Night.

Rel. Aug. 20; © Aug. 20, 1917; LP 11286.

Story: Joe Roach. Scenario Editor: Herbert Warren. Photog.: George Peters.

Cast: Alice Mann, Arthur Earle.

Summary: Fatty is a soda clerk in a country drugstore (Koff & Kramp Druggists). Gags include: Fatty juggles egg & milk, strains through a comb, and brushes off foam with a hairbrush; provides beer for a customer with a wink; gives charcoal to a Negress who comes in for powder. At the gas station, different prices for a Rolls-Royce and a Ford. Fatty overcomes a rival suitor who then plans to kidnap the bride (*MPW*, September 8, 1917; p. 1,523).

Oh Doctor.

Rel. Sept. 30; © Sept. 19, 1917; LP 11430.

Scenario: Jean Havez. Scenario Editor: Herbert Warren. Photog.: George Peters.

Cast: Alice Mann.

Summary: An adventure among thieves and race track gamblers. In the capacity of a doctor, Fatty visits (unknown to his wife) a beautiful vampire who finally becomes the possessor of his wife's necklace through an accomplice (*MPW*, December 22, 1917, p. 1,808).

Fatty at Coney Island.

Rel. Oct. 29; © Oct. 11, 1917; LP 11535.

Scenario Editor: Herbert Warren. Photog.: George Peters.

Cast: Alice Mann, Agnes Neilson, James Bryant, Joe Bordeau.

A Country Hero.

Rel. Dec. 10; © Dec. 13, 1920; LP 15929.

Scenario Editor: Herbert Warren. Photog.: George Peters.

Cast: Alice Lake, Joe Keaton.

Summary: Fatty plays a village blacksmith in "Jazzville," an imaginary rural village. Rivalry between Fatty and Cy Klone, the garage owner, over the affections of a pretty schoolteacher. A city chap unites the two rivals when he tries to steal the girl. At annual village ball, amateur talent in vaudeville stunts: Keaton as a wriggling Fatima who charms a long black stocking from a cigar box like a snake. (*MPW*, Nov. 24, 1917, p. 1,205; Dec. 1, 1917, p. 1,359; Dec. 8, 1917, p. 1,483).

1918

Out West.

Rel. Jan. 20; © Feb. 20, 1918; LP 12211.
Scenario: Natalie Talmadge. Scenario Editor: Herbert Warren.
Photog.: George Peters.
Cast: Alice Lake.

The Bell Boy.

Rel. Mar. 18; © Mar. 7, 1918; LP 12194.
Scenario Editor: Herbert Warren. Photog.: George Peters.
Cast: Alice Lake, Charles Dudley, Joe Keaton.

Moonshine.

Rel. May 13; © May 6, 1918; LP 12398.
Scenario Editor: Herbert Warren. Photog.: George Peters.
Cast: Charles Dudley, Alice Lake, Joe Bordeau.

Good Night, Nurse!

Rel. July 8; © June 22, 1918; LP 12589.
Scenario Editor: Herbert Warren. Photog.: George Peters.
Cast: Alice Lake, Kate Price, Joe Bordeau, Joe Keaton.

*The Cook.

Rel. Sept. 15; © Aug. 20, 1918; LP 12764.
Cast: Alice Lake, Glen Cavender.
Summary: Restaurant setting that ends in a chase to a Pacific Coast
Luna Park setting (*MPW,* September 14, 1918, p. 1,609).

1919

*Back Stage.

Rel. Sept. 7; Color (tinted), © Aug. 20, 1919; LP 14114.
Scenario: Jean Havez.
Cast: Molly Malone, John Coogan.
Summary: Burlesque of stage life. Roscoe and Buster do a dance
together (*MPW,* Dec. 20, 1919, p. 1,013).

The Hayseed.

Rel. Oct. 26; © Oct. 13, 1919; LP 14307.
Scenario: Jean Havez.
Cast: Molly Malone.

1920

The Garage.

Rel. Jan. 11; © Dec. 15, 1919; LP 14555.
Scenario: Jean Havez. Photog.: Elgin Lessley.
Cast: Molly Malone, Harry McCoy, Daniel Crimmins, Luke.

Silent Keaton Shorts, 1920–23

Except where noted, all films were written and directed by Keaton and Eddie Cline.

On all shorts, Elgin Lessley is the cameraman; Fred Gabourie, the technical director; Joseph M. Schenck, the producer.

For Metro shorts, the release date given is from the MGM production records; date in parentheses is that given in the trades. For the First National Shorts, release date is that reported in trade publications. Metro Pictures Corp. is the original copyright holder on all the Metro releases.

1920
One Week. 2 reels. Metro.
  Rel. Sept. 7 (Sept. 1); © Sept. 3, 1920; LP 15503.
  Cast: Keaton, Sybil Seely, Joe Roberts.
Convict 13. 2 reels. Metro.
  Rel. Oct. 27; © Oct. 4, 1920; LP 15633.
  Cast: Keaton, Sybil Seely, Joe Roberts, Eddie Cline, Joe Keaton.
  Some filmographies list the rest of the Keaton clan as cast members. Surviving prints are missing approximately one reel.
The Scare Crow. 2 reels. Metro.
  Rel. Nov. 17 (Dec. 22); © Nov. 12, 1920; LP 15806.
  Cast: Keaton, Sybil Seely, Joe Roberts, Joe Keaton, Al St. John, Luke.
Neighbors. 2 reels. Metro.
  Rel. Dec. 22 (Jan., 1921); © Dec. 20, 1920; LP 15947.
  Cast: Keaton, Joe Keaton, Joe Roberts, Virginia Fox, Eddie Cline, James Duffy. Also known as *Backyard; Mailbox.*
  1921
The Haunted House. 2 reels. Metro.
  Rel. Feb. 10 (Feb. 7); © Feb. 7, 1921; LP 16116.
  Cast: Keaton, Virginia Fox, Joe Roberts, Eddie Cline.
*Hard Luck. 2 reels. Metro.
  Rel. March 16; © Mar. 14, 1921; LP 16274.
  Cast: Keaton, Virginia Fox, Joe Roberts.
The High Sign. 2 reels. Metro.
  Rel. Apr. 12; © Apr. 11, 1921; LP 16388.
  Cast: Keaton, Al St. John.
The Goat. 2 reels. Metro.
  Rel. May 18; © May 17, 1921; LP 16562.
  Director/Script: Keaton, Mal St. Clair.
  Cast: Keaton, Joe Roberts, Virginia Fox, Mal St. Clair.

The Play House. 2 reels. First National.
    Rel. October; © Joseph M. Schenck, Oct. 6, 1921; LP 17060.
    Cast: Keaton, Virginia Fox, Joe Roberts.
The Boat. 2 reels. First National.
    Rel. November;© Comique Film Corp., Nov. 10, 1921; LP 17411.
    Cast: Keaton, Sybil Seely, Eddie Cline.
1922
The Paleface. 2 reels (1,960 ft.). First National.
    Rel. January; © Comique Film Corp., Dec. 17, 1921; LP 17487.
    Cast: Keaton, Joe Roberts.
Cops. 2 reels (1,725 ft.). First National.
    Rel. March; © Comique Film Corp., Inc., Feb. 15, 1922; LP 17630.
    Cast: Keaton, Virginia Fox, Joe Roberts, Eddie Cline.
My Wife's Relations. 2 reels (2,096 ft.). First National.
    Rel. May; © Comique Film Corp., Inc., June 12, 1922; LP 17975.
    Cast: Keaton, Kate Price, Monty Collins, Wheezer Dell, Tom Wilson.
The Blacksmith. 2 reels (1,764 ft.). Wash amber. First National.
    Rel. July; © Comique Film Corp., Inc., July 21, 1922; LP 18143.
    Director/Script: Keaton, Mal St. Clair.
    Cast: Keaton, Virginia Fox, Joe Roberts.
The Frozen North. 2 reels (2,049 ft.). First National.
    Rel. Aug.;© Buster Keaton Productions, Inc., Aug. 3, 1922; LP
    18111.
    Cast: Keaton, Bonnie Hill, Freeman Wood, Joe Roberts.
The Electric House. 2 reels (2,231 ft.). Associated–First National.
    Rel. Oct.;© Buster Keaton Productions, Inc., Oct. 19, 1922; LP
    18329.
    Cast: Keaton, Virginia Fox, Joe Roberts. Also listed as being in the
    cast are Joe, Myra, and Louise Keaton.
Day Dreams. 3 reels (2,483 ft.). First National.
    Rel. Nov.;© Buster Keaton Productions, Inc., Sept. 28, 1922; LP
    18735.
    Cast: Keaton, Renée Adorée, Joe Roberts. Existing prints are incomplete.
1923
The Balloonatic. 2 reels (2,152 ft.). Associated–First National.
    Rel. Jan. 22;© Buster Keaton Productions, Inc., Jan. 22, 1923; LP
    18604.
    Cast: Keaton, Phyllis Haver.
The Love Nest. 2 reels (1,975 ft.). Associated–First National.
    Rel. Mar.;© Buster Keaton Productions, Inc., Mar. 6, 1923; LP
    18752.
    Director/Script: Keaton.
    Cast: Keaton, Virginia Fox, Joe Roberts.

Silent Keaton Feature Films, 1920–29

Joseph M. Schenck, who was Keaton's producer up through *Steamboat Bill, Jr.*, is listed in the credits alternately as the producer or as "presenting Keaton in . . ."

1920

The Saphead. 7 reels. Metro.
Rel. Oct. 18; © Oct. 11, 1920; LP 15662.
Presented by John L. Golden and Winchell Smith, in conjunction with Marcus Loew.
Director: Herbert Blaché. Producer: Winchell Smith.
Scenario: June Mathis, based on *The New Henrietta* by Winchell Smith and Victor Mapes, adapted from *The Henrietta,* a play by Bronson Howard. Photog.: Harold Wenstrom.
Cast: Keaton (Bertie Van Alstyne), William H. Crane (Nicholas Van Alstyne), Irving Cummings (Mark Turner), Carol Holloway (Rose Turner), Beulah Booker (Agnes Gates), Jeffery Williams (Hutchins), Edward Jobson (Rev. Murray Hilton), Edward Alexander (Watson Flint), Jack Livingston (Dr. George Wainwright), Edward Connelly (Musgrave), Odette Tyler (Mrs. Cornelia Opdyke), Katherine Albert (Hattie), Helen Holte (Henrietta Reynolds), Alfred Hollingsworth (Hathaway), Henry Clauss (Valet).

1923

Three Ages. 6 reels (5,252 ft.). Metro.
Rel. Sept. 24; © July 25, 1923; LP 19231.
Director: Keaton, Eddie Cline. Script: Clyde Bruckman, Joseph Mitchell, Jean Havez. Photog.: William McGann, Elgin Lessley. Technical Director: Fred Gabourie.
Cast: Keaton (the hero, the boy), Margaret Leahy (the girl), Wallace Beery (the villain), Joe Roberts (the father), Horace Morgan (the emperor), Lillian Lawrence (the mother), Lionel Belmore.
Our Hospitality. 7 reels (6,220 ft.). Metro.
Rel. Nov. 19; © Nov. 20, 1923; LP 19675.
Director: Keaton, John Blystone. Script: Clyde Bruckman, Joseph Mitchell, Jean Havez. Photog.: Elgin Lessley, Gordon Jennings. Technical Director: Fred Gabourie.
Cast: Keaton (William McKay), Natalie Talmadge (Virginia Can-

field), Buster Keaton, Jr. (William McKay as a baby), Joseph Keaton (Lem Doolittle), Kitty Bradbury (Aunt Mary), Joe Roberts (Joseph Canfield), Leonard Clapham (James Canfield), Craig Ward (Lee Canfield), Ralph Bushman (Clayton Canfield), Edward Coxen (John McKay), Jean Dumas (Mrs. McKay), Monty Collins (Rev. Benjamin Dorsey), James Duffy (Sam Gardner).

1924

Sherlock, Jr. 5 reels (4,065 ft.). Metro.
  Rel. Apr. 21; © April 22, 1924; LP 20125.
  Director: Keaton, Roscoe Arbuckle (?). Script: Clyde Bruckman, Jean Havez, Joseph Mitchell. Photog.: Byron Houck, Elgin Lessley. Technical Director: Fred Gabourie. Costumes: Clare West.
  Cast: Keaton (Sherlock, Jr.), Kathryn McGuire (the girl), Ward Crane (the rival), Joseph Keaton (her father), Horace Morgan, Jane Connelly, Erwin Connelly, Ford West, George Davis, John Patrick, Ruth Holley.

The Navigator. 6 reels (5,600 ft.), tinted. Metro-Goldwyn.
  Rel. Oct. 13; © Oct. 14, 1924; LP 20689.
  Director: Keaton, Donald Crisp. Script: Clyde Bruckman, Joseph Mitchell, Jean Havez. Photog.: Elgin Lessley, Byron Houck. Technical Director: Fred Gabourie. Electrician: Denver Harmon.
  Cast: Keaton (Rollo Treadway), Kathryn McGuire (Betsy O'Brien), Frederick Vroom ("Cappy" John O'Brien, her father), Noble Johnson, Clarence Burton, H. M. Clugston, the liner *Buford*.

1925

Seven Chances. 6 reels (5,113 ft.), Technicolor sequences. Metro-Goldwyn.
  Rel. Mar. 16; © Apr. 22, 1925; LP 21376.
  Director: Keaton. Script: Jean Havez, Clyde Bruckman, Joseph Mitchell, based on Roi Cooper Megrue's *Seven Chances*, a comedy in three acts, produced by David Belasco. Photog.: Elgin Lessley, Byron Houck. Technical director: Fred Gabourie. Electrician: Denver Harmon.
  Cast: Keaton (Jimmy Shannon), T. Roy Barnes (his partner), Snitz Edwards (a lawyer), Ruth Dwyer (the girl), Frankie Raymond (her mother), Jules Cowles (hired man), Erwin Connelly (clergyman), Loro Bara, Marion Harlan, Hazel Deane, Pauline Toler, Judy King, Eugenie Burkette, Edna Hammon, Barbara Pierce, Jean Arthur, Connie Evans, Rosalind Mooney.

Go West. 7 reels (6,256 ft.). Metro-Goldwyn.
  Rel. Nov. 1; © Nov. 23, 1925; LP 220481.
  Director/Story: Keaton. Script: Raymond Cannon. Photog.: Elgin Lessley, Bert Haines.

Cast: Keaton (Friendless), Howard Truesdale (owner of the Diamond Bar Ranch), Kathleen Myers (his daughter), Ray Thompson (the foreman), Brown Eyes (herself/a cow).

1926

Battling Butler. 7 reels (6,970 ft.). MGM.

Rel. Sept. 19; © Aug. 30, 1926; LP 23068.

Director: Keaton. Script: Paul Gerard Smith, Albert Boasberg, Lex Neal, Charles Smith, based on the musical play *Battling Butler* (Book: Stanley Brightman and Austin Melford; Music: Philip Brabham; Lyrics: Douglas Furber). Photog.: Dev Jennings, Bert Haines.

Cast: Keaton (Alfred Butler), Sally O'Neil (the girl), Snitz Edwards (his valet), Francis McDonald (Alfred "Battling Butler"), Mary O'Brien (his wife), Tom Wilson (his trainer), Eddie Borden (his manager), Walter James (the girl's father), Buddy Fine (the girl's brother).

1927

The General. 8 reels (7,500 ft.). United Artists.

Rel. Feb. 5; © Dec. 22, 1926; LP 23453.

Director: Keaton, Clyde Bruckman. Script: Al Boasberg, Charles Smith. Photog.: Dev Jennings, Bert Haines. Technical Director: Fred Gabourie. Electrician: Denver Harmon. Editor: J. S. Kell. Assistant Director: Harry Barnes.

Cast: Keaton (Johnnie Gray), Glen Cavender (Capt. Anderson), Jim Farley (Gen. Thatcher), Frederick Vroom (a Southern general), Marian Mack (Annabelle Lee), Charles Smith (her father), Frank Barnes (her brother), Joseph Keaton, Mike Donlin, Tom Nawn (Union generals), Ross McCutcheon (one of the Northern raiders).

Remade as *A Southern Yankee* (1948, MGM).

College. 6 reels (5,916 ft.). United Artists.

Rel. Sept. 10; © Sept. 10, 1927; LP 24409.

Director: James W. Horne. Supervisor: Harry Brand. Script: Carl Harbaugh, Bryan Foy. Photog.: Dev Jennings, Bert Haines. Technical Director: Fred Gabourie. Editor: J. S. Kell.

Cast: Keaton (Ronald), Ann Cornwall (the girl), Flora Bramley (her friend), Harold Goodwin (a rival), Buddy Mason, Grant Withers (his friends), Snitz Edwards (the dean), Carl Harbaugh (crew coach), Sam Crawford (baseball coach), Florence Turner (Ronald's mother), Paul Goldsmith, Morton Kaer, Bud Houser, Kenneth Grumbles, Charles Borah, Leighton Dye, Lee Barnes, Shorty Worden, Robert Boling, Erick Mack, University of Southern California baseball team.

1928

Steamboat Bill, Jr. 7 reels (6,400 ft.). United Artists.

Rel. May 12; © June 2, 1928; LP 25362.

Director: Charles F. Reisner. Script: Carl Harbaugh. Photog.: Dev Jennings, Bert Haines. Technical Director: Fred Gabourie. Editor: J. S. Kell. Assistant Director: Sandy Roth.

Cast: Keaton (Steamboat Bill, Jr.; William Canfield, Jr.), Ernest Torrence (Steamboat Bill), Tom Lewis (Tom Carter, his first mate), Tom McGuire (John James King, his rival), Marion Byron (Mary King, his daughter).

The Cameraman. 8 reels (6,995 ft.). MGM.

Rel. Sept. 22; © Sept. 15, 1928; LP 25722.

Director: Edward Sedgwick. Script: Richard Schayer. Story: Clyde Bruckman, Lew Lipton. Titles: Joseph Farnham. Photog.: Elgin Lessley, Reggie Lanning. Technical Director: Fred Gabourie. Editor: Hugh Wynn, Basil Wrangell (sources disagree on editor credit).

Cast: Keaton (Luke Shannon), Marceline Day (Sally), Harold Goodwin (Stagg), Harry Gribbon (cop), Sidney Bracy (editor), Edward Brophy (dressing room companion), William Irving (photographer), Vernon Dent (man in tight bathing suit).

All circulating prints are missing footage and run approximately 70 min.

Remade as *Watch the Birdie* (1950, MGM).

1929

Spite Marriage. 9 reels (7,047 ft., version with synchronized sound effects; 6,500 ft., silent version). MGM.

Rel. Apr. 6; © Apr. 22, 1929; LP 329.

Director/Producer: Edward Sedgwick. Story: Lew Lipton. Adaptation: Ernest S. Pagano. Continuity: Richard Schayer. Titles: Robert Hopkins. Photog.: Reggie Lanning. Art Director: Cedric Gibbons. Editor: Frank Sullivan. Costumes: David Cox. Supervisor: Lawrence Weingarten.

Cast: Keaton (Elmer), Dorothy Sebastian (Trilby Drew), Edward Earle (Lionel Denmore), Leila Hyams (Ethyle Norcrosse), William Bechtel (Nussbaum), John Byron (Giovanni Scarzi), Hank Mann (stage manager), Pat Harmon (ship captain).

Remade as *I Dood It* (1943, MGM).

Sound Feature Films Starring Keaton, 1929–1968

1929

The Hollywood Revue of 1929. (11,669 ft.). B & W, with color sequences. MGM.

Rel. Nov. 23; © Sept. 23, 1929; LP 800.

Director: Charles Reisner. Producer: Harry Rapf. Dialogue: Al Boasberg, Robert E. Hopkins. Photog.: John Arnold, Irving G. Ries, Maximilian Fabian, John M. Nickolaus. Editor: William S. Gray, Cameron K. Wood. Art Director: Cedric Gibbons, Richard Day. Recording Engineer: Douglas Shearer.

Cast: Keaton as an Oriental dancer in "The Dance of the Sea." Also appears with other principals in the finale, "Singing in the Rain." Other stars include John Gilbert, Norma Shearer, Joan Crawford, Marion Davies, Cliff Edwards, Laurel & Hardy, etc.

Current running time approximately 113 min.

Wir Schalten Um Auf Hollywood (German version: *The Hollywood Revue*).

Director: Frank Reicher. Adaptation: Paul Morgan.

1930

Free and Easy. 93 min. (8,413 ft.; 5,240 ft., silent version). MGM.

Rel. Mar. 22; © April 2, 1930; LP 1193.

Director/Producer: Edward Sedgwick. Scenario: Richard Schayer. Dialogue: Al Boasberg. Adaptation: Paul Dickey. Photog.: Leonard Smith. Editor: William Le Vanway, George Todd. Art Director: Cedric Gibbons. Recording Engineer: Douglas Shearer.

Cast: Keaton (Elmer Butts), Anita Page (Elvira Plunkett, "Miss Gopher City"), Trixie Friganza (Ma Plunkett), Robert Montgomery (Larry), Fred Niblo (director), Edgar Dearing (officer), David Burton (director), Edward Brophy (stage manager); playing themselves: Gwen Lee, John Miljan, Lionel Barrymore, in bedroom scene; William Collier, Sr., as a master of ceremonies; William Haines, as a guest; Dorothy Sebastian, Karl Dane, in cave scene; Jackie Coogan; Cecil B. De Mille; Arthur Lange; Joe Farnham.

Working title: *On the Set.* Television title: *Easy Go.*

Le Metteur en Scene (French version: *Free and Easy*).

Titles: Alexander Stein, Allen Byre.

Estrellados (Spanish version: *Free and Easy*).

Cast: Keaton, Raquel Torres, Don Alvarado, Maria Calvo, Emile Chautard.

Doughboys. 81 min. (7,325 ft.). MGM.

Rel. Aug. 30; © Sept. 8, 1930; LP 1540.

Director: Edward Sedgwick. Scenario: Richard Schayer. Dialogue: Al Boasberg, Schayer. Story: Boasberg, Sidney Lazarus. Photog.:

Leonard Smith. Editor: William Le Vanway. Art Director: Cedric Gibbons. Recording Engineer: Douglas Shearer.

Cast: Keaton (Elmer Stuyvesant), Sally Eilers (Mary), Cliff Edwards (Nescopeck), Edward Brophy (Sergeant Brophy), Victor Potel (Svendenburg), Arnold Korff (Gustave), Frank Mayo (Captain Scott), Pitzy Katz (Abie Cohn), William Steele (Lieutenant Randolph).

Working Title: *The Big Shot.*

De Fronte, Marchen (German version: *Doughboys.* Spanish version: *Doughboys;* title unknown).

Cast: Keaton, Conchita Montenegro, Juan de Landa, Romualdo Tirado.

1931

Parlor, Bedroom and Bath. 73 min. (6,563 ft.). MGM.

Rel. Feb. 28; © May 1, 1931; LP 2185.

Director: Edward Sedgwick. Adaptation: Richard Schayer, Robert E. Hopkins, from the play by Charles W. Bell and Mark Swan. Photog.: Leonard Smith. Editor: William Le Vanway. Recording Engineer: Karl Zint.

Cast: Keaton (Reginald Irving), Charlotte Greenwood (Polly Hathaway), Reginald Denny (Jeffery Haywood), Cliff Edwards (bellhop), Dorothy Christy (Angelica Embrey), Joan Peers (Nita Leslie), Sally Eilers (Virginia Embrey), Natalie Moorhead (Leila Crofton), Edward Brophy (detective), Walter Merrill (Frederick Leslie), Sidney Bracy (butler).

Keaton used his own home in this film. Previous film version: Metro, 1920.

Buster se Marie (French version: *Parlor, Bedroom and Bath*). 80 min. MGM.

Director: Edward Brophy, Claude Autant-Lara. French Dialogue: Yves Mirande. Dialogue Director: André Luguet.

Cast: Keaton (Reggie), André Luguet (Jef), Jeanne Helbling (Virginia), Françoise Rosay (Angelique), André Berley (le commissaire de police), Mona Goya, Mireille, Georgette Rhodes, Lya Lys, Rolla Norman, George Davis, Paul Morgan.

Casanova Wider Willen (German version: *Parlor, Bedroom and Bath*).

Director: Edward Brophy. Cast: Keaton, Paul Morgan, Marion Lessing, Egon von Jordan, Françoise Rosay, Leni Stengel, Gerda Mann, George Davis, Wolfgang Zilzer.

Sidewalks of New York. 70 min. MGM.

Rel. Sept. 26; © Sept. 21, 1931; LP 2490.

Director: Jules White, Zion Myers. Story/Scenario: George Landy, Paul Gerard Smith. Dialogue: Robert E. Hopkins, Eric Hatch. Photog.: Leonard Smith. Editor: Charles Hochberg.

Cast: Keaton (Harmon), Anita Page (Margie), Cliff Edwards (Poggle), Frank Rowan (Butch), Norman Phillips, Jr. (Clipper), Frank La Rue (sergeant), Oscar Apfel (judge), Syd Saylor (Mulvaney), Clark Marshall (Lefty).

1932
The Passionate Plumber. 73 min. MGM.
  Rel. Feb. 6; © Feb. 8, 1932; LP 2826.
  Director: Edward Sedgwick. Adaptation: Laurence E. Johnson, from *Her Cardboard Lover,* a play by Jacques Deval. Dialogue: Ralph Spence. Photog.: Norbert Brodine. Editor: William S. Gray.
  Cast: Keaton (Elmer Tuttle), Jimmy Durante (McCracken), Irene Purcell (Patricia Alden), Polly Moran (Albine), Gilbert Roland (Tony Lagorce), Mona Maris (Nina), Maude Eburne (Aunt Charlotte), Henry Armetta (bouncer), Paul Porcasi (Paul Le Maire), Jean Del Val (chauffeur), August Tollaire (General Bouschay), Edward Brophy (unbilled bit outside beauty parlor).
  Other film versions: *The Cardboard Lover* (MGM, 1928); *Her Cardboard Lover* (MGM, 1942).
Le Plombier Amoureux (French version: *The Passionate Plumber*).
  Director: Claude Autant-Lara.
  Cast: Keaton, Purcell, Durante, Maris, Moran, Jeanette Ferney, Barbara Leonard, Eburne, Del Val, George Davis, Fred Perry.
Speak Easily. 80 min. MGM.
  Rel. Aug. 13; no U.S. copyright.
  Director: Edward Sedgwick. Adaptation: Ralph Spence, Laurence E. Johnson, from the six-part story, "Footlights," by Clarence Budington Kelland. Photog.: Harold Wenstrom. Editor: William Le Vanway. Costumes: Arthur Appell.
  Cast: Keaton (Professor Timoleon Zanders Post), Jimmy Durante (James), Ruth Selwyn (Pansy Peets), Thelma Todd (Eleanor Espere), Hedda Hopper (Mrs. Peets), William Pawley (Griffo), Sidney Toler (stage director), Lawrence Grant (Dr. Bolton), Henry Armetta (Tony), Edward Brophy (Reno).
  Originally published in the *Saturday Evening Post;* later published as a novel under title *Speak Easily* (Harper & Brothers, 1932).

1933
What! No Beer? 70 min. MGM.
  Rel. Feb. 10; © March 13, 1933; LP 3711.
  Director: Edward Sedgwick. Script: Carey Wilson. Story: Robert E. Hopkins. Additional dialogue: Jack Cluett. Photog.: Harold Wenstrom. Editor: Frank Sullivan.
  Cast: Keaton (Elmer J. Butts), Jimmy Durante (Jimmy Potts), Ros-

coe Ates (Schultz), Phyllis Barry (Hortense), John Miljan (Butch Lorado), Henry Armetta (Tony), Edward Brophy (Spike Moran), Charles Dunbar (Mulligan), Charles Giblyn (chief).

1934

Le Roi des Champs Elysees. 7 reels (70 min.). Nero Film Production, released in France by Paramount. No U. S. release.
Director: Max Nosseck. Producer: Seymour Nebenzal. Supervisor: Robert Siodmak. Script: Arnold Lipp, with dialogue by Yves Mirande. Photog.: Robert Le Febvre. Art Director: Hugues Laurent, Jacques-Laurent Atthalin. Music: Joe Hajos.
Cast: Keaton (Buster Garnier/Jim Le Balafre), Paulette Dubost (Germaine), Colette Darfeuil (Simone), Madeline Guitty (Mme. Garnier), Jacques Dumesnil, Pierre Pierade, Gaston Dupray, Paul Clerget, Frank Maurice, Pitouto, Lucien Callamand.

See: William K. Everson. "Rediscovery: Keaton, *Le Roi des Champs Elysées,*" *Films in Review.* 27, No. 10 (December 1976).

1936

The Invader. 61 min. British & Continental (MGM). Released in U. S. by J. H. Hoffberg under the title *An Old Spanish Custom.*
Rel. Jan. 2; no U. S. copyright.
Director: Adrian Brunel. Producers: Sam Spiegel, Harold Richman.
Script: Edwin Greenwood. Photog.: Eugene Schuftan.
Editor: Dan Birt. Music: John Greenwood, George Rubens. Recording Engineer: Scanlan.
Cast: Keaton (Leander Proudfoot), Lupita Tovar (Lupita Malez), Esme Percy (José), Lyn Harding (Gonzalo Gonzalez), Webster Booth (serenader), Andrea Malandrinos (Carlos), Hilda Moreno (Carmita), Clifford Heatherley (David Cheeseman). Filmed at Interworld Studios, Worton Hall, Isleworth.

1946

El Moderno Barba Azul. 90 min. Alsa Films (Mexico).
Not rel. in the U. S.
Director: Jaime Salvador.
Cast: Keaton, Angel Garasa, Virginia Seret, Luis Bareiro, Fernando Sotto.

1968

The Great Stone Face. 93 min. 16mm. Funnyman Productions, Inc.
Director/Script: Vernon P. Becker. Editor: William C. Dalzell. Narrator: Henry Morgan.

Cast: Keaton in a compilation film that covers his life and films from age three until the late twenties. Includes excerpts from *Coney Island, Cops, Day Dreams, The Balloonatic,* and *The General.*

Sound Feature Films with Keaton in Subordinate Roles, 1939–74

1939

Hollywood Cavalcade. 96 min. Twentieth Century–Fox.
Rel. Oct. 13; © Oct. 13, 1939; LP 9213.
Director: Irving Cummings. Producer: Darryl F. Zanuck. Script: Ernest Pascal. Story: Hilary Lynn, Brown Holmes, based on idea by Lou Breslow. Photog.: Allen M. Davey, Ernest Palmer. Editor: Walter Thompson. "Keystone Kops" sequences directed by Mal St. Clair; Technical Advisor: Mack Sennett.
Cast: Keaton as himself, Alice Faye, Don Ameche, and others.

1940

The Villain Still Pursued Her. 65 min. Franklin-Blank Productions, released by RKO.
Rel. Oct. 11; © Oct. 4, 1940; LP 10044.
Director: Edward Cline. Producer: Harold B. Franklin. Script: Elbert Franklin. Additional Dialogue: Ethel La Blanche. Photog.: Lucien Ballard. Editor: Arthur Hilton.
Cast: Keaton (William), Hugh Herbert (Healy), Anita Louise (Mary), Alan Mowbray (Cribbs), Richard Cromwell (Edward), and others.
Based on the play *The Fallen Saved,* presented for most of this century as *The Drunkard.*
Li'l Abner. 78 min. Vogue Pictures, released by RKO.
Rel. Nov. 1; © Nov. 1, 1940; LP 10126.
Director: Albert S. Rogell. Script: Charles Kerr, Tyler Johnson. Story: Ben Oakland, Milton Drake, Milton Berle, based on the comic strip by Al Capp. Editor: Otto Ludwig, Donn Hayes.
Cast: Keaton, Granville Owen, Martha O'Driscoll, Mona Ray.

1943

Forever and a Day. 104 min. Anglo-American Productions, released by RKO.
Rel. Mar. 26; © March 19, 1943; LP 11962.
Director: Cedric Hardwicke, and others.
Cast: In the second episode, Keaton and Hardwicke as plumbers

installing a bathtub. With Charles Laughton as the butler, and Jessie Matthews.

1944

San Diego, I Love You. 83 min. Universal.

Rel. Sept. 29; © Sept. 15, 1944; LP 12905.

Director: Reginald Le Borg. Producer/Script: Michael Fessier, Ernest Pagano, based on a story by Ruth McKenney and Richard Branstein. Photog.: Hal Mohr. Editor: Charles Maynard.

Cast: Keaton (bus driver), Jon Hall, Louise Allbritton, Edward Everett Horton, Eric Blore, and others.

1945

That's the Spirit. 93 min. Universal.

Rel. June 1; © Apr. 24, 1945; LP 13254.

Director: Charles Lamont. Producer/Script: Michael Fessier, Ernest Pagano. Photog.: Charles Van Enger. Editor: Fred R. Reitshans, Jr.

Cast: Keaton (as L. M.), Peggy Ryan, Jack Oakie, and others.

That Night with You. 84 min. Universal.

Rel. Sept. 28; © Sept. 21, 1945; LP 13496.

Director: William A. Seiter. Executive Producer: Howard Benedict. Producer/Script: Michael Fessier, Ernest Pagano, based on a story by Arnold Belgard. Photog.: Charles Van Enger. Editor: Fred R. Reitshans, Jr.

Cast: Keaton, Franchot Tone, Susanna Foster, David Bruce, and others.

1946

God's Country. 7 reels. Color. Action Pictures, released by Screen Guild Productions.

Rel. Apr.; © May 18, 1946; LP 607.

Director/Script: Robert Tansey. Producer: William B. David. Photog.: Carl Wester.

Cast: Keaton, Robert Lowery, Helen Gilbert.

1949

The Loveable Cheat. 74 min. Skyline Pictures, released by Film Classics, Inc.

Rel. May 11; © May 11, 1949; LP 2317.

Director: Richard Oswald. Producer/Script: Richard Oswald, Edward Lewis. Photog.: Paul Ivano. Editor: Douglas Bagier.

Cast: Keaton, Charles Ruggles, Peggy Ann Garner, Richard Ney, Alan Mowbray. Based on comic play by Balzac about a rogue who manages to forestall a horde of creditors until a long-lost partner reappears with a fortune.

In the Good Old Summertime. 102 min. Color. MGM.
  Rel. July 29; © June 23, 1949; LP 2370.
  Director: Robert Z. Leonard. Producer: Joe Pasternak. Script: Samson Raphaelson. Adaptation: Albert Hackett, Frances Goodrich, Ivan Tors, based on a play by Miklos Laszlo. Photog.: Henry Stradling. Editor: Adrienne Fazan.
  Cast: Keaton (Hickey), Judy Garland, Van Johnson, S. Z. "Cuddles" Sakall.
  Previous film version: *The Shop Around the Corner* (1940, MGM).
You're My Everything. 94 min. Color. Twentieth Century–Fox.
  Rel. Aug.; © July 16, 1949; LP 2568.
  Director: Walter Lang. Producer: Lamar Trotti. Script: Lamar Trotti, Will H. Hays, Jr. Original story: George Jessel. Photog.: Arthur E. Arling. Editor.: J. Watson Webb, Jr.
  Cast: Keaton (butler), Dan Dailey, Anne Baxter, Anne Revere, and others.

  1950
Sunset Boulevard. 110 min. Paramount.
  Rel. Aug.; © Aug. 4, 1950; LP 260.
  Director: Billy Wilder. Producer: Charles Brackett. Script: Brackett, Wilder, D. M. Marshman, Jr., from short story "A Can of Beans." Photog.: John F. Seitz. Editor: Doane Harrison, Arthur Schmidt.
  Cast: Keaton (as himself) in bridge game with Anna Q. Nilsson, H. B. Warner, and Gloria Swanson. Also stars William Holden, Erich von Stroheim.

  1953
Limelight. 143 min. Celebrated Films Corp., rel. by United Artists.
  Rel. Feb. 6; © Oct. 23, 1952; (in notice: 1951); LP 2006.
  Director/Producer/Script: Charles Chaplin.
  Cast: Keaton as piano accompanist in sketch with Chaplin. Claire Bloom.
L'incantevole Nemica. 86 min. Orso Film (Rome), Lambar Film (Paris).
  Not rel. in U. S.
  Director: Claudio Gora.
  Cast: Keaton, Robert Lamoureux, Carlo Campanini, Raymond Bussieres, Silvana Pampanini.

  1956
Around the World in 80 Days. 148 min. Color, 70 mm. Todd A-O.
  Michael Todd Co., rel. by United Artists.
  © Oct. 17, 1956; LP 9127.

Director: Michael Anderson. Script: S. J. Perelman, James Poe, John Farrow, based on the Jules Verne novel. Photog.: Lionel Lindon.
Cast: Keaton, David Niven, Cantinflas, Robert Newton, Shirley MacLaine.

1960
When Comedy Was King. 81 min. Ro-Co Productions, rel. by Twentieth Century–Fox.
 Rel. Mar.; © Dec. 31, 1959; LP 15646.
Producer/Script: Robert Youngson. Assoc. Producer: Herman Gelbspan. Narrator: Dwight Weist. Musical Conductor: Sylvan Levin. Music: Ted Royal. Music arr.: Ted Royal, Charles L. Cooke. Music supervision: Herman Fuchs, Louis Turchin.
Cast: Keaton, Chaplin, Laurel and Hardy, and others in a compilation of silent comedy sequences from Sennett (1914) to Roach (1928).
The Adventures of Huckleberry Finn. 107 min. Color, CinemaScope. MGM.
 Rel. June 17; © Mar. 7, 1960; LP 15872.
Director: Michael Curtiz. Producer: Samuel Goldwyn, Jr. Script: James Lee, from the Mark Twain novel. Photog.: Ted McCord. Editor: Frederic Steinkamp.
Cast: Keaton as lion tamer, Tony Randall, Eddie Hodges.

1962
The Great Chase. 79 min. Color (tinted). Janus Films.
 Rel. Dec. 20; no copyright.
A Saul J. Turell–Paul Killiam Presentation. Producer: Harvey Cort. Script: Cort, with Turell, Killiam. Editor: Cort, Turell. Narrator: Frank Gallop.
Cast: Keaton in scenes from *The General,* Douglas Fairbanks, Sr., William S. Hart, Lillian Gish, and others. A Mack Sennett and a Mabel Normand sequence added in 1975.
Ten Girls Ago. Color, CinemaScope. Am-Can Productions.
 Never rel.
Director: Harold Daniels. Producer: Edward A. Gollin. Script: Peter Farrow, Diane Lampert. Photog.: Lee Garmes, Jackson M. Samuels. Music Director: Joseph Harnell. Music/Lyrics: Diane Lampert, Sammy Fain. Choreography: Bill Foster.
Cast: Keaton, Bert Lahr, Eddie Foy, Jr., Dion, Austin Willis, Jan Miner, Jennifer Billingsley, Risella Bain.

See: Peter Morris, ed. *Canadian Feature Films, 1913–69.* Ottawa: Canadian Film Institute, 1974.

1963

30 Years of Fun. 85 min. Twentieth Century–Fox.
Rel. Feb. 12; © Dec. 31, 1962; LP 23683.
Producer/Script: Robert Youngson. Music: Bernard Green, Jack Shaindlin. "Bring Back the Laughter": words, Youngson; orchestrations, Green, Milton Weinstein.
Cast: Keaton in excerpts from *Cops, Day Dreams, The Balloonatic.* Chaplin, Laurel and Hardy, Langdon, and others.

It's a Mad, Mad, Mad, Mad World. 192 min. Color, 35 & 70 mm (Ultra Panavision, Cinerama). United Artists.
Rel. Nov. 7; © Nov. 7, 1963; LP 28452.
Producer/Director: Stanley Kramer. Script/Original story: William and Tania Rose. Photog.: Ernest Lazlo. Editor: Fred Knudtson.
Cast: Keaton, as Jimmy the crook. Spencer Tracy, Milton Berle, Sid Caesar, and others.

The Sound of Laughter. 75 min. A Union Films Release.
Rel. Dec. 17; no copyright.
Director: John O'Shaughnessy. Producer: Barry B. Yellen, Irvin S. Dorfman. Script: Fred Saidy. Music: Robert Waldman. Narrator: Ed Wynn.
Cast: Keaton in excerpts from two Educational shorts: a baseball game skit (*One-Run Elmer*) and competing on Major Crow's Amateur Hour (*Grand Slam Opera*). Danny Kaye, Bing Crosby, Bob Hope.

1964

Pajama Party. 85 min. Color. American International.
Rel. Nov. 11; © Nov. 11, 1964; LP 29677.
Director: Don Weis. Producer: James H. Nicholson, Samuel Z. Arkoff. Script: Louis M. Heyward. Photog.: Floyd Crosby. Editor: Fred Feitshans, Eve Newman.
Cast: Keaton as Chief Rotten Eagle. Tommy Kirk, Annette Funicello, Elsa Lanchester, and others.

1965

Beach Blanket Bingo. 98 min. Color. American International.
Rel. Apr. 15; © April 14, 1965; LP 30614.
Director: William Asher. Producer: James H. Nicholson, Samuel Z. Arkoff. Script: Asher, Leo Townsend. Photog.: Floyd Crosby. Editor: Fred Feitshans, Eve Newman.
Cast: Keaton as himself. Frankie Avalon, Annette Funicello, Deborah Walley, and others.

How to Stuff a Wild Bikini. 90 min. Color. American International.
Rel. July 14; © July 14, 1965; LP 31862.
Director: William Asher. Producer: James H. Nicholson, Samuel Z.

Arkoff. Script: Asher, Leo Townsend. Photog.: Floyd Crosby. Editor: Fred Feitshans, Eve Newman.
Cast: Keaton as the witch doctor Bwana. Annette Funicello, Dwayne Hickman, Brian Donlevy, Mickey Rooney, and others.

Sergeant Deadhead. 90 min. Color. American International.
Rel. Aug. 18; © Aug. 11, 1965; LP 31861.
Director: Norman Taurog. Producer: James H. Nicholson, Samuel Z. Arkoff. Script: Louis M. Heyward. Photog.: Floyd Crosby. Editor: Ronald Sinclair, Fred Feitshans, Eve Newman.
Cast: Keaton as Private Blinken. Frankie Avalon, Deborah Walley, Cesar Romero, and others.

1966
A Funny Thing Happened on the Way to the Forum. 99 min. Color. United Artists.
Rel. Oct. 16; © Oct. 15, 1966; LP 37133.
Director: Richard Lester. Producer: Melvin Frank. Script: Frank, Michael Pertwee, from a play by Burt Shevelove, Larry Gelbart. Photog.: Nicholas Roeg. Editor: John Victor Smith.
Cast: Keaton as Erronius. Zero Mostel, Phil Silvers, Jack Gilford.

1967
War Italian Style. 84 min. Color. Techniscope. American International.
Rel. Jan. 18; © Jan. 11, 1967; LP 34004.
Director: Luigi Scattini. Producer: Fulvio Lucisano. Script: Franco Castellano, Pipolo. Photog.: Fausto Zuccoli.
Cast: Keaton in a silent role as General Von Kassler. Franco Franchi, Ciccio Ingrassia, Martha Hyer, Fred Clark.
Italian title: *Due Marines e Uno Generale.*

1970
Four Clowns. 97 min. Twentieth Century–Fox.
Rel. Sept.; © Dec. 31, 1969; LP 39199.
Producer/Script: Robert Youngson. Assoc. Producer: Raymond Rohauer. Asst. Producer: Herbert Gelbspan, Alfred Dahlem. Narrator: Jay Jackson.
Cast: Keaton in *Seven Chances.* Laurel and Hardy, Charley Chase.

1974
The Three Stooges Follies. 116 min. Columbia.
Rel. Nov.
A compilation of Columbia shorts from the thirties and forties, mainly starring the Three Stooges, but also Vera Vague, Krazy Kat, and Keaton in *Nothing but Pleasure* (1940).

Miscellaneous Shorts, 1922–66

1922

Screen Snapshots—#3. 2 reels. Silent. Pathé Exchange.
© June 26, 1922; LU 17999.
Produced by Jack Cohn and Louis Lewyn.

1929

The Voice of Hollywood. 1 reel. Silent. Produced by Tiffany Productions.
Keaton performs some visual gags in a Hollywood night club.

1931

The Stolen Jools. 2 reels. Presented by National Variety Artists, distributed by Paramount and National Screen Service.
Rel. Apr.
Director: William McGann. Producer: Pat Casey. Supervisor: E. K. Nadel.
Cast: All-star, including Norma Shearer, Wallace Beery, Joan Crawford, and others in a benefit short for what is now the Will Rogers Memorial Hospital for Respiratory Diseases. Keaton as a Keystone Kop.
Alternate title: *The Slippery Pearls.*

1936

La Fiesta de Santa Barbara. 2 reels. MGM Musical Revue.
© Apr. 2, 1936; LP 6294.
Producer: Louis Lewyn. Script: Alexander Van Dorn.
Cast: Keaton, Chester Conklin, and others, at a carnival.

1950

Un Duel à Mort. Films Azur, Paris.
Not rel. in U. S.
Director: Pierre Blondy. Script: Keaton, Blondy.
Cast: Keaton, Antonin Berval.

1952

Paradise for Buster. 39 min., 16mm. Deere and Co., produced by Wilding Picture Productions.
© Oct. 15, 1952; LP 2029.
Director: Del Lord. Script: J. P. Prindle, John Grey, Hal Goodwin. Music: Albert Glasser. Editor: William Minnerly. Supervisors: H. M. Railsback, G. M. Rohrbach.
Cast: Keaton in a pantomime comedy about an unsuccessful book-

keeper who inherits a run-down farm and solves his financial difficulties by turning his well-stocked lake into a fisherman's paradise.

1960

The Devil to Pay. 28 min., 16mm. Produced by Education Research Films for the National Association of Wholesalers.
Director: Herb Skoble. Production: Rodel Productions, Inc. Script/Editor: Cummins-Betts. Video: Del Ankers, Fritz Roland. Audio: Nelson Funk. Art Director: Peter Masters, Joseph W. Swanson.
Cast: Keaton (Diablos), Ralph Dunne (the furnace man), Ruth Gillette (Minnie), Marion Morris (Esther), John Rodney (the druggist).

1961

Sad Clowns. 27 min., 16mm. Sterling Educational Films.
Producer/Narrator: Saul J. Turell, Paul Killiam. Research: William K. Everson. Supervising Editor: Ray Angus. From *The History of Motion Pictures* series. Also televised as an episode of *Silents, Please.* Discusses the widely different styles and techniques of Chaplin, Keaton, and Langdon, showing examples of their comedy, both slapstick and subtle.

1963

The Triumph of Lester Snapwell. 22 min. Color, 16mm. Eastman Kodak Co. © March 25, 1963; MU 7288.
Cast: Keaton in an updated version of a two-reel silent comedy which traces the highlights in the development of the camera. Includes historical sequences that deal with the period 1868–88, the 1920s, and the period from 1950 to today to illustrate the operating case of the modern camera as compared with its predecessors.

1965

Buster Keaton Rides Again. 56 min. National Film Board of Canada.
Director/Photog.: John Spotton. Producer: Julian Biggs. Commentary: Donald Brittain.
Cast: Keaton, Eleanor Keaton. Informal view of Keaton: how he relaxes, plots the next day's action for his motion picture, and recalls gags he employed in the past. Filmed during the making of *The Railrodder.*

Film. 22 min., 16mm. Grove Press.
Director: Alan Schneider. Producer: Evergreen Theatre. Script: Samuel Beckett. Photog.: Boris Kaufman. Editor: Sydney Meyers.
Cast: Keaton in a one-character drama without dialogue based on Berkeley's theory that "to be is to be perceived." As in all of Beck-

ett's work, elements of comedy surround the philosophical founda-
tion.

The Railrodder. 21 min. Color. National Film Board of Canada.
Director/Script: Gerald Petterton. Producer: Julian Biggs. Photog.:
Robert Humble. Editor: J. Kirkpatrick. Music: Eldon Rathburn.
Cast: Keaton on a journey from Atlantic to Pacific coasts of Canada
aboard a small motorized handcart on the railway.

1966

The Scribe. 30 min. Color, 16mm. Association Instructional Materials,
made by Construction Safety Association of Ontario, Toronto.
Director: John Sebert. Producer: Ann and Kenneth Heeley-Ray.
Exec. Producer: Raymond Walters, James Collier. Script: Paul
Sutherland, Clifford Braggins. Photog.: Mike Lente. Music: Quar-
tet Productions, Ltd. Film/Sound Editor: Kenneth Heeley-Ray. A
Film-Tele Production.
Cast: Keaton as cleaning man turned newspaper reporter who
visits a large construction job to do a story on safety.

Educational Films, 1934–37

All films (except where noted): Presented by E. W.
Hammons; Producer, E. H. Allen; Director, Charles
Lamont; Rel. by Twentieth Century–Fox. Where
only the © date is listed, that is also the rel. date.

For descriptions of the Educational and Columbia
shorts, see Leonard Maltin, *The Great Movie Shorts*
(Crown, 1972).

1934

The Gold Ghost. 2 reels (22 min.).
© March 16, 1934; LP 4555.
Story: Ewart Adamson, Nick Barrows. Adaptation/Continuity: Er-
nest Pagano, Charles Lamont.
Cast: Keaton, Dorothy Dix, William Worthington, Lloyd Ingraham,
Warren Hymer, Leo Willis, Joe Young, Al Thompson, Billy Engle.

Allez Oop. 2 reels.
© May 31, 1934; LP 4728.
Story: Ernest Pagano, Ewart Adamson.
Cast: Keaton, Dorothy Sebastian, Harry Myers, George Lewis.

1935

Palooka from Paducah. 2 reels (20 min.).
Rel. Jan. 11; © Jan. 10, 1935; LP 5230.

Story: Glen Lambert.

Cast: The Keatons (Buster, Joe, Myra, Louise), Dewey Robinson, Bull Montana.

One-Run Elmer. 1,753 ft. (19 min.).

© Feb. 22, 1935; LP 5355.

Story: Glen Lambert.

Cast: Keaton, Lona André, Dewey Robinson, Harold Goodwin.

Hayseed Romance. 2 reels (20 min.).

© Mar. 15, 1935; LP 5418.

Story: Charles Lamont. Dialogue/Continuity: Glen Lambert.

Cast: Keaton, Jane Jones, Dorothea Kent.

Tars and Stripes. 1,830 ft. (20 min.).

Rel. May 3; © May 2, 1935; LP 5510.

Story: Charles Lamont. Adaptation: Ewart Adamson.

Cast: Keaton, Vernon Dent, Dorothea Kent, Jack Shutta.

The E-Flat Man. 2 reels (21 min.).

© Aug. 9, 1935; LP 5717.

Story: Charles Lamont, Glen Lambert.

Cast: Keaton, Dorothea Kent, Broderick O'Farrell, Charles McAvoy, Si Jenks, Fern Emmett, Jack Shutta.

The Timid Young Man. 1,786 ft. (20 min.).

© Oct. 25, 1935; LP 5899.

Producer/Director: Mack Sennett.

Cast: Keaton, Lona André, Tiny Sandford, Kitty McHugh, Harry Bowen.

1936

Three on a Limb. 2 reels (19 min.).

© Jan. 3, 1936; LP 6038.

Story: Vernon Smith

Cast: Keaton, Lona André, Harold Goodwin, Grant Withers, Barbara Bedford, John Ince, Fern Emmett, Phyllis Crane.

Grand Slam Opera. 1,860 ft. (21 min.).

© Feb. 21, 1936; LP 6190.

Story: Keaton, Charles Lamont.

Cast: Keaton (Elmer Butts), Diana Lewis, Harold Goodwin, John Ince, Melrose Coakley, Bud Jamison, Eddie Fetherstone.

Blue Blazes. 2 reels (19 min.).

© Aug. 21, 1936; LP 6550.

Director: Raymond Kane. Story: David Freedman.

Cast: Keaton, Arthur Jarrett, Rose Kessner, Patty Wilson, Marlyn Stuart.

The Chemist. 2 reels (19 min.).

© Oct. 9, 1936; LP 6648.

Director/Producer: Al Christie. Story: David Freedman.

Cast: Keaton (Elmer "Happy"), Marlyn Stuart, Earl Gilbert, Don McBride, Herman Lieb.

Mixed Magic. 2 reels (17 min.).
© Nov. 20, 1936; LP 6737.
Director: Raymond Kane. Story: Arthur Jarrett, Marcy Klauber. Photog.: George Webber.
Cast: Keaton (Elmer "Happy" Butterworth), Eddie Lambert, Marlyn Stuart, Eddie Hall, Jimmie Fox, Walter Fenner, Pass Le Noir.

1937
Jail Bait. 2 reels (19 min.).
© Jan. 8, 1937; LP 6854.
Story: Paul Gerard Smith.
Cast: Keaton, Harold Goodwin, Bud Jamison, Matthew Betz, Betty Andre.

Ditto. 1,537 ft. (17 min.).
© Feb. 12, 1937; LP 6927.
Story: Paul Gerard Smith.
Cast: Keaton, Barbara and Gloria Brewster, Harold Goodwin, Lynton Brent, Al Thompson, Bob Ellsworth.

Love Nest on Wheels. 1,604 ft. (18 min.).
Rel. Mar. 26; © Mar. 24, 1937; LP 7000.
Story: William Hazlett Upson. Adaptation: Paul Gerard Smith.
Cast: The Keatons (Buster, Myra, Louise, Harry), Al St. John, Lynton Brent, Diana Lewis, Bud Jamison.

Columbia Shorts, 1939–41

Director (except where noted): Jules White.

1939
Pest from the West. 2 reels.
Rel. June 16; © June 7, 1939; LP 8898.
Director: Del Lord. Script: Clyde Bruckman.
Cast: Keaton, Lorna Gray, Gino Corrado, Richard Fiske, Bud Jamison, Eddie Laughton, Ned Glass, Forbes Murray.
Based on *The Invader.*

Mooching through Georgia. 2 reels.
Rel. Aug. 11; © Aug. 14, 1939; LP 9062.
Script: Clyde Bruckman.
Cast: Keaton, Monty Collins, Bud Jamison, Jill Martin, Lynton Brent, Jack Hill, Stanley Mack, Ned Glass.

1940

Nothing but Pleasure. 1,580 ft.
Rel. Jan. 19; © Dec. 18, 1939; LP 9323.
Script: Clyde Bruckman.
Cast: Keaton, Dorothy Appleby, Beatrice Blinn, Bud Jamison, Richard Fiske, Robert Sterling, Jack Randall.
Reworks the putting-his-wife-to-bed gag from *Spite Marriage.*

Pardon My Berth Marks. 2 reels.
Rel. Mar. 22; © Mar. 18, 1940; LP 9502.
Script: Clyde Bruckman. Photog.: Benjamin Kline.
Cast: Keaton (Elmer), Dorothy Appleby (Mary Christman), Richard Fiske, Vernon Dent.

The Taming of the Snood. 2 reels.
Rel. June 28; © May 28, 1940; LP 9711.
Script: Ewart Adamson, Clyde Bruckman. Photog.: Henry Freulich.
Cast: Keaton, Dorothy Appleby, Elsie Ames, Richard Fiske, Bruce Bennett.

The Spook Speaks. 2 reels.
Rel. Sept. 20; © Aug. 31, 1940; LP 9875.
Script: Ewart Adamson, Clyde Bruckman.
Cast: Keaton, Elsie Ames, Dorothy Appleby, Orson (the penguin), Don Beddoe, Bruce Bennett.

His Ex Marks the Spot. 1,610 ft.
Rel. Dec. 13; © Feb. 3, 1941; LP 10280.
Script: Felix Adler.
Cast: Keaton, Elsie Ames, Dorothy Appleby, Matt McHugh.

1941

So You Won't Squawk. 2 reels.
© Feb. 21, 1941; LP 10478.
Director: Del Lord. Script: Elwood Ullman.
Cast: Keaton, Eddie Fetherstone, Matt McHugh, Bud Jamison, Hank Mann, Vernon Dent, Edmund Cobb.

General Nuisance. 1,603 ft.
© Sept. 18, 1941; LP 11028.
Script: Felix Adler, Clyde Bruckman.
Cast: Keaton, Elsie Ames, Dorothy Appleby, Monty Collins, Bud Jamison, Lynton Brent, Nick Arno, Harry Semels.

She's Oil Mine. 1,586 ft.
© Nov. 20, 1941; LP 11359.
Script: Felix Adler.
Cast: Keaton, Elsie Ames, Monty Collins, Eddie Laughton, Bud Jamison.

Television Credits

Keaton made numerous appearances on TV (including many on variety and quiz shows). Among them were guest shots on: "B. F. Goodrich Celebrity Time" (Conrad Nagel, host), "Masquerade Party," "Colgate Comedy Hour," "James Melton Show," "Jack Carter Show," "Steve Allen Show," "Faye Emerson Show," "I've Got a Secret," "The Garry Moore Show" (daytime), "What's My Line?," "Candid Camera," This Is Your Life," "Ed Sullivan Show" (Toast of the Town), "The Ed Wynn Show," "The Arthur Murray Dance Party."

Keaton also had his own thirty-min. series ("The Buster Keaton Show") on KTTV in Hollywood, televised on Wednesdays at 7:30 P.M. during 1951. Consolidated Television Products was the distributor of the series. Other credits: Director, Arthur Hilton; Producer, Carl Hittleman; Writers, Hittleman, Jay Sommers, Clyde Bruckman.

For all the following TV appearances, the times are Eastern Standard.

1954

The Awakening ("Douglas Fairbanks, Jr., Presents: The Rheingold Theatre").
Televised: NBC, Wed., July 14, 10:30 P.M., 30 min.
Based on Gogol's "The Overcoat"; Keaton plays an individual "swamped in an ocean of totalitarianism."

The Man Who Came to Dinner ("Best of Broadway").
Televised: CBS, Wed., Oct. 13, 10:00 P.M., 60 min. Color.
Director: David Alexander. Producer: Martin Manulis. Adaptation: Ronald Alexander, from a play by Kaufman and Hart. Music: David Broekman.
Cast: Keaton (Dr. Bradley), Sylvia Field (Mrs. Stanley), Zasu Pitts (Miss Preen), Frank Tweddell (John), Margaret Hamilton (Sarah), Howard St. John (Mr. Stanley), Merle Oberon (Maggie Cutler), Monty Woolley (Sheridan Whiteside), Catherine Doucet (Harriet Stanley), William Prince (Bert Jefferson), Joan Bennett (Lorraine Sheldon), Reginald Gardiner (Beverly Carlton), Bert Lahr (Banjo).

1955

Eddie Cantor Theatre.
Televised: ABC, Mon., Oct. 10, 10:00 P.M., 30 min.
Cast: Keaton (Alonzo Pennyworth), Christine Larsen. Keaton as a

travel agent who has never been anywhere. He also strikes out with his girl. Too bashful to ask for a date, he daydreams of faraway lands and lands in trouble.

The Silent Partner ("Screen Director's Playhouse").
Televised: NBC, Wed., Dec. 21, 8:00 P.M., 25 min. (Retelevised: Mar. 21, 1956). © Dec. 21, 1955; LP 7499.
Director: George Marshall. Producer: Hal Roach.
Cast: Keaton (Kelsey Dutton), Joe E. Brown (Arthur Vail), Zasu Pitts (Selma), Evelyn Ankers (Miss Loving), Jack Kruschen (Ernie), Jack Elam (Shanks), Percy Helton (Barney), Joseph Corey (Arnold), Lyle Latell (Ernie's friend), Charles Horvath (barber).
Famed producer (Brown) receives a special Oscar on TV and reminisces about the man (Keaton) who is the real reason for the award and who is a forgotten man watching the presentation on a café TV set. Includes silent comedy sequences done in flashback.

1956

Martha Raye Show.
Televised: NBC, Tues., March 6, 8:00 P.M., 60 min.
Guests: Keaton, Paul Douglas, Harold Arlen, the Baird Marionettes. Keaton and Raye in a parody of *Limelight.*

The Lord Don't Play Favorites ("Producers Showcase").
Televised: NBC, Sept. 17, 8:00 P.M., 90 min. Color.
Producer: Hal Stanley. Adaptation: Jo Swerling, based on a story by Patrick H. Maloy. Music/Lyrics: Hal Stanley. Choreography: Tony Charmoli.
Cast: Keaton (Joey), Robert Stack (Duke), Kay Starr (Jessie), Dick Haymes (Doc), Louis Armstrong (Satch), Nejla Ates (Little Egypt), Mike Ross (Maxie), Arthur Q. Bryan (Mayor), Oliver Blake (sheriff), Barry Kelley (Rev. Willis), Jerry Maren (Speck).
Musical about a small traveling circus that gets stranded in a Kansas town in 1905.

1958

The Innocent Sleep ("Playhouse 90").
Televised: CBS, Thurs., June 5, 9:30 P.M., 90 min.
Director: Franklin Schaffner. Script: Tad Mosel.
Cast: Keaton (Charles Blackburn), Hope Lange (Alex Winter), Dennis King (Clyde Winter), John Ericson (Leo), Hope Emerson (Mrs. Downey).
Keaton plays the town character who was struck deaf and dumb at the trial in which he was accused of killing his father.

A Very Merry Christmas ("Donna Reed Show").
Televised: ABC, Wed., Dec. 24, 9:00 P.M., 30 min.

Cast: Keaton (Charlie), Donna Reed, Carl Betz, Shelley Fabares, Paul Petersen.

Keaton as Santa Claus: a benevolent man who provides the money for the annual Christmas party in the children's ward at the hospital and who is coaxed by Donna into playing Santa.

1960

After Hours ("Sunday Showcase").

Televised: NBC, Sun., Feb. 7, 8:00 P.M., 60 min. Color.

Director: Alex March. Script: Tony Webster.

Cast: Keaton (Santa Claus), Christopher Plummer (Steve Elliott), Sally Ann Howes (Susan Chambers), Robert Emhardt (Dr. Werner), Philip Abbott (Alan Buckman), Natalie Schafer (Edith Chambers), Paul McGrath (Harry Chambers), John Fiedler (congressman).

Elliott quits his job to avoid going to the office Christmas party. Instead, he goes to a psychiatrist where another patient, Susan, mistakes him for the doctor.

1961

Once Upon a Time ("Twilight Zone").

Televised: CBS, Fri., Dec. 15, 10:00 P.M., 30 min. © Dec. 12, 1961; LP 21470.

Director: Norman Z. McLeod. Producer: Buck Houghton. Script: Richard Matheson. Photog.: George T. Clemens. Host: Rod Serling.

Cast: Keaton (Janitor Woodrow Mulligan), Stanley Adams (Prof. Rollo), Milton Parsons (Prof. Gilbert), Jesse White (repairman), Gil Lamb, James Flavin, Michael Ross, George E. Stone, Warren Parker.

Discontented with the time (1890) he lives in, Janitor Mulligan experiments with a time machine and transports himself to 1962. Includes reprise of Keaton-Arbuckle gag ("stealing the pants") from *The Garage.*

1962

Journey to Nineveh ("Route 66").

Televised: CBS, Fri., Sept. 28, 8:30 P.M., 60 min. © Sept. 21, 1962; LP 31903.

Script: William Cox.

Cast: Keaton (Jonah Butler), George Maharis (Buz), Martin Milner (Tod), Joe E. Brown (Sam Butler), Gene Raymond (Constable), Jenny Maxwell (Susie), John Astin (gas station attendant), John Davis Chandler (Frank), John Durren (Charlie).

Keaton as the town jinx.

1963
Think Mink ("Mr. Smith").

Televised: ABC, Sat., Jan. 19, 8:30 P.M., 30 min.

Cast: Keaton (Si Willis), Fess Parker (Smith), Sandra Warner (Pat), Jesslyn Fax (Abigail).

Si and Abigail Willis have a secret for producing thousands of mink a week—by feeding them Abigail's middlin' stew.

Today Show

Televised: NBC, Fri., Apr. 26, 7:00 A.M., 120 min.

Host Hugh Downs devotes the show to a tribute to Keaton, who joins him in viewing clips from his silent film comedies.

1964
You're All Right Ivy ("The Greatest Show on Earth").

Televised: ABC, Tues., Apr. 28, 9:00 P.M., 60 min. © Mar. 27, 1964; LP 29347.

Director: Jack Palance.

Cast: Keaton (Pippo), Jack Palance (Slate), Stuart Erwin (King), Lynn Loring (Ivy Hatch), Ted Bessell (Loring Wagner), Joe E. Brown (Diamond "Dimey" Vine), Joan Blondell (T. T. Hill), Betsy Jones-Moreland (Louella Grant), Barbara Pepper (Fat Woman), Larry Montaigne (Felix).

Blondell, Keaton, and Brown portray a trio of veteran performers now reduced to handling menial chores around the circus.

Who Killed ½ of Glory Lee? ("Burke's Law").

Televised: ABC, Fri., May 8, 8:30 P.M., 60 min. © May 8, 1964; LP 31090.

Script: Harlan Ellison.

Cast: Keaton (Mortimer Lovely), Gene Barry (Burke), Gary Conway (Tilson), Regis Toomey (Les), Joan Blondell (Candy Sturtevant), Nina Foch (Anjanette Delacroix), Anne Helm (Sable), Betty Hutton (Carlene Glory), Gisele McKenzie (KeeKee Lee).

Burke discovers that the elevator accident that killed couturier Benjamin Glory was caused by sabotage, and the only suspect is KeeKee Lee, the victim's business partner.

Hollywood Palace.

Televised: ABC, Sat., June 6, 9:30 P.M., 60 min.

Host: Gene Barry.

Keaton and Gloria Swanson offer a Sennett comedy version of Cleopatra and join Barry in a dance routine.

1965
The Man Who Bought Paradise (Original title: *Hotel Paradise*).

Televised: CBS, Sun., Jan. 17, 9:00 P.M., 60 min. © Jan. 17, 1965 (in notice: 1963); LP 31389.

Director/Producer: Ralph Nelson. Script: Richard Alan Simmons. Cast: Keaton (knife-wielding Mr. Bloor), Robert Horton (runaway financial wizard), Angie Dickinson (his wife), Paul Lukas (Col. Von Rittner), Ray Walston (lawyer), Hoagy Carmichael (Mr. Leoni), Dolores Del Rio (Mona Meyerling, three times a widow), Cyril Ritchard (hotelkeeper), Walter Slezak (Capt. Meers, local police chief). Fugitives hole up in a decaying hotel in a country with no extradition treaties with any major powers.

Now You See It, Now You Don't ("Donna Reed Show").
Televised: ABC, Thurs., Feb. 11, 8:00 P.M., 30 min. © Feb. 4, 1965 (in notice: 1964); LP 30730.
Director: Gene Nelson.
Cast: Keaton (Mr. Turner), Donna Reed, Ann McRea (Midge), Carl Betz (Alex), Bob Crane (Dave), Paul Petersen (Jeff), Darryl Richard (Smitty).
Strange things happen to the rear fender of the family car when Midge borrows it for a shopping trip.

Director/Writer Credits

1938
Life in Sometown, U.S.A. 1 reel (11 min.). An MGM Miniature.
Rel. Feb. 26; © Feb. 18, 1938; LP 7847.
Director: Keaton. Script: Carl Dudley, Richard Murphy. Narrator: Carey Wilson.
Hollywood Handicap. 1 reel (10 min.). MGM.
Rel. May 28; © June 2, 1938; LP 8075.
Director: Keaton. Producer: Louis Lewyn.
Streamlined Swing. 1 reel (9 min.). Sepia. MGM.
Rel. Sept. 10; © Sept. 7, 1938; LP 8302.
Director: Keaton. Producer: Louis Lewyn. Script: Marian Mack. Dialogue: John Krafft.

1939
The Jones Family in Hollywood. 5,300 ft. Twentieth Century–Fox.
Rel. June 2; © June 2, 1939; LP 9250.
Director: Mal St. Clair. Original story: Joseph Hoffman, Keaton, based on characters created by Katharine Kavanaugh. Script: Harold Tarshis.
Cast: Jed Prouty, Spring Byington.
The Jones Family in Quick Millions. 5,300 ft. Twentieth Century–Fox.
Rel. Aug. 25; © Aug. 25, 1939; LP 9371.
Director: Mal St. Clair. Original Story: Joseph Hoffman, Keaton,

based on characters created by Katharine Kavanaugh. Script: Hoffman, Stanley Rauh.
Cast: Jed Prouty, Spring Byington.

Uncredited Work by Keaton

1920
The Round Up. Paramount.
    Director: George Melford.
    Cast: Roscoe Arbuckle.
    Keaton as an Indian extra.

1931
Splash. MGM.
    Director: Zion Myers, Jules White.
    Swimming short. Keaton worked one day on it.

1938
Fast Company. MGM.
    Director: Edward Buzzell.
    Cast: Melvin Douglas.
    Keaton turned in a routine for Douglas.
    TV title: *The Rare Book Murder.*
Too Hot to Handle. MGM.
    Director: Jack Conway.
    Cast: Clark Gable, Myrna Loy.
    Keaton gags.

1939
At the Circus. MGM.
    Director: Edward Buzzell.
    Cast: Marx Brothers.
    Keaton gags.

1942
Tales of Manhattan. Twentieth Century–Fox.
    Director: Julien Duvivier.
    Keaton worked on a W. C. Fields skit that was cut from film.

1943
I Dood It. MGM.
    Director: Vincente Minnelli.

Cast: Red Skelton, Eleanor Powell.
Keaton gags. Based on *Spite Marriage*.

1944
Casey G.I. Jones. MGM. (Never filmed).
Keaton submitted an incomplete story outline.
Bathing Beauty. MGM.
Director: George Sidney.
Cast: Red Skelton, Esther Williams, Basil Rathbone.
Keaton gags.

1945
Nothing but Trouble. MGM.
Director: Sam Taylor.
Cast: Laurel & Hardy.
Keaton gags.
Working title: *The Home Front.*
She Went to the Races. MGM.
Director: Willis Goldbeck.
Cast: Ava Gardner, James Craig.
Keaton gags. Bit as bellboy.

1946
The Equestrian Quiz. MGM.
A Pete Smith Specialty. What's Your I.Q.? No. 11.
Keaton-directed running gag.

1947
Cynthia. MGM.
Director: Robert Z. Leonard.
Cast: Elizabeth Taylor.
Keaton submitted five pages of script.
It Happened in Brooklyn. MGM.
Director: Richard Whorf.
Cast: Frank Sinatra, Kathryn Grayson.
Keaton gags.
Merton of the Movies. MGM.
Director: Robert Alton.
Cast: Red Skelton.
Keaton: Technical Advisor.

1948
A Southern Yankee. MGM.
Director: Edward Sedgwick.

Cast: Red Skelton.
Keaton gags. Based on *The General.*

1949
Neptune's Daughter. MGM.
 Director: Edward Buzzell.
 Cast: Esther Williams, Ricardo Montalban, Red Skelton, Betty Garrett.
 Keaton worked on a thirty-one-page section of dialogue.
In The Good Old Summertime. MGM.
 Director: Robert Z. Leonard.
 Cast: Judy Garland, Van Johnson, Keaton.
 Keaton gags.

1950
Watch the Birdie. MGM.
 Director: Jack Donohue.
 Cast: Red Skelton.
 Keaton gags. Based on *The Cameraman.*

1951
Excuse My Dust. MGM.
 Director: Roy Rowland.
 Cast: Red Skelton.
 Keaton gags.

1957
The Buster Keaton Story. Paramount.
 Director: Sidney Sheldon.
 Cast: Donald O'Connor (as Keaton), Ann Blyth, Rhonda Fleming.
 Keaton: Technical Advisor.

NOTES AND SOURCES

Chapter 1

Page
1 "Joseph Frank Keaton . . ." Buster's middle name was not Francis as has been variously reported. Eleanor Keaton states the name was that of an uncle.
2 ". . . all over the stage." Friedman transcript, 2.
6 ". . . mining towns of Kansas." *Pittsburgh* (Kansas) *Leader,* July 14, 1907, 7.
7 ". . . a natural clown." Bob and Joan Franklin interview with Keaton, New York, October 1958.
8 ". . . ten dollars a week . . ." Feinstein, 392.
9 ". . . wiping of the stage floor." Scrapbook.
10 ". . . call it experience." Friedman transcript, 30.
11 ". . . the audience didn't . . ." Ibid., 6.
11 ". . . I *couldn't* smile . . ." Blesh, 38.
11 ". . . *not even whimper* . . ." Keaton, "Why I Never Smile," 20.
12 ". . . fun out of the Keatons . . ." *Variety,* January 9, 1911, 3.
13 ". . . week of September 7th." Scrapbook.
14 ". . . it names everything . . ." Friedman transcript, 4.
15 ". . . six times a year . . ." Ibid., 5.
17 "KEEP YOUR EYE ON THE KID." Scrapbook.
18 ". . . with a broom . . ." Friedman transcript, 3.
19 "BUSTER IS SIXTEEN." Scrapbook.
20 ". . . put me in irons." Joe Keaton, "London: 'Mr. Butt and Co.'," 40.
22 ". . . in the stalls." Ibid.
22 ". . . next boat sailing . . ." Ibid.
22 "BUTT . . . BUTT . . . BUTT." Scrapbook.
23 "This yours?" interview with Harold Goodwin, Woodland Hills, August 1976.
24 ". . . played out anyway . . ." Keaton, "Why I Never Smile," 26.

Chapter 2

25 ". . . and joined them . . ." *Moving Picture World,* July 2, 1921, 37.
25 ". . . will eventually be." Pratt, *Spellbound in Darkness,* 43.
26 ". . . could not endure . . ." Hampton, 57.
26 ". . . for a nickel." Ibid., 46.
27 ". . . waves came too close . . ." Pratt, *Spellbound,* 16.

Page
29 ". . . that is our tendency." Ibid., 50.

29 ". . . *the Bijou Dream.*" Ibid., 54.

30 ". . . *the Keatons?*" Interview with Louise Keaton, Los Angeles, August 1976.

30 ". . . how you like it." Friedman transcript, 8–9.

30 All information about Arbuckle's filmmaking in New Jersey supplied by William K. Everson, New York, October 1978.

34 ". . . a girl tumbler . . ." Yallop, 38.

36 ". . . about comedy?" Blesh, 151.

36 ". . . put you at the Shuberts." Pratt, "Anything Can Happen," 20.

37 ". . . I'm startin' tomorrow." Ibid.

37 ". . . so that was it." Ibid.

37 ". . . tell him afterwards!" Friedman transcript, 9.

38 ". . . fascinated me." Ibid.

38 ". . . do on the stage." Feinstein, 393.

38 ". . . wanted 'em in there . . ." Pratt, "Anything," 20.

40 ". . . recruited from Brooklyn." Talmadge, 135.

41 ". . . PICKFORD HAS ARRIVED." Latham, 37.

42 ". . . Just-So Girl." Talmadge, 42.

42 ". . . full of good humour . . ." Samuels, 94.

44 ". . . about six two-reelers . . ." Pratt, "Anything," 20.

Chapter 3

45 ". . . too young a business . . ." Franklin, Sutherland transcript, 132.

45 ". . . ever seen before." Samuels, 109.

46 ". . . invited to the party . . ." Franklin, Keaton transcript, 39.

47 "REGARDS TO SAM. CECIL." De Mille, 79.

47 "JESSE AND SAM." Ibid.

47 ". . . as Edendale itself." Chaplin, 149.

47 ". . . the harness-room." Ibid., 151.

48 ". . . the nostrils smart." Ibid., 213.

48 ". . . revelers from roadhouses." Ibid.

48 ". . . pealing of little bells." Ibid., 214.

49 ". . . 'Bus' or 'Bussy.' " Interview with Louise Keaton, June 1977.

51 ". . . in and around that." Franklin, Keaton transcript, 9.

56 ". . . if it happened to them." Feinstein, 398.

59 ". . . for him that night." The details of this prank have been assembled from Samuels, 113–17, Zukor, *The Public Is Never Wrong,* in addition to information supplied by Louise Keaton, June 1977.

60 ". . . chief Hollywood prankster." This story is included in Zukor.

60 ". . . the other victims." Samuels, 118–19.

61 ". . . a pleasant end." Ibid., 119–20.

Page
Chapter 4
63 ". . . looks were deceptive . . ." Capra, 268.

63 ". . . calls him Daddy." Talmadge, 141, 146.

64 ". . . end of the thirties." Interview with Louise Brooks, Rochester, New York, March 1977.

65 All information about Arbuckle's salary and contracts was obtained from the files of Buster Keaton Productions, Inc.

66 ". . . called Metro." Feinstein, 394.

66 ". . . I did that . . ." Ibid.

66 ". . . So I did." Franklin, Keaton transcript, 11.

68 ". . . know what we are talking about." Hemingway, 63.

70 ". . . without a little ferocity . . ." Franklin, Sutherland transcript, 73.

73 ". . . 'a mail order romance' . . ." Talmadge, 173.

80 ". . . his future ruined . . ." Franklin, Zukor transcript, 25.

82 ". . . was an accident." Ibid., 26.

82 ". . . never got over that experience." Samuels, 160.

84 ". . . contributing $33,000 apiece." All information about Reel Comedies was obtained from the files of Buster Keaton Productions, Inc.

Chapter 5
85 ". . . really needed was affection." Interview with William Collier, San Francisco, June 1977.

87 ". . . enforced by Natalie herself." Interview with Louise Keaton, August 1976, and with Buster Collier, Eleanor Keaton, and Harold Goodwin, June 1977.

89 ". . . just like the previous one." Interviews with Louise Keaton and William Collier, August 1976 and June 1977.

94 ". . . make it all legal." All information about Keaton's earnings was obtained from the files of BK Productions.

95 ". . . a five-reel picture." American Film Institute interview with Harold Lloyd, Beverly Hills, September 23, 1969, T1A, 10.

95 ". . . believe our story." Franklin, Keaton transcript, 15.

96 ". . . to see my way . . ." *Moving Picture World,* July 21, 1921, 38.

96 ". . . Let's play it out." AFI, Lloyd transcript, 10.

97 ". . . ridin' that railroad." Pratt, "Anything," 24.

99 ". . . I was safe . . ." Ibid.

100 ". . . then you really got it." Gillett and Blue, 28.

100 ". . . a great many people." In the early days of silent film the cameras were all hand-cranked; after about 1924 motor-driven ones became standard. Hand-cranked films were shot at varying speeds of between 12 and 18 frames per second, the speed often depending on how much action the director needed to cram into the thousand feet of film he usually had to work with. These early

Page

films require a projection speed roughly equivalent to the way they were originally shot, with a speed of about 16 to 18 frames serving for most films. After 1924 the films were shot at speeds nearing the standard one for sound films: 24 frames per second. Buster's *The General* can be shown at sound speed without too much damage, a situation that does *not* apply to his two-reelers or his feature films up through *The Navigator*. It is the fact of being shown at the wrong speed that causes the annoyingly jerky, speeded-up movements in the silent films that are shown on TV. Most archive houses have silent-speed projectors, but they are not used for TV presentations because of the medium's demand for sound accompanying the images.

102 ". . . you fit them." *Moving Picture World,* March 15, 1924, 27.
102 ". . . so that's that." Franklin, Keaton transcript, 27.
102 ". . . out of the minds of screenwriters." *New York Times Magazine,* July 10, 1977, 26.
102 ". . . not word guys at all." Samuels, 130–31.
103 ". . . an audience would accept . . ." Gillett and Blue, 27.
104 ". . . a strict point of view." Blesh, 150.
104 ". . . an eyebrow." Ibid., 149.
105 ". . . or both . . ." Ibid., 150.
105 ". . . with my own hands." Franklin, Sutherland transcript, 85.
108 ". . . floors below . . ." Friedman transcript, 15–16.
109 ". . . got our start . . ." Ibid., 20.
109 ". . . a story about it . . ." Pratt, "Anything," 26.
110 ". . . that's *The Navigator* . . ." Ibid., 20.
111 ". . . bit of timing." Agee, 19.
112 ". . . to the floor." Ibid.
113 All gross earning figures for Keaton's films were obtained from MGM files.
113 ". . . $1,000." Information about Keaton's contract and the shareholders in BK Productions was obtained from the files of BK Productions, courtesy of Leopold Friedman.

Chapter 6

116 ". . . was a set." Interview with Louise Brooks, March 1977.
116 ". . . and governess." Samuels, 182.
120 ". . . a bad loser." Brooks interview.
120 ". . . inventing scenes . . ." Ibid.
121 ". . . Peter Pan's ship." Louise Brooks to TD, March 20, 1977.
122 ". . . for a cow." Wilson, 77.
124 ". . . no good for me at all . . ." Pratt, "Anything," 27.
124 ". . . to do about it." Friedman transcript, 17.
124 ". . . get away from them . . ." Ibid.

Page

125 ". . . out and out accident." Ibid., 18.

128 ". . . What's his name?" Interview with Ben Pearson, Santa Monica, June 1977.

129 ". . . then get comfortable . . ." Louise Brooks to TD, April 9, 1977.

129 ". . . a long lost son." Harold Goodwin to TD, April 29, 1976.

130 ". . . melancholia." Agee, 16.

130 ". . . natural way of workin' . . ." Franklin, Keaton transcript, 27.

132 ". . . a portable kitchen." Pratt, "Anything," 27.

132 ". . . stampede at all . . ." Ibid.

133 ". . . didn't care for it." Ibid.

133 ". . . worked out swell." Ibid.

Chapter 7

135 ". . . laughs with it." Gillett and Blue, 29.

135 ". . . worry about it . . ." Pratt, "Anything," 27.

135 ". . . a business man." *PM* (New York), April 2, 1941.

137 ". . . loved challenges." Balio, Chapter 5.

138 ". . . army supply route." Gillett and Blue, 29.

139 ". . . way it happened." Ibid.

139 ". . . out of the South." Ibid.

140 ". . . refused him permission," Wead, *American Film*, 20.

140 ". . . was 'Texas.' " Brownlow, 491.

140 ". . . fought the war . . ." Pratt, "Anything," 28.

145 ". . . only $474,264." All costs and grosses of Keaton's United Artists releases were obtained from the Wisconsin Center for Film and Theater Research.

146 ". . . those hangovers! . . ." Interview with Collier, June 1977.

146 ". . . wretched reality." Interview with Louise Brooks, March 1977.

146 ". . . no known cure." Except, of course, total abstinence. The latest medical opinion now seems inclining toward a genetic theory of alcoholism, with men inheriting a biochemical predisposition to alcoholism much more commonly than women. See "Born to Drink?" *Lancet*, 1979, i, 24–5.

147 ". . . did *College*." Brownlow, 491.

148 ". . . was on salary." Ibid.

152 ". . . public accepts it . . ." *New York Herald Tribune*, September 11, 1932, 7.

152 ". . . started to deteriorate . . ." Franklin, Sutherland transcript, 86.

152 ". . . have Metro risk them." Interview with Leopold Friedman, New York, May 1977.

Page
153 "The conclave . . ." *Variety,* August and September 1927.
154 ". . . without interruption." Interview with Louise Keaton, Los Angeles, June 1977.

Chapter 8
158 ". . . as far as I know . . ." Pierre Sauvage interview with Weingarten, Beverly Hills, June 1972.
158 ". . . choosing to possess . . ." Louise Brooks to TD, October 26, 1977.
159 ". . . MGM agreed to pay . . ." Robert J. Rubin to Joseph Moscowitz, United Artists, October 9, 1928 and October 14, 1930.
159 ". . . shall be final." All information about Keaton's contract was obtained from MGM files.
159 ". . . piss ice water." Marx [vii].
160 ". . . never changed. Never." Interview with Collier, June 1977.
161 ". . . top of the industry." *The Distributor,* May 17, 1928, 6.
162 ". . . Some thinking! . . ." Harold Goodwin to TD, March 7, 1977.
163 ". . . those extra things." Feinstein, 405.
166 ". . . cost of $362,565 . . ." All film costs and earnings for Keaton's MGM films were obtained from MGM files.
169 ". . . what happens in here." Brooks interview, March 1977.
169 ". . . still an employee." Collier interview, June 1977.
170 ". . . became good friends . . ." Harold Goodwin to TD, March 7, 1977.
171 ". . . a problem with him." Sauvage interview, June 1972.
171 ". . . find him someplace . . ." Ibid.
175 ". . . to deliver them." Brooks interview, March 1977.
176 ". . . away in disgust." Interview with Louise Keaton, June 1976.
177 ". . . go to the verbal . . ." AFI interview with Harold Lloyd, September 23, 1969, T1A, 23.
177 ". . . anything to say." Parrish, 143.
177 ". . . get any older . . ." Collier interview, June 1977.
177 ". . . find the material." Sauvage interview, June 1972.
178 ". . . and Lew Lipton . . ." Ibid.
178 ". . . the times were changing . . ." Ibid.
178 ". . . the blank face . . ." Ibid.
182 ". . . literally breathtaking." *The Distributor,* March 22, 1930.
183 ". . . complete financial independence." De Mille, 289.
183 ". . . rush for destruction." Ibid., 290.
184 ". . . roaring at these things . . ." Harold Lloyd interview, T1A, 23.
184 ". . . cutting them in . . ." Ibid.
187 ". . . was a problem . . ." American Film Institute interview with Weingarten, Beverly Hills, January 23, 1974, T1B, 38.

Page
187 ". . . to combine both . . ." Sauvage interview, June 1972.
188 ". . . You didn't avoid it." Franklin, Keaton transcript, 30.
188 ". . . fighting that, see . . ." Ibid., 31.
188 ". . . fighting with them?" Ibid., 33.
189 Telegram, Thalberg to Keaton, June 3, 1930.
189 ". . . we did it anyhow . . ." Franklin, Keaton transcript, 31.
190 ". . . Charlotte Greenwood's salary . . ." Sauvage interview, June 1972.
191 All information about the duck hunt obtained from interview with Collier, June 1977.

Chapter 9
194 ". . . school kept or not . . ." Franklin, Keaton transcript, 33.
194 ". . . just too nice . . ." Phone conversation with Roland, May 1976.
194 ". . . $20,000, He Charges." *New York Times,* February 6, 1931, 18:1.
195 Kathleen Key appeared in the role of Tirza in the 1926 MGM production of *Ben Hur.* She was paid $10,000 by MGM in February 1931 through the law firm of Lord, Wacker and Lord.
195 ". . . a black eye." Samuels, 225.
196 ". . . in the 'Kennel.' " *Movie Classic,* March 1932.
198 ". . . hysterical easily . . ." Franklin, Keaton transcript, 32.
198 ". . . ever in a school . . ." Sauvage interview, June 1972.
200 ". . . absolutely impossible." Franklin, Keaton transcript, 31.
201 ". . . French-Spanish accent . . ." Ibid., 34.
202 ". . . destroy Buster . . ." Sauvage interview, June 1972.
202 Information supplied by Roland, May 1976.
205 ". . . I don't know . . ." Franklin, Keaton transcript, 31.
206 ". . . greet me in San Diego." *Los Angeles Times,* April 6, 1932, 1.
206 ". . . I guess." Ibid., 2.
207 Telegram, March 29, 1932.
207 ". . . your said contract . . ." April 8, 1932.
209 ". . . suspension without pay . . ." Memo, M. E. Greenwood to Mayer, Thalberg and Mannix, May 2, 1932.
210 ". . . bourbon in his hand." Interview with Louise Keaton, August 1976.
213 ". . . of her sister." *New York Post,* September 25, 1936, 3.
215 ". . . $36,000 to $25,000." All information about Keaton's divorce was obtained from the Los Angeles Hall of Records.
216 ". . . look after Buster?" Interview with Louise Keaton, August 1976.
218 ". . . had never liked." Mayer's quarrel with Thalberg is detailed in both Crowther and Thomas.
219 ". . . turned it down." Samuels, 242–43.

Page
225 ". . . would like to omit . . ." Memo, M. E. Greenwood to George Cohen, August 12, 1932.
225 ". . . no longer required." Samuels, 241.

Chapter 10
228 ". . . skids under you." Franklin, Keaton transcript, 33.
229 ". . . house in the rain." Interview with Louise Keaton, June 1977.
231 ". . . good men friends." Interview with Louise Keaton, August 1976.
234 ". . . nothing came of it." Interview with Harold Goodwin, August 1976.
234 ". . . walk in the apple orchard . . ." Phone conversation with Charles Lamont, Hollywood, August 1976.
236 ". . . listing liabilities of $308,332." Information obtained from Los Angeles Hall of Records.
238 William K. Everson: see Bibliography.
239 *The Invader:* This was the name of Joe Schenck's yacht.
239 "DON'T LET HIM DRINK!" Note supplied by Christopher Brunel, London, January 1977.
240 ". . . this galere." Brunel, 177.
240 ". . . disturbing addictions . . ." Ibid., 176.
241 ". . . throughout the film . . ." Ibid., 178.
241 ". . . the defendant to pay . . ." Los Angeles Hall of Records.
242 ". . . another drink." Interview with Louise Keaton, June 1977.
242 ". . . psychopathic ward . . ." Samuels, 258.
243 ". . . Buster's $5,000 checks . . ." Los Angeles Hall of Records.
245 ". . . take another drink." *New York Post,* September 28, 1936, 3.
245 ". . . whatever you need." Interview with Harold Goodwin, August 1976.
253 ". . . . a screaming judge." Information about the wedding supplied by Eleanor Keaton, August 1976 and June 1977.
254 ". . . work was work." A standard myth about Buster's employment at MGM from 1937 through 1951 is that he was hired for reasons of charity or to ease the conscience of his employers. When the studio wished to raise Buster's weekly salary from $100 per week to $250 in 1944 it was necessary to obtain the approval of the Wage Stabilization Board. Benjamin Thau, a studio executive, was responsible for explaining to the board the background of Buster's position at the studio:

Mr. Thau explained . . . his prior employment by us at a salary of $3000.00 per week. He also explained that it had always been his practice to work with the director and the

Page

> writers in comedy routines, gags, etc., in any picture in
> which he appeared and that his contributions along this line
> were very valuable to the picture. Mr. Thau further ex-
> plained that it was because of drink that he could no longer
> be used in pictures and eventually he came to the point of
> being destitute, at which time we put him on salary at
> $100.00 per week. For the past year Keaton has not been
> drinking and consequently has made very valuable sugges-
> tions to our directors and writers in the way of gags, etc. We
> therefore wish to compensate him for his increased value to
> us and it is our desire to pay him $250.00 per week.

The board agreed to the raise, but

> . . . Mr. Thau explained that Keaton also has to assume the
> burden of taking care of his father who has been in the hospi-
> tal for some time and as a result has contracted bills of
> around $1000 to $1500, we desire to make his salary retroac-
> tive to give him a lump sum payment of an amount suf-
> ficient to take care of these bills. . . . (Interoffice memo,
> April 3, 1944)

Chapter 11

256 ". . . seen him do." Wilson, 73.

257 ". . . has been responsible." Ibid.

257 ". . . in hysterics." Gallico, 108.

258 ". . . the show continued." Interview with Eleanor Keaton, June 1977.

261 ". . . brought in to help." All information on Buster's work in TV obtained from interview with his agent, Ben Pearson, Santa Monica, Cal., June 1977.

261 ". . . literally bloody." Interview with Garry Moore, New York, October 1976.

261 ". . . in his own film." Interview with Mia Agee, New York, June 1975.

264 ". . . so awful!" Interview with Eleanor Keaton, May 1976.

265 ". . . barbecue again." Interview with Harold Goodwin, August 1976.

265 ". . . always working!" Interviews with Jane Dula, Hollywood, August 1976 and June 1977. Also interview with Carol DeLuise, Hollywood, August 1976.

267 ". . . Good-bye now, Nat!" Interview with Louise Keaton, June 1977.

267 ". . . in a hurry." Gilliatt, 54.

271 ". . . delight on his face." All information about the making

Page
    of *Film* obtained from Alan Schneider, New York, September 1978.
272 ". . . their own films." Leopold Friedman to Ben Menliker, MGM, January 12, 1971.
273 ". . . make some money." Joseph M. Schenck to Buster Keaton Productions, Inc., September 10, 1948.
275 ". . . where I am . . ." Gillett and Blue, 26.
275 ". . . Ma and Pa." Unpublished memoir, "If You Hang Around Long Enough What You Get Is Lonely," by William Cox.
277 ". . . heat can't help." Interview with William Cox, Sherman Oaks, Cal., August 1976.
277 ". . . knew the truth." Interview with Eleanor Keaton, June 1977.
277 ". . . Why don't I?" Interview with Jane Dula, Los Angeles, June 1977.
278 ". . . He's gone." Eleanor Keaton interview, June 1977.
278 ". . . permanent legacy." Buster is buried in Forest Lawn Cemetery, not far from the grave of Stan Laurel.

BIBLIOGRAPHY

Agee, James. *Agee on Film: Reviews and Comments.* New York: McDowell, Obolensky, Inc., 1958.

Balio, Tino. *United Artists: The Company Built by the Stars.* Madison: The University of Wisconsin Press, 1976.

Beckett, Samuel. *Film.* New York: The Grove Press, 1969.

Bishop, Christopher. "An Interview with Buster Keaton." *Film Quarterly* 12, no. 1 (Fall 1958): 15–22.

Blesh, Rudi. *Keaton.* New York: The Macmillan Company, 1966; London: Allen & Unwin, 1967.

Brownlow, Kevin. *The Parade's Gone By.* New York: Alfred A. Knopf; London: Secker & Warburg, 1969.

Brunel, Adrian. *Nice Work.* London: Forbes & Robertson, 1947.

Capra, Frank. *The Name Above the Title.* New York: The Macmillan Company, 1970.

Chaplin, Charles. *My Autobiography.* London: The Bodley Head, 1964; New York: Simon & Schuster, 1964.

Coursodon, Jean-Pierre. *Buster Keaton.* Paris: Cinema Club/Edition Seghers, 1973.

Crowther, Bosley. *Hollywood Rajah: The Life and Times of Louis B. Mayer.* New York: Holt, Rinehart & Winston, 1960.

De Mille, Cecil. *Autobiography.* Englewood Cliffs, N.J.: Prentice-Hall, Inc., 1963.

Denis, Michel. *Buster Keaton, 1895–1966.* Anthologie du Cinema, vol. 7, no. 62. Paris: Edition Avant-Scene du Cinema, 1971.

Everson, William K. "Rediscovery: Le Roi des Champs Elysees." *Films in Review* 27, no. 10 (December 1976): 629–32.

Feinstein, Herbert. "Buster Keaton: An Interview." *Massachusetts Review* 4, no. 2 (Winter 1966): 392–407.

Friedman, Arthur B. "Buster Keaton: An Interview." *Film Quarterly* 19, no. 4 (Summer 1965): 2–5.

Gallico, Paul. "Circus in Paris." *Esquire* 42, no. 2 (August 1954): 108–13.

Geduld, Harry. *Birth of the Talkies From Edison to Jolson.* Bloomington and London: Indiana University Press, 1975.

Gillett, John, and Blue, James. "Keaton at Venice." *Sight and Sound* 35, no. 1 (Winter 1963): 26–30.

Gilliatt, Penelope. *Unholy Fools: Wits, Comics, Disturbers of the Peace: Film & Theatre.* New York: The Viking Press, 1973.

Hampton, Benjamin. *A History of the Movies.* New York: Covici-Friede, 1931.

Hemingway, Ernest. *Death in the Afternoon*. New York: Charles Scribner's Sons, 1932.

Keaton, Buster. "Why I Never Smile." *Ladies' Home Journal*, June 1926, p. 20.

Keaton, Buster, with Samuels, Charles. *My Wonderful World of Slapstick*. New York: Doubleday, 1960; London: Allen & Unwin, 1967.

Keaton, Joe. "London: 'Mr. Butt and Co.'" *Variety*, December 11, 1909, pp. 40, 106.

Kerr, Walter. *The Silent Clowns*. New York: Alfred A. Knopf, 1976.

Latham, Aaron. *Crazy Sundays: F. Scott Fitzgerald in Hollywood*. New York: The Viking Press, 1971.

Lebel, Jean-Patrick. *Buster Keaton*. Paris: Editions Universitaires, 1964; New York: A. S. Barnes, 1967; London: A. Zwemmer, 1967. (English translation by P. P. Stovin.)

Loos, Anita. *The Talmadge Girls*. New York: The Viking Press, 1978.

Marx, Samuel. *Mayer and Thalberg: The Make-Believe Saints*. New York: Random House, 1975.

Moews, Daniel. *Keaton: The Silent Features Close Up*. Berkeley: University of California Press, 1977.

Oms, Marcel. *Buster Keaton*. Lyon: Société d'Etudes Recherches et Documentation Cinematographiques, (Premier Plan no. 31).

Parrish, Robert. *Growing Up in Hollywood*. New York: Harcourt Brace Jovanovich, 1976.

Pratt, George C. "'Anything Can Happen—And Generally Did!': Buster Keaton on His Silent Film Career." *Image* 17, no. 4 (December 1974): 19–29.

―――. *Spellbound in Darkness*. Greenwich: The New York Graphic Society Ltd., 1973.

Robinson, David. *Buster Keaton*. 2d ed. London: Secker and Warburg; Bloomington: University of Indiana Press, 1970.

Rubinstein, Elliott. *Film Guide to The General*. Bloomington: University of Indiana Press, 1973.

[Samuels, Charles.] *See* Keaton, *My Wonderful World of Slapstick*.

Talmadge, Margaret. *The Talmadge Sisters*. Philadelphia: J. B. Lippincott, 1924.

Thomas, Bob. *Thalberg: The Life and Legend*. New York: Doubleday, 1969; London: W. H. Allen, 1971.

Wead, George. "The Great Locomotive Chase." *American Film* 2, no. 9 (July–August 1977), 18–24.

―――, and Lellis, George. *The Film Career of Buster Keaton*. Boston: G. K. Hall, 1977.

Wilson, Edmund. *The American Earthquake*. New York: Doubleday Anchor Books, 1958.

Yallop, David A. *The Day the Laughter Stopped: The True Story of Fatty Arbuckle*. New York: St. Martin's Press, 1976.

Zukor, Adolph, and Kramer, Dale. *The Public Is Never Wrong.* New York: G. P. Putnam's Sons, 1953.

Unpublished Material

Photocopies of Myra Keaton's *Scrapbook* are available at the Charles K. Feldman Library of the American Film Institute in Beverly Hills and at the Margaret Herrick Library of the Academy of Motion Picture Arts and Sciences in Los Angeles.

A transcript of Arthur Friedman's taped interview with Keaton in 1958 is on deposit at the library of the University of California at Los Angeles.

Transcripts of the taped interviews of Joan and Bob Franklin with Keaton, A. Edward Sutherland, and Adolph Zukor in 1958 are in the Oral History Project of Columbia University, New York City.

Transcripts of the taped interviews of the American Film Institute with Harold Lloyd and Lawrence Weingarten, 1969 and 1974, are on deposit at the Charles K. Feldman Library of the American Film Institute, Beverly Hills.

INDEX

Illustration page numbers are *italicized*.